DRUG
WARRIOR

DRUG WARRIOR

INSIDE THE HUNT FOR EL CHAPO AND THE RISE OF AMERICA'S OPIOID CRISIS

JACK RILEY
WITH MITCH WEISS

hachette
BOOKS

New York   Boston

Hachette Books
Hachette Book Group
1290 Avenue of the Americas
New York, NY 10104
hachettebookgroup.com
twitter.com/hachettebooks

First Edition: February 2019

Hachette Books is a division of Hachette Book Group, Inc.
The Hachette Books name and logo are trademarks of Hachette Book Group, Inc.

The publisher is not responsible for websites (or their content) that are not owned by the publisher.

The Hachette Speakers Bureau provides a wide range of authors for speaking events. To find out more, go to www.hachettespeakersbureau.com or call (866) 376-6591.

Library of Congress Cataloging-in-Publication Data
Names: Riley, Jack, 1958– author.
Title: Drug warrior : inside the hunt for El Chapo and the rise of America's opioid crisis / Jack Riley.
Description: First edition. | New York : Hachette Books, [2019]
Identifiers: LCCN 2018041368| ISBN 9781602865839 (hardcover) | ISBN 9781549167720 (audio download) | ISBN 9781602865846 (ebook)
Subjects: LCSH: Chapo, 1957– | Riley, Jack, 1958– | Drug dealers—Mexico. | Drug traffic—Mexico—History. | Fugitives from justice—Mexico. | United States. Drug Enforcement Administration—Officials and employees—Biography. | Drug enforcement agents—United States—Biography. | Drug control—United States—History. | Opioid abuse—United States—History.
Classification: LCC HV5805.C485 R55 2019 | DDC 363.25/93365092—dc23
LC record available at https://lccn.loc.gov/2018041368

Printed in the United States of America

LSC-C

10 9 8 7 6 5 4 3 2 1

To my wife, Monica, and son, Kevin, for their unwavering love and support.

CONTENTS

AUTHOR'S NOTE

This is the story of a group of extraordinary men and women who not only hunted down and captured one of the world's most dangerous drug lords, but fight every day to keep us safe at home and around the globe. The events depicted in this book are seen through my eyes and based on my extensive experience in the Drug Enforcement Administration. The story is told as honestly and faithfully as I can. I can do no more than that. And in honor of my fallen law enforcement comrades, I can do no less.

Many people have heard of Joaquín "El Chapo" Guzmán Loera and the dangerous drug cartels that threaten our nation's security. But few know the behind-the-scenes details of the manhunt, or the partisan politics, that impede our nation's ability to effectively deal with the drug crisis that has destroyed so many families.

This book is intended to tell that story.

The secret is to work less as individuals and more as a team.
As a coach, I play not my eleven best, but my best eleven.

—Knute Rockne

THE CHASE, 2007

My brand-new Chevy roared north through the dark toward Las Cruces and home, the Notre Dame fight song blasting on the CD player:

Cheer, cheer for Old Notre Dame,
Wake up the echoes cheering her name!

But it was hard to concentrate on the song. My eyes kept shifting between the dark road and the pickup truck and SUV tailing me.

I was driving a 2007 Chevrolet Impala, black. In my rearview mirror I saw a late-model Ford F-150 pickup truck, navy blue. And a Ford Explorer, black. Ours were the only six headlights along this lonely stretch of Interstate-10.

I pushed the accelerator toward the floor and watched the needle pass one hundred miles an hour.

Intelligence reports said Joaquín "El Chapo" Guzmán Loera, infamous drug lord, head of the deadly Sinaloa cartel, had put a price on my head shortly after I had taken over as the DEA special agent in charge of El Paso.

Now I had hit men on my tail.

My headlights didn't reach far into the darkness. I couldn't remember how far it was to the next exit. All I knew was I had to keep driving until I came up with a plan. My family's life might be at stake.

My own life depended on it.

El Chapo was the most dangerous drug trafficker in the world, and I'd been busting his balls since I got to El Paso, one of the biggest Drug Enforcement Administration territories in the United States. I'd been tracking Guzmán since my days with a DEA special operations unit. I wanted the job in El Paso so I'd be on the front lines in the fight against Guzmán's massive organization. So why did I think he wouldn't come after me?

I was already in a hurry when I left my office. My wife and son were waiting for me at home. For security's sake we didn't live in El Paso. Instead, we'd moved to a quiet neighborhood in Las Cruces, New Mexico, about forty miles northwest of the border. It was a long commute, but I wanted my family as far from the action as I could keep them.

The move was hard. My son was getting ready to start high school in St. Louis, Missouri, and we'd taken him from his friends. But I knew things were getting better when he burned a CD for me with all my favorite country artists: Merle Haggard, Willie Nelson, Waylon Jennings. And right toward the middle, Kevin added a surprise: the Notre Dame fight song. I popped in my custom CD every night on the long drive home.

I first spotted the pickup truck and Ford Explorer as I approached the interstate on-ramp. They sat side by side in the parking lot of a fast-food place, their vehicles pointed in opposite directions so the drivers could talk to each other. Cops in unmarked cars, I thought. But as soon as I got onto the highway, they rolled out of the parking lot and followed me.

It just didn't look right, I thought.

No one heads north that time of night. There's nothing between El Paso and Las Cruces, except a couple of bullshit gas-and-burrito exits.

Something didn't feel right.

I punched the accelerator, and felt the big engine kick in. Soon I was going one hundred miles an hour, but the pickup truck and Ford Explorer were right on top of me. Every time I slowed down, they slowed down. Every time I accelerated, they accelerated. When the pickup truck sped by, I noticed it had no license plates.

"Whoaaaa. Holy shit," I said. Then the fight song came on the stereo.

Rah, rah, for Notre Dame
We will fight in every game,
Strong of heart and true to her name!

I grabbed my BlackBerry and fumbled with the keyboard until I somehow managed to punch in the number for Mike, one of my agents who lived close to my neighborhood. He answered his phone, and all he could hear was the Notre Dame fight song.

"What the hell?" he said.

I paused the music.

"Mike, get to my house. Get to the front of my house. I don't want my wife to know you're there, but *they* gotta know that you're there."

I didn't have to say another word. Mike understood that my family might be in danger.

"Got it."

I hung up and called my best friend, Tony, who had just retired from the DEA. We'd been together as agents on the streets of Chicago. He was the godfather of my only child. Tony answered on the second ring.

"You've only been there a couple of months. How'd you piss these people off that fast?" he said in a thick Chicago accent.

"I don't know. I guess I move fast."

"You must be doing something right," he said.

But this wasn't a time to catch up. I told Tony about the Ford Explorer on my back bumper and the pickup truck in the lane in front of me.

"Look, you gotta get to the police station," he said.

"You don't get it. I got thirty miles of desert on each side and these scumbags are on me. This isn't Chicago where you drive a few blocks and you're at a police station. There's nothing I can do."

"Turn your lights and sirens on."

"They haven't installed them in this car yet. I don't even have a police radio."

"What the hell are you driving that for?"

"Because it's brand-new."

I could tell Tony was worried.

"Listen, I really don't know the area, but I think the Doña Ana County Sheriff's Department is somewhere up the road, past Las Cruces," I said.

"How far?"

"Twenty-five, thirty miles."

"Just keep driving. Get to the sheriff's department. Get to the damn sheriff's department."

I placed my BlackBerry on the passenger seat, pushed the PLAY button on the stereo, and focused on the road. The Ford Explorer pulled a little closer to my back bumper, almost hitting me. It held steady there, while the pickup truck in the lane in front of me started slowing down.

My mind went to the Glock strapped to my left ankle and one spare magazine with eight rounds in my glove compartment.

Not a lot of firepower.

I pulled hard on the wheel, hit the gas, and accelerated past the pickup. I was jumping off the next exit and taking these bastards for a ride. At the stop sign at the end of the exit ramp, I turned left and headed west on Road Runner Drive toward a cluster of homes. I glimpsed in the rearview mirror and the headlights were still behind me.

I was driving sixty miles an hour, zigzagging up and down streets in residential neighborhoods, but I just couldn't shake them. When I spotted a playground parking lot, I pulled to the back.

There was no outrunning them.

What though the odds be great or small,
Old Notre Dame will win over all

I shut off the music, killed the headlights. The lot was dark. I grabbed the extra magazine from the glove box—wishing I had my shotgun—and jumped out of the car.

I squatted behind the engine block and waited. I knew I was out-gunned, outmanned, but I wasn't going to let these jagoffs take me down without a fight.

CHAPTER 1

GLORY DAYS, 1986

This was it. After days of careful planning, everything was set: the location, the drugs, the money. I hung up the phone on the nightstand and took a deep breath. Time to get ready. I slipped on a white Ralph Lauren shirt and crisp khaki pants. I tugged on the shoelaces of my topsider boat shoes to make sure they were tight. I stepped in front of the mirror. My face was shaved smooth, and every strand of my short reddish-brown hair was in place. I put on my fake Rolex and Ray-Bans, and became John Lynch.

It was close to 6 p.m. on a crisp autumn night in 1986. I was an undercover street agent for the Drug Enforcement Administration, so most of my days started when everybody else was headed home. For weeks, I had been hanging around seedy beer-and-a-shot bars in the working-class Chicago suburb of Roselle, Illinois, trying to buy cocaine. That's how I met Mike Rizzo, a burly laborer with a big black pompadour and a porno mustache. He introduced himself one night while I was sitting at a bar, nursing a Miller Lite. Rizzo was a roofer, divorced. He sold drugs on the side to help make ends meet.

"Got three kids. You know how that is, right?" he said, before lifting a cold bottle of Budweiser to his lips.

I nodded. I started small, buying nickel and dime bags of cocaine from Rizzo. When I had earned his trust, I confessed that I was looking for a bigger score. Not a problem, he bragged. And he kept his promise. Now I was about to drive an hour west to downtown Roselle to meet him in a furniture store parking lot. He had five ounces of Colombian cocaine, and I had a gym bag with $10,000 inside.

I'd been on the job for a year. Undercover work was risky, so I planned every detail in advance. No surprises. I had to know where the deal was going to take place. My team had to know the signal I'd use to alert them to arrest the dealer after I bought the dope (something as simple as putting on my sunglasses, or taking off my baseball cap).

And I had to stick to the script. So, like Robert De Niro in *Taxi Driver*, I recited my lines over and over in front of my bathroom mirror until I slipped into character. Forget about Jack Riley, a tough-talking hotshot DEA agent. I was John Lynch, a trust-fund yuppie. My father was a millionaire lawyer, and I was in the real estate business. I'd heard how lucrative cocaine was, and I was preparing to do a little dealing myself, just among my friends.

But the act was more than just remembering my backstory. I had to constantly remind myself of the little things. I had to pay attention to what I said. No cop phrases. Let the drug dealer talk as much as possible. Stay alert, and be aware of the surroundings. And, most importantly, remember that dealers are scumbags who'll cut your throat and steal your money if they get a chance. I could get killed for even the smallest amount of dope. Most of the bad guys I met were unstable. Many were addicts, supporting their habit by selling drugs.

I glanced at my watch. It was getting late. I had to be in Roselle by 7 p.m. When I stepped out of the bathroom, my wife Monica was waiting with a pained look on her face that I had seen a dozen times before. We had been married a year, and she understood how much I loved my job. She never complained, but she didn't stop worrying. She knew my job was dangerous. She knew I had been in fistfights with bad guys in dark alleys. She knew I had been jumped by gun-toting drug dealers. She was afraid of that call in the middle of the night, the summons to a hospital, the nightmare of every spouse of every cop and soldier and warrior in the world.

"This isn't going to take long," I assured her.

"Be careful, Jack," she whispered.

I hugged her and gently kissed her cheek. Then it was all business. I opened my dresser drawer, removed an old, rusty, five-shot revolver from its holster and carefully placed it in a small black leather bag. (When you're working undercover, you never carry a police-issue gun. If you do—and it's discovered—that's a good way for the deal to go sideways.) I grabbed the green Nike gym bag stuffed with Rizzo's dough, and bounded out the front door into the dusk. Neighbors in my western Chicago suburb walked their dogs or jogged down the respectable neighborhood street at this hour. I tossed the green gym bag in the trunk of my black Pontiac Firebird, a macho sports car right out of a *Smokey and the Bandit* movie. I jumped in the car and stuffed my black satchel under the passenger seat.

In those days before cell phones, the only way to communicate with my team was by two-way radio. So I picked up the microphone hidden under my seat and called my partner and best friend, Tony.

"307, you there?" I asked. (Working undercover we had to use call numbers assigned to us by our supervisors.)

"Yeah. What took you so long?"

"I had to get ready."

"Get ready? Are you going to a fucking party?"

I smiled. "Don't worry. I'm on my way, looking fine. The question is: Will he be there? He's a bullshit artist."

"He'll be there," Tony predicted. "Just do me a favor."

"What?"

"Don't take all night. Let's get this shit over with so I can watch the Bulls."

I laughed. "Piece of cake."

All kidding aside, we really didn't know much about Rizzo. We wondered about his supplier. Probably a Colombian. At that point in our careers, none of that really mattered, at least to our immediate supervisors: Jack Brison and Joe Lopez. Tony and I were in our mid-twenties, running fast and hard. We were badasses, taking down every drug dealer on every street corner in the Chicago area we could.

Brison and Lopez loved us. The more guys we busted, the more dope and money we seized, the better they looked to their bosses. So they encouraged us and the other young agents in the Chicago DEA office to be aggressive. "I'm going to need five or six more arrests from you by the end of the month," they'd say. Tony and I were having fun. We loved going undercover.

These were the Pablo Escobar days, when the drug boss was a folk hero in his country, thumbing his nose at the world. His Medellín cartel moved all the cocaine that ended up in those nickel and dime bags flooding Chicago streets. Back then, you didn't have to be a DEA agent to know Escobar's backstory. US journalists had been writing about him for years. At first, that's how I gleaned much of my information about him.

His real-life narrative was straight out of a Hollywood gangster movie. Escobar was born in a mountainous village outside of Medellín, Colombia. His father was a hardworking cattle farmer, while his mother was a schoolteacher. From an early age, Escobar was ambitious. Young Pablo told his friends he wanted to be president of Colombia. But as a teenager, he tossed his books and turned to bullets.

He was a petty street thief, stealing cars, before moving into the cocaine smuggling business. For Escobar, it was perfect timing. As the cocaine market flourished in the 1970s, Colombia's geographical location proved to be its biggest asset. Colombia was situated at the northern tip of South America, between the thriving coca cultivation epicenters of Peru and Bolivia and the United States—the biggest market for the drug.

Escobar's big break came when he murdered his boss—Fabio Restrepo, Colombia's first cocaine kingpin. He took over his business and expanded Restrepo's business into something the world had never seen. Pablo controlled every step of the operation. He bought cultivation farms and processing plants. He bribed law enforcement agencies, developing a ruthless policy known as *plato o plomo*—silver or lead. If officials didn't accept his bribe, they'd end up dead.

Within years, his Medellín cartel provided most of the cocaine smuggled into the United States. Escobar's ruthlessness made him one of the wealthiest, most powerful, and most violent criminals in the world. He tried to soften his image by positioning himself as a Robin Hood–like figure, spending millions to build schools and soccer fields. He was even elected as an alternate member of Colombia's Congress, but was later forced to resign after his notorious background was exposed by Justice Minister Rodrigo Lara. (Lara was later assassinated by Escobar's men.)

By 1982, President Ronald Reagan had had enough of Pablo Escobar. He created a cabinet-level task force to coordinate the fight against drug smuggling into the United States. It was the beginning of Escobar's serious problems with the United States. Since then, he had been engaged in a cat-and-mouse game with the United States and the DEA.

And that only enhanced Escobar's cachet—and influence. Every dirtbag dealer said they had a Colombian connection. They all wanted to be like Escobar, or his alter ego, Tony Montana, Scarface, a powerful drug lord with the beachfront mansion and trophy girlfriend. Us? We wanted to be the Irish version of Sonny Crockett and Rico Tubbs, the two Metro-Dade police detectives from the television show *Miami Vice*. Tony and I argued about who was Crockett. I'd joke that I was the Don Johnson character because I was better looking.

Traffic was thick as the office-worker crowd headed home. I turned the dial on my radio. I needed a little music to get pumped up. When I heard the opening chords to "The Heat Is On" by Glenn Frey, I cranked up the volume. I tapped my hand in rhythm against the steering wheel, singing out loud and off-key. Undercover karaoke. I didn't care. Anything to break the tension. By the time the song was over, I had pulled into a parallel parking spot across the street from the furniture store lot. I glanced at my watch. I'd made it with a few minutes to spare, but Rizzo wasn't there. I picked up the microphone and called Tony, who was leading the surveillance team: "Everyone in position?"

"We got you covered," he said.

There was nothing to do but wait. Tony and I had been on dozens of stakeouts, and in those few months I'd learned to trust him with my life. Hell, Tony was like a brother to me. We hit it off from the beginning.

I first met him in the lobby of the Federal Building on South Dearborn Street in downtown Chicago the summer of 1985. I had just gotten married and was waiting to meet with a supervisor to find out when I'd be heading to Quantico, Virginia, for training. Nearby a young, barrel-chested agent with a shock of red hair sat fidgeting in his seat. He nodded at me, then said, "Man, what did we get ourselves into?"

I smiled. "Yeah, I hear you."

He reached out his hand and introduced himself. It doesn't take me long to decide if I'm going to like someone, and Tony and I clicked immediately. And why not? We'd find out later that we both grew up in big Irish families. His father was a Chicago cop, my grandfather was one, too. We were both sarcastic, tough, outgoing, and loved to drink and bullshit.

Tony said he had only been on the job for a few weeks, and was in the lobby waiting for an informant. "He should've been here by now. I don't think he's gonna show up," he said, his eyes scanning the lobby. I told him I was about to begin training. He waved his hand dismissively and said he had just finished "sixteen weeks of hell" at Quantico, but there was "nothing to it." He volunteered to give me a quick rundown on the office I was about to join.

He said the DEA's Chicago office was divided into groups. There were ten supervisors and about 150 agents. Tony explained that when I was done with my training I'd go through a hazing, just like all new agents.

"It's like a college fraternity. It happens to everyone," he warned. "The agents are going to make you do all kinds of shit. Washing their cars. Getting their coffee and food. Organizing thousands of cassette tapes from wiretaps. Grunt work.

"But they're cool," he said. He laughed about a few older guys who really didn't want to do much. "I've seen some of them get down on their knees at 5 o'clock and crawl on the floor past the supervisors' office so they won't be seen heading out the door."

"Really?"

"Yeah. They don't want to do shit. But then you have the younger agents, guys who are aggressive. We're out all the time busting these dirtbags. That's why we're in the business, right?"

I nodded in agreement. "Right."

We traded stories about our pasts and how we had decided the DEA was the place to be. The allure certainly wasn't the money—new agents only made about $15,000 a year, not enough to support a family in a major city. But we both shared a strong sense that, more than at any other agency, a job at the DEA would be about making a difference.

We were still bullshitting when a supervisor came down to the lobby and escorted me upstairs to the DEA offices, up on the twelfth to fifteenth floors of the Federal Building. Tony decided to tag along.

The place was a dump. Agents sat at dented metal desks that had seen far better days. The floor was covered in worn-out, coffee-stained, green shag carpet. The equipment in the workout gym looked like it was from the 1940s. A thick haze of cigarette smoke rose from dozens of ashtrays and blanketed the office ceilings. Each DEA group shared one computer. Agents had to fight to get time on the machines. Senior agents were supposed to mentor their younger colleagues, but Tony said that wasn't happening.

"You're pretty much on your own," he said. "But when you get back, we'll team up. You gotta get assigned to Group 3. We'll kick ass."

And that's what happened.

Now here I was, waiting in my yuppie persona to take down another bad guy. I knew Tony's red Buick Regal was parked a few cars in back of me. Across the street, members of our surveillance team were waiting in a Chevy van.

I heard Tony's voice crackle over the radio. "He's coming down the street. Just do me a favor."

"What?"

"Make sure this guy doesn't start crying," he joked. "He'll smear your makeup."

Wise guy, I thought.

In my driver's side mirror, I glimpsed Rizzo's white work van heading in my direction. His vehicle made a sharp left into the parking lot. He stopped at the far end of the lot, but kept the motor running.

I didn't waste any time. I bounded out of the Firebird, and looked both ways before crossing the street. I made a beeline to the van. With each step, everything slowed in my mind. I was calm, collected, confident. I could handle anything.

It was a far cry from my first undercover operation, when I almost lost my pants.

A few weeks after I started, an older agent set up a deal for me to buy cocaine from an Italian guy named Vito. We met up for the deal in a bar on the South Side of Chicago, in the shadow of elevated train tracks. Vito was big, about six-foot-four, three hundred pounds, with black, greasy hair and more gold on him than Mr. T. My hands were sweating as I approached him. I couldn't catch my breath. I had taken my big, heavy, brand-new SIG Sauer 9mm handgun with me, tucked between my waistband and the small of my back. It was so heavy it kept pulling my pants down. When I sat on the barstool next to Vito the gun nearly fell on the floor, so I had to stand.

"Why won't you sit down, pal?" Vito asked, and I had to come up with something fast.

"Hemorrhoids," I told him, tugging at my waistband. I didn't know if that was going to fly. I was tense, expecting the worst.

"Oh my God, yeah, kid, I got those, too," Vito said. "Barstools are definitely out. I understand. Here, have a beer. It's good for you." We talked, drank a beer. Over the next few days I bought a few bags of cocaine from him. And just when we were getting ready to bust him, he dropped dead of a heart attack.

As I approached Rizzo's van, I could see that his driver's side window was rolled down. Rizzo saw me but stayed in his vehicle.

"Do you have the cash?" he asked.

"Yeah," I said. "But I need to see the package first."

He showed me the dope. I smiled. "I have the money in the car. I'll go get it."

I wheeled around and headed to my Firebird. I opened my trunk—the signal for my guys to move in. Then I turned around and watched the scene unfold.

A wave of DEA agents rushed the van. With their guns drawn, they dragged Rizzo from the vehicle and tossed him to the ground. "Don't move, motherfucker!" one of the agents yelled at him.

Just as Tony had predicted, Rizzo burst into tears. "Come on, man. Please don't do this. I'm gonna lose my job."

"Tough guy," said Tony, sarcastically.

Usually, I didn't have any compassion for drug dealers. My adrenaline would kick in and I'd turn to Tony and say, "Let's get another one." But this time was different. I don't know why, but I actually felt sorry for Rizzo. I became philosophical: In the scheme of things, what did Rizzo's arrest mean? Were we really making a difference? We'd busted how many Rizzos? Dozens. There had to be a better way of dealing with the flow of drugs. I didn't say anything to Tony or the other guys on the team, but I started thinking.

We handcuffed Rizzo and took him to a holding cell in the Federal Building. During interrogation, Rizzo broke down. He couldn't stop bawling. He pleaded with us to let him go, promised he'd help us. If we released him, he said he'd become a confidential informant. He said he'd give up his Colombian suppliers, the guys smuggling the dope.

I pulled Tony to the side. "What are we doing?"

Tony was puzzled. "Huh?"

"We're just locking people up," I said.

"Isn't that the point?"

Yes, I said. Then I tried to articulate what I was thinking. We had been arresting guys all over Chicago. But before the ink was dry on the paperwork, they were out on the street again, dealing drugs. These were small-time dealers. We weren't going after the big fish, the guys running the operation.

"It's like a game of whack-a-mole," I said. "We get one guy and another one is already out on the street taking his place. We're just spinning our wheels. To have any kind of impact, we have to take down the entire organization, not some low-level dealers."

To my surprise, Tony agreed with me. But what were we going to do? Our supervisors encouraged us to bust as many dirtbags as possible. They wanted us to seize drug money. It looked good on their monthly and annual reports. That's how they got promoted. That's how they got funding.

But that night, Tony and I decided to take a radical approach. We'd talk to our supervisor and get permission to let Rizzo go—on one condition: He'd have to call us on a regular basis with updates. He'd have to provide us with information about his sources, guys higher up the food chain. We were no longer going to bust small-time drug dealers and call it a day. Instead, we'd use those dealers to catch the bigger fish, to bring down entire criminal organizations.

What I didn't know then was that, within days, I'd come under the tutelage of a hard-charging supervisor who saw things the same way. He would change the trajectory of my career.

CHAPTER 2

THE MENTOR

Joe Corcoran was a larger-than-life figure in the office. Of all the group supervisors, his agents seemed to handle the biggest cases. They went after criminal organizations, not small-time drug dealers. Corcoran was the only supervisor in the Chicago office who didn't focus on "metrics," the number of arrests or the amount of money seized by his men. No, he was a big-picture guy.

Tony and I had talked a lot about what life would be like if we worked for Corcoran. We said hello to him in the office, but we didn't have much interaction with him. He wasn't our supervisor. And the DEA, like so many government agencies, was a bureaucracy. Your supervisor was your supervisor. Case closed.

Rizzo had called several times since his arrest. He said he'd tried to get the names of big-time drug dealers—the Colombian suppliers and the smugglers—but none of his leads panned out.

"This is bullshit," Tony said. "We should just go lock him up now."

I knew Tony was frustrated. So was I. We were stuck.

But then one day Corcoran stopped me in the hallway. "You got a minute?" he asked me.

I said yes. I was anxious to talk to him, pick his brain. Tony and I wanted to do more. I followed Corcoran into his office. He told me to close the door.

Corcoran leaned back in his chair, but he wasn't relaxed. He was in his early forties, a legend in the office. An Irish guy from the Bronx in New York, Corcoran only operated on one speed: fast. He moved fast. He talked fast. He ate fast. The guy was a dynamo.

Corcoran was also a screamer: When you did something wrong, he'd yell so loud that his pale white face would turn beet-red. But moments later, he'd hug you. It wasn't personal. He just wanted to get the best out of you. His moral compass was right on. He respected the truth. I never met anyone with more integrity. He was not a politically gifted guy. He was blunt. He said what was on his mind. But if you worked for him and did the right thing, he had your back. That's why agents loved him.

They also loved him because he was a real character. He was nearly six feet tall and about 250 pounds, draped in an ill-fitting suit. He was always talking about some new diet or workout he was trying as a way to lose weight. He wore big-ass brown wingtip shoes—Frankenstein shoes. Corcoran's nickname was Cruiser, because he loved classic cars, especially old Chevys, like the 1957 Bel Air. He liked doo-wop music, songs like "In the Still of the Night" and "I Only Have Eyes for You." He knew every word to every classic doo-wop song, like he was a teenager hanging out on a street corner in the Bronx.

After I closed the office door, Corcoran didn't waste any time. He looked me in the eye. He said he had been following Tony and me. He said our supervisors praised us in their daily briefings. "You guys have potential," he said.

"Thank you, sir," I said.

"It's Joe. Call me Joe." He paused for a moment and then got down to business. "You're doing a great job. You and Tony are kicking ass. But I want to give you guys some advice," he said.

"You're taking out drug dealers, but they're small-time hoods. That's not getting to the root of the problem," he said. His group was successful because they were targeting entire criminal organizations.

I jumped in. I told Corcoran about Rizzo, how we held off charging him because he wanted to cooperate. "That's something we wouldn't have done before," I said. I explained that we wanted to take a new approach. I said we wanted to go after the guys who supplied Rizzo, and then we'd work our way up to the top.

Corcoran smiled. "That's the way to do it. That's how we do it. My guys always ask: 'Who's the supplier? Where are the drugs coming from? How are they getting into the Chicago area?'"

But Corcoran didn't stop there. He said we should build organizational flowcharts and follow the flow of the money. And, most importantly, we had to work with other agencies: the Federal Bureau of Investigation; the Internal Revenue Service; the Bureau of Alcohol, Tobacco and Firearms; and federal prosecutors. Too many times, the agencies operated in their own little worlds. They didn't share information or communicate with one another. "If we're ever going to bring down criminal organizations, we have to cooperate with each other," he said.

That was a refreshing change. I can't tell you how many times I heard that you couldn't trust the FBI guys or the IRS—or anyone who worked in other agencies. The prevailing feeling among DEA agents was that the agencies were all out to take credit for major busts. Even Tony sometimes felt that way—especially about the FBI. But here was Corcoran, taking the opposite approach, preaching that we all had to work together. We had to trust each other.

"I just wanted to share some of this shit with you, Jack, because you have the potential to be a great agent. Because of office politics, I'm not sure I can get you into my group. Your supervisors ain't gonna give you or Tony up, that's for sure. But if you have any questions, I want you to come to me anytime. Use me as a resource," he said.

With that, he got up, shook my hand, and escorted me to the door. As I walked out of his office, I was on cloud nine. Everything he said made sense.

My desk faced Tony's. He was on the telephone, but when he hung up, I signaled that I needed to talk to him.

"Take a break?" I asked.

"Yeah. Let's go outside."

I was quiet as we took the elevator to the lobby. We walked outside the building, where the streets were bustling with the suit-and-tie lunch crowd from the office buildings.

"What's up?" he asked.

I recounted my conversation with Corcoran. Tony listened closely to every word. When I finished, he shook his head in disbelief. "Damn. I wish he was our boss."

"I know. But we're on the right track. From now on we target organizations. If we arrest dirtbags selling nickel and dime bags, we have to get them to flip. And, as we work our way up, we have to get other agencies involved."

"Huh?"

I could tell by Tony's immediate reaction that he wasn't totally onboard with that idea—at least not yet. But I understood what Corcoran was saying. You can't operate in a silo.

After that, I started to study how Corcoran built a case. At times, he must have thought I was a stalker. I'd go into his office and ask a shitload of questions. One of the biggest things I learned was that you had to involve the US attorney's office as soon as possible. They were the guys who were going to help you build the case. They were the ones who were going to help you get the wiretaps.

I saw how closely Corcoran built consensus with guys like Gary O'Hara, a special agent who was his point man. I watched how Corcoran lobbied DEA officials in Washington to get money to help with cases. I watched how he schmoozed with FBI agents and Chicago police officials.

It got to a point that I'd ask to attend his meetings with agents or prosecutors. I was like a sponge—I wanted to absorb everything I could from him. He'd always offer advice. He would tell me who to stay away from because he was worthless, or who I needed to talk to because he would help. He could be loud and obnoxious, like the times he'd walk by my desk and say, "Hey, kid. What did you fuck up today?"

Unlike my supervisors, he never asked his agents for more arrests. But Corcoran loved to test me. For a while, he asked me the same question:

"Who's the biggest drug dealer in Chicago?" The first time, I threw out a name and said, "But we'll never get him." I learned quickly that was the wrong answer. He jabbed a finger at me and snapped, "Bullshit. You'll get him." I can't tell you how many times I heard an agent say, "It's too dangerous. We can't get him" and Corcoran would scream, "Don't ever say that. You can find a way!"

With Corcoran's leadership, I began to find my voice. When I was growing up, I wasn't sure what I wanted to do with my life. Now I knew the DEA was the right career choice for me, even though my parents had been against that decision. They thought law enforcement was too dangerous, too stressful, but, in a way, that direction was inevitable. Fighting bad guys was in my blood. My grandfather, Ralph Riley, was a hard-drinking, burly Irish cop in Chicago's downtown vice district. The boys called him "Big Hands" because, it was said, "he put his fists on people."

I grew up listening to tales of those long-ago days before DUI laws and Miranda rights. Ralph liked to go to bars after work. Grandmother could tell what kind of night he had by how far he parked his police car from the curb. "If it was out in the middle of the road, he had a good night," she'd say.

My dad, Ralph Riley Jr., was his father's opposite, a quiet, serious man who grew up in the Depression. He joined the Navy during World War II, but never saw action. As he put it, he "fought in the battle of Navy pier," because he never left Chicago's shoreline.

After his discharge, he went to the University of Notre Dame, an achievement that filled his old man with pride. The subsequent medical degree from St. Louis University Medical School didn't make much of an impression on old Ralph. For him, Notre Dame was as good as you could get.

My dad was a hospital pathologist, a real middle-class American dream achiever. My mother, Jane, was outgoing, a people person, into arts and culture. She'd walk into a room and make a thousand friends. She was a nurse, but she became a housewife after she married my dad and had children—two girls and a boy.

I was born in 1958, and grew up in Flossmoor, an upscale Chicago suburb. My dad was honest and respectful to the point of being a pain in the ass, and he expected everyone else to be the same. He was also frugal. He bought himself a Mercedes one time, then took it back to the dealer. He just couldn't let himself pay that much money for a car.

And he could be tough as nails, something he inherited from old Ralph. To him, everything was black and white, good and evil. My dad kept me on the straight and narrow and I was terrified of him. Not that I didn't do some dumb-ass things. Just before I started eighth grade, I took some cash out of my mother's purse. When my dad heard about that, he went nuts. He pulled me out of Flossmoor Junior High and sent my ass to a military school about two hundred miles away. At Roosevelt Military Academy, you wore a uniform and a crew cut. You got up at 6:40 a.m. and marched.

What my father didn't know was that 30 percent of the kids at Roosevelt were sent there by the courts. For them, it was Roosevelt or prison. And there wasn't always a lot of difference. I was only there for a year, but that place toughened me up. That's where I learned to fight. My parents thought it was going to straighten me out, and they were right. It scared the hell out of me. And it opened up the world to me.

Flossmoor was a lily-white suburb. Before Roosevelt, I hardly ever saw a black person. About half the students at Roosevelt were black kids from the city who got into trouble, or whose parents had put together some money to get them out of Chicago and give them a chance.

That was my first contact with black kids. We lived together, so we had to try to understand each other. I think that helped me down the road. I learned to look beyond race and language, and just judge people by whether or not they were assholes. I played basketball at Roosevelt, on the varsity team. We were terrible. I wasn't great. But basketball helped me fit in, and I learned to love the game.

Once back home, I went to Homewood Flossmoor High, and made the junior varsity team. My coach, Don Laketa, was a former US Marine, an old-school coach, a strict disciplinarian who loved to bust my balls. From a coaching standpoint, it was all defense, defense, defense. He had a bunch of rules off the court, too. If you wanted to play, you had to cut your hair. I couldn't swallow that. Coming out of the military school nightmare, I was just trying to play ball. I didn't want to deal with all the rules. By the time I was a junior, I couldn't take any more. I quit.

My dad backed the coach. "If I had known that you were having problems with him, I would have taken you off the team myself," he told me. It didn't take me long to miss playing, and, as I grew older, I realized I got more of an education on the basketball court than I ever did in the classroom. Basketball gave me an idea of what rules are for, and how they're best used.

I learned that somebody's got to be the boss and draw the line, but there's a way to do that without bashing people over the head. I also learned that leadership is all about relationships. I don't think my father, or the people from his era, understood that. For them it was "This is it. You must do this, and you cannot do that."

But not everybody is OK with that black-and-white bullshit. You have to spend a little more time with some kids, find out what makes them tick, see how they respond to reason. You just can't say, "Do it my way, or I'm going to kick your ass."

I graduated from high school in 1976 without any idea of what to do with my life. My sisters had gone to college. I figured I'd just go, too. There was no Notre Dame for me. I didn't have a lot of choice, because I was a mediocre student. I ended up going to Bradley University in Peoria, mostly because they accepted me. I majored in criminal justice, mostly because of my grandfather. I went on after graduation and got a master's of public administration at the University of Illinois at Springfield in 1982. I did an internship with the state legislature during the day and went to classes at night.

After class, I'd hang out at student bars, and that's where I met Tom Steele, a fifty-something guy who was getting another degree to prepare for life after he retired from the Secret Service. We drank a lot of beer and slung a lot of bullshit. And one night in 1983, he said I ought to apply to the DEA.

"They haven't hired for years, but they're getting ready to fire up," he said. "If you want to have fun and kick ass and travel, sign on with the DEA."

I did a little research. Before 1973, federal drug enforcement was scattered over several agencies, like the Bureau of Drug Abuse Control and the Bureau of Narcotics. The hippies brought marijuana and then heroin to public consciousness in the late 1960s and early 1970s, so President Richard Nixon, with a single executive order, combined America's antidrug effort into a single agency to tackle the problem.

Back then, drug trafficking was a pretty casual, small-time affair, with a few regional growers and shippers smuggling the goods to big-city distributors. Well-organized international drug syndicates in Colombia and Mexico had not yet stepped onto the world stage.

I applied to the DEA. It took two years for the DEA to finally hire me.

Meantime, I worked at the American Hospital Association in Chicago, putting on continuing education programs for hospital-based doctors. There I met Monica Sherry, a pretty brunette who ran employee health promotions. We had some things in common: childhood in suburban Illinois, university education, second-generation Irish families. On our first date I took her to see Deluxury, my favorite bar band, at Southside Johnny's, a dirty old blues dive. I fell in love. And a year later, we were married in a big wedding at St. Clement Church. My wedding was the best party I ever went to. All my college buddies were there, along with my high school friends, dancing and celebrating into the night at an Italian restaurant.

I was set to start DEA training right after the honeymoon, and just then I got another call: from the Federal Bureau of Investigation. I had taken the FBI test, and now they wanted me to come and work for them. I was torn. My parents, especially my father, wanted me to join the FBI. They thought the FBI job would be safer, maybe more respectable. Back then, few people knew anything about the DEA. And what they knew wasn't flattering. DEA agents were considered cowboys—they liked to kick in doors but didn't know how to build cases. I talked to people in both agencies. I discovered that DEA agents had gotten a bum rap. They went after drug traffickers worldwide and did a lot of undercover work. In the FBI, very few agents did street work, went undercover, or even arrested bad guys. The pay was the same and I saw what drugs were doing to my community. I wanted to make a difference, so I decided to stay with the DEA. My parents didn't approve. Still, I knew from the first day of training that I'd made the right choice. I had found my people.

We trained at the FBI Academy at Quantico, Virginia, a place with a military feel. We wore black shirts, camouflage pants, and army boots, and we did a lot of marching. We mingled with the FBI guys, who wore nice pants and polo shirts.

DEA recruits fell into categories. We had "coppers," guys who had worked narcotics and organized crime before joining the DEA. They were great in all the training exercises that involved taking down bad guys on the streets. There were "brainiacs," accountants and chemists and scholars with advanced degrees and linguistic abilities.

I fell into the "other" group: college graduates with no specialty. We stayed in the middle of the pack, but I mixed with all the groups. I could hang out and talk with anyone, just like my mom.

When they sent me back to Chicago, I became a street agent. I was assigned to Group 3, and Tony and I became good friends. Our desks faced each other in the middle of the office on the twelfth floor. Like schoolkids, we laughed and played practical jokes on each other. We were like two brothers who shared the same room. Hell, we spent more time with each other than with our wives. Everything seemed to click. We were the same age. We had just gotten married, but had no kids. We had strong police ties. His father was a legendary Chicago police officer, a "cop's cop." He had four sisters and three brothers. His mom was like mine—and many of our generation—she stayed at home and raised the kids. When Tony was young, his father taught him to box. And he played linebacker on his high school football team. His ability to knock heads was an asset during undercover operations when we had to take down drug dealers in back alleys, and things got a little crazy.

At the DEA, we had both jumped at the chance to work undercover. Some of our success depended on acting skills, but most of it was a cultivated awareness. You had to understand who you were dealing with, and where your surveillance was set up. You had to protect your money. And, most importantly, you had to protect yourself. There were tricks I learned along the way: Never bring money with you. You have to make the bad guys understand that. If they think you carry cash, they'll rob you.

You have to really plan, and you have to really keep track as you go along. If you're doing prolonged undercover work, your story had to be straight for every one of those transactions. You had to remember just what you said to this mutt or that one, because it couldn't be different from what the guy remembers, when he finally starts to talk.

You're dealing with criminals, drug dealers. All you really have to do is prove you can come up with the money. Money blinds them to everything else. They're greedy, grabby bastards. They don't want to know you; they don't make friends.

They don't teach this at Quantico. We didn't have senior agents hanging around giving advice on how to do undercover. This is the stuff I learned with Tony. We sometimes learned on the fly.

And now, with Corcoran's help, we were making bigger busts. When we bought cocaine from street dealers, we'd tell them we were agents, and that we could either bust them or work with them. And we started getting them to flip. Some started giving up their suppliers, and we started going to federal prosecutors to build bigger cases. We made organizational charts. No matter how well we thought we were doing, Corcoran kept pushing us. But we were feeling really good about our careers. We were on a roll. But then we uncovered a corruption case that hit too close to home.

CHAPTER 3

GOOD COPS BAD COPS

By now, Tony and I had been working as street agents for several years. Cocaine was still the drug of choice on the streets, but the Chicago landscape had changed. Users weren't just snorting cocaine. They were buying more and more of a crystallized, smokable version of cocaine called "crack." The drug was extremely addictive, and cheaper than powdered cocaine. The high was quick and more intense, causing hallucinations, seizures, and paranoia. Crack cocaine was fueling explosive violence in Chicago and cities across the United States. Crack addicts would rob people at gunpoint, or break into homes to steal valuables, money—anything for their next high. Gang members selling Colombian cocaine were killing each other as they carved out their own territories.

But not even the escalating violence in his biggest market—the United States—or in Colombia could hurt Pablo Escobar's bottom line. He was making so much money that *Forbes* magazine named him one of the ten richest people on earth. Escobar spent millions bribing Colombian police officials and politicians. And he didn't hesitate to kill anyone who got in his way, including members of the rival Cali cartel.

The DEA had been working for years to stop the flow of cocaine into the United States by choking off Escobar's key smuggling routes in the Caribbean. Our agents had been seizing all kinds of vessels used to move dope—from slow-moving fishing crafts to high-powered speed-boats. Nothing seemed to work. The cocaine kept coming. And once the dope was in the United States, the Colombians would sell to anyone who had money, including groups like the Outfit, a traditional Italian-American organized crime syndicate with deep Chicago roots. The Outfit was responsible for much of the crack cocaine and heroin on Chicago streets in the 1980s. And the Outfit was known for having cops on their payroll.

Tony and I were building such a good reputation in Chicago that other law enforcement agencies began turning to us for help. In fact, it was an FBI agent who broke the news to us: Someone was selling a lot of dope out of the Washington Pines Hotel on the West Side of Chicago. It was a sweet operation. A secretary in the hotel office took orders over the phone, and when the customer arrived, she directed him to a particular hotel room.

"We think the guy running the operation is the building super-intendent, and lives there for free," the FBI agent said.

That was it. The FBI didn't know much else, except for a possible tie to the Outfit. The FBI usually takes the lead in police corruption cases, and the DEA offers assistance if there are drugs involved. But this time, they handed us the tip and kept walking.

The FBI agent gave us the phone number for the woman in the office. "We probably should get a wire for the phone," I said to the FBI agent.

"Look, I don't have time for that. I'm doing a lot of white-collar crime. This is drugs. That's why I turned to you guys," he said.

The FBI agent, sitting facing me, didn't see it, but I saw Tony roll his eyes in disgust.

"OK. We'll take over from here," I told him.

When the FBI guy left, Tony closed the door a little too hard. "What the fuck—do we have to do everything for those bastards?" he said.

"Hey, don't worry about it. You know these guys don't want to get their nice suits dirty," I joked.

After getting the green light from our supervisors, we began working our informants and staking out the hotel. It was clearly a big-time drug operation that had been going on for a while.

Neighbors had complained to cops for years that dealers had set up shop in the old seven-story hotel, later turned into cheap apartments. Men hung out day and night in the lobby, and business was so brisk the kids called the place "Crack City."

The longer we watched the hotel, the more clear it became that crooked cops might be involved.

We knew someone in the hotel was cutting and packaging shipments of cocaine and heroin. But when Chicago cops arrived to investigate complaints, the dope always vanished minutes before they arrived—a sure-fire sign that dirty cops were tipping off the dealers.

"We gotta find out where the leaks are coming from," Tony said.

We didn't have enough proof yet to get a judge to approve a wiretap. We needed someone to get inside the building and find out who was running the operation.

One of our sources told us about Alvin Carvill, an informant who went by the name Top Cat. Carvill knew some of the players in the Washington Pines. He could get in, buy dope, and help us identify the key players. Only one problem, though: Top Cat was in a county jail outside Detroit, doing time for brandishing a weapon and not paying child support.

We drove to Michigan and had a chat with Top Cat, who listened to our sales pitch, looked at the gloomy gray prison walls, and agreed to help. But there was a condition: He wanted a car. A Lincoln Town Car.

We agreed. We asked the state attorney's office to release Top Cat. "He's all yours," he said.

Top Cat took full advantage of his new lease on life, and his DEA expense account. When he hit the streets in Chicago again, he looked like a pimp character from a 1970s blaxploitation movie—the shiny Lincoln, a long coat with a fur collar, gold chains, a purple velvet hat tilted sideways, even a walking cane. The only thing missing were the women.

We set him up in an apartment in Presidential Towers, an upscale building on the city's West Side. Within a few days he'd made so many contacts that he had the mutts bringing dope to him, delivering right to the door. Top Cat could bullshit with the best of them. I had no doubt he was going to get us inside the Washington Pines operation.

Top Cat wore a wire the first day he went to the hotel, with an undercover DEA agent tagging along. Top Cat was to introduce the agent Van Quarles—a guy he called Little Wolf—to the bosses, so they could start doing business.

And so they did. In Apartment 103, Little Wolf gave $5,000 to a guy named Nedrick "Rick" Miller, the leader of the operation. Miller told our undercover guy that his son had the cocaine, but was on his way back from Indiana. He'd call them when his son got there. So Top Cat and Little Wolf left. Without the money and without the drugs.

You never front money. You give a dealer money in exchange for drugs. I was pissed off. I knew if we lost the money, my boss would be all over my ass. But I also knew that sometimes an undercover agent has to make a quick decision. You didn't have time to call a supervisor to ask for permission. Plus, I knew Little Wolf was a really good undercover agent. I trusted his judgment. Still, we got some blowback.

"What the fuck are you doing? You're never going to see the money again," a couple of the agents told us.

But we needed to get this prick to trust us. It was close to midnight, so we went to Top Cat's apartment to wait for the call.

I was anxious and began pacing like a worried parent. I was concerned about the deal falling through—and losing the money. But I was really worried about the danger. These were thugs. This was a dangerous operation. Anything could happen. I could tell I was getting on Tony's nerves. The apartment building had a swimming pool, so he decided to take a swim.

"Call me if anything happens," he said.

"Yeah, right. I'll do that, darling," I said sarcastically. "You go on and enjoy yourself."

About a half hour after Tony left, the phone rang. It was Miller. "Come on over. We got it," Miller said.

So we had to scramble. At that point, it was just me, Tony, and Little Wolf. Everyone else on the surveillance team had gone home. I ran up to the pool and shouted to Tony, "It's on!" He jumped out and we bounded back to the apartment to get ready and go over the plans. I knew sending Little Wolf back to the hotel alone was very dangerous. At that time of night in that part of the city, Tony and I would stick out. The lookouts protecting the drug dealers would eventually spread the news that two white cops were sitting on the hotel. So we set a time limit for Little Wolf to be in the building: If we didn't see him in fifteen minutes, Tony and I would barge into the building with our guns blazing.

We drove back there in two cars, and we watched as Little Wolf walked into the hotel. Tony and I were tense, but ready. We didn't say a word. We both knew this had the potential of going sideways quickly. A few minutes later, we heard Miller's voice on the wire: "Here's the dope," he said to Little Wolf.

And so our undercover operation was off and running.

After the meeting, Tony quickly discovered that Miller was a cop. Tony's old man had just retired from the Chicago police department. He knew all about Miller.

"Miller is a West Side badass," Tony told me. "Everyone knows he's corrupt, but they can't prove it. Now he's an enforcer for Mario Lettieri."

Fuck, I thought.

Lettieri, owner of Mario's Butcher Shop, was a man of many talents. He was a meat cutter, a gangster, and a drug dealer—part of the Sicilian mob.

Miller was doing all sorts of shit for Lettieri—breaking legs for his loan-sharking business, allegedly even whacking people. And now he was moving large quantities of his cocaine and heroin.

Lettieri had a good man in Miller, because nobody would fuck with him. Not only was he a cop, but he was six feet tall and built like Arnold Schwarzenegger.

This new information changed everything. Now, we had to get the FBI and the US attorney's office involved in the investigation. One of our first moves was getting a warrant to tap the hotel phones, a practice that wasn't widely used in drug investigations at the time.

➤ If Miller was dirty, we were afraid other police officers were involved as well.

Little Wolf bought a bunch of cocaine from Miller over the following few weeks. Whenever Miller needed a kilo or more, he phoned the butcher shop and told them, "I need some rib eyes."

As the investigation expanded, it became clear that Miller was the Outfit's muscle in the black community.

"A lot of police officers like him because if you had an issue on the West Side he could fix it," Tony told me.

We couldn't share information with Chicago cops because we didn't know which of them was rotten. Tony came up with a "test" to see who might be involved.

"Mention Rick Miller's name to a cop. If he hates the guy, he's straight," Tony said. "If he tells you 'Hey, Rick's a good guy,' you know he's probably on his payroll."

Our worst fears were confirmed when Little Wolf went into Miller's room at the Washington Pines one afternoon and saw six cops in uniform there, playing cards. Little Wolf bought the drugs right in front of them.

This was much bigger than anyone thought, and hiding in plain sight. Just about anyone could get inside the hotel at any hour—strangers off the street, gang members with guns, drug addicts desperate for a fix. They entered freely, buzzed in without question by whoever manned the front desk.

But if a squad car swung by and slowed down, or if an unmarked police car pulled up and unknown officers jumped out, cries, shouts, and wolf whistles resounded through the lobby and the first floor as the officers headed toward the exit.

Lookouts shouted to appointed runners. The runners, all in tennis shoes, scattered in every direction up the various stairways and down the halls, shouting warnings and disappearing from view while the police officers were left pounding on the front door.

Eventually, someone in the lobby would buzz them in. (Obviously, the buzzer system wasn't meant to protect tenants, but to keep cops out, or at least slow them down.) By the time the police got through the lobby and up the stairs, no drugs or drug sellers could be found. Apartments stood empty, doors half-open, TVs on, cigarettes still burning in the ashtrays. But the caches of drugs and the people who sold them had disappeared into the labyrinth of seedy hallways.

"Why didn't we find out about this sooner?" I asked Tony.

He didn't answer. We both knew why: police protection.

Soon, our wiretaps began paying dividends. Not only were we finding dirty cops, but we learned that three Cook County correctional officers were part of Miller's crew, selling dope to jail inmates.

Finally, we had enough evidence to bring them down.

The US attorney got arrest warrants and on April 20, 1989, more than two hundred FBI and DEA agents, and other enforcement officials, began rounding up the suspects. Tony and I wanted to arrest Miller ourselves. Early that morning we found Miller at his post at a hospital on the West Side of the city, in uniform, working his "day job." We took him into custody, but because he was a police officer we weren't supposed to talk to him until the US attorney got there. We put him in the holding cell at the DEA office.

Miller was unhappy. He stripped off his uniform and threw it on the floor. Then he squatted down and took a shit, right on his clothes. He didn't want to go anywhere in his uniform. That's what a sick fuck he was.

I remember the news conference announcing the arrests. Assistant US Attorney Michael Mullen said Miller, a thirty-three-year police veteran, had for more than two years received $10,000 a month from a dope dealer to provide him with drugs and protect his drug operation.

Miller was also responsible for the death of Debra Foster, a thirty-two-year-old drug addict. Miller wanted to test the strength of a new shipment of heroin, so he used her as a human guinea pig. She died of an overdose.

Even after everyone in Miller's operation was arrested, Tony and I kept working the case. We got court permission to listen to the cell phones of several cocaine distributors tied to Miller, a groundbreaking technological development.

The men turned out to be underlings of a top mobster named Anthony "Tony the Hat" Zizzo. One of them was a Chicago police officer who made trips to Florida to pick up cocaine from a Colombian source. Others were also trafficking in stolen goods and overseeing gambling operations. Business owners were told their legs would be broken if they didn't cooperate.

The US attorney's office would later indict nine of Zizzo's men for distributing cocaine.

As for Miller, he pleaded guilty that same month to drug conspiracy charges and was sentenced to twenty-four years in prison.

Meanwhile, some cops were trying to justify the corruption, saying they were underpaid for the work they did. So what if they made a little money on the side? They called it a "Christmas bonus." That really pissed me off, and it stuck with me.

This case made an impression, probably because Tony's dad was a righteous cop, and my grandfather was, too. If you're a cop, you have to do right. None of this bullshit.

The Miller investigation showed me the nasty underbelly of drug trafficking, and how important it is to have a moral compass. If you didn't have that, the bad guys with all that easy money could suck you in. And once you were in, you couldn't turn back.

Days after the case was over, Corcoran called me into his office again. I sat down. He broke the news: He was being transferred to headquarters. I wasn't surprised. If you spent any time with Corcoran you knew he was headed for great things. Still, I felt gut-punched.

"Jack, I'm proud of you. You've turned into one helluva agent," he said.

That meant a lot. Corcoran didn't offer praise casually. He told me that if I wanted to advance in my career, the day would come when I, too, would have to do a stint in Washington. Maybe we'd work together again in the future.

Tony and I were both bummed out. We'd learned so much from Corcoran. He'd offer solid, timely advice when our cases got complicated. But at this point in our careers, we were cocky. We believed we could handle anything—even a bunch of scumbag bikers who'd cut your throat for looking at them the wrong way.

CHAPTER 4

THE BROTHERS

After the Miller case, Tony and I were riding high. We were involved in more and more dangerous undercover operations. So far, I had been lucky. I was never seriously hurt, but sooner or later my luck was going to run out, Monica told me.

"Jack, you're taking too many chances," she'd say.

"John Lynch is taking too many chances," I'd joke.

She'd shake her head sadly. "You're not John Lynch. You're Jack Riley. Please don't forget that."

Monica was worried. She read the newspapers, magazines. She watched the nightly news. And Pablo Escobar was still the star of everyone's show. Everybody knew his name. He was the world's biggest drug trafficker, with an empire worth billions and a pop-culture persona.

What concerned her the most was the flip side of the narco-glamour. With the United States pushing for Escobar's capture and extradition, he had turned to extreme violence—so-called narco-terrorism. He was responsible for the killing of thousands of people, including politicians, civil servants, journalists, and ordinary citizens to subvert the Colombian government. The drug lord unleashed his fury on his enemies in hopes of influencing Colombian politics. His goal was a no-extradition clause and amnesty for drug lords. Escobar's terror was starting to turn public opinion against him.

The violence in Colombia didn't stop US criminal organizations from jumping into the cocaine business. For the Brothers motorcycle gang, there was too much money at stake. The bikers were ruthless thugs. They'd commit armed robberies and brag about whacking people. The Brothers were in the drug business, too, but they were small-time players. They mostly sold a little weed on the side. But now they were determined to compete with the Hells Angels and Outlaws for a share of the booming cocaine market.

We found out about the Brothers when a small-time cocaine dealer named Robert Blessing flipped after he got busted by the Chicago cops. They turned to us to handle the case. Blessing bought dope from Dan Taglia and Oscar DeLisle, but the real leader of the Brothers was a psychotic biker named Paul Born II. Blessing was scared shitless of Born.

But not John Lynch. He didn't know any better.

Blessing arranged for me to buy coke from DeLisle. We met at the ABC Lounge in Streamwood, a down-at-the-heels Chicago suburb struggling with decayed buildings, crime, and corrupt officials—a common mix in Cook County.

ABC Lounge was a typical beer-and-a-shot kind of joint: dimly lit, smoky, with cigarette burns along the Formica bar. Guys in their factory overalls sat at the bar, their eyes glued to the Chicago Bulls and Michael Jordan on the television.

Blessing introduced me to DeLisle and Taglia, and John Newell, an obese old biker with greasy red hair. And the boss was there, too: Mr. Born, president of the Brothers Motorcycle Club, decked out in full gang colors.

I could see why everyone was terrified of him. Born was huge, about six-foot-two, 260 pounds, a bushy beard, tattoos. Strapped to his hip was a Desert Eagle .357 Magnum, the most powerful handgun you could get at that time. The back of his denim jacket, in red letters outlined in black, read "Brothers MC Illinois." In the middle grinned a flaming Grim Reaper.

I shook everyone's hands and made small talk. They looked at me suspiciously, like I was wearing a wire.

"You a cop?" DeLisle asked me.

"Yeah, sure. Do I look like a cop?" I said, trying to stay calm.

He turned away. The three dealers huddled, then motioned for me and Blessing to follow them to a storeroom in the back. DeLisle opened a cabinet and handed me a plastic bag with two ounces of coke inside. I gave him $3,200 in cash, which I had counted out before I got to the bar.

I made a couple dozen more of these small-time buys in the next few months, mostly at bars and restaurants in the neighborhood. Sometimes, Born sent Jimmy Westerman, one of his enforcers, to make the drop. Guys like Westerman and Newell were the scum of the earth—stupid, racist assholes. They wouldn't think twice about cutting my throat. I was careful not to prolong any meeting, because the longer I spent with them, the better chance they had to see my cover team. Each time an undercover cop moves, his cover team moves. That's why bad guys are always changing the meeting spot.

I was building up to a big buy, one that would put away Born and key members of his gang for a long time.

So one summer morning I met up with Taglia on a street corner, and didn't waste any time. "Look, I just inherited $300,000. I'd like to make a big buy because I want to move it outside of Chicago. I don't feel comfortable here anymore," I said.

"How much do you want?"

"Twenty-two kilos."

He cocked his head back and looked at me with alarm. "Twenty-two kilos?"

"Yeah."

At the time, a hand-to-hand transfer of twenty-two kilos in Chicago was unheard of. Still, I could see him counting out those thousands of dollars...the wheels were turning.

"Let me see what I can do," he said.

We talked a couple of times on the phone before he agreed to a deal.

"I think I can do it, but my guy wants to make sure you have the money," he said.

"OK, I'll be happy to show it. Let's figure out a place to meet."

The guy's name was Taglia, after all, so he set up the meeting at Nancy's Pizza, in Addison, a village west of Chicago. He lived over there, so it made sense.

But first I had to convince Mullen, the US attorney in Chicago, to let me do this. He'd already said no. The situation was too dangerous, he said. It was a great setup for a simple robbery and execution—no cocaine, they just shoot me and take the money. The Brothers were known to do that. I had never seen them kill anyone, or even get violent, but they talked about it all the time.

Still, I was determined to go through with it. So many agents in my office—especially the older ones—said I should give up, cut my losses. "You'll never get Born," a few of them said. *Bullshit,* I thought. I channeled my inner Corcoran. If there was a chance to get Born, the scumbag leader, I was going to do it. I didn't give a fuck about the danger.

"I've been building a case for months. We have to do it. I know what I'm in for," I told Mullen. "How many times have I done this before, right? Nothing's happened."

He finally agreed.

Then we made a plan.

Tony would be the money guy. When I got to the meeting, I would ask Taglia to show me the dope. Once he did, I'd tell him I had to go to a pay phone to call my cousin, who had the money. Once Tony showed up, we'd finish the deal and get the hell out of there. Then the other agents would move in and make the arrests.

We rehearsed our moves. I was vulnerable, no doubt about it.

"These guys are going to rob me," I said to Tony. "I don't think they'll kill me. It's not like I could go crying to the police and say, 'I was all set to buy all this dope, and they took my drug money.'"

I really didn't know what they had planned.

"Whatever happens, we got your back," Tony said.

We were all set to go, and Taglia called to change the plans. Instead of Nancy's Pizza, he wanted me to bring the cash to his condo in Addison.

"Look, if you want to do this thing, I gotta feel comfortable," he said.

Fuck, I thought. They're worried about me wearing a wire.

At that point, I hadn't told him about Tony. He still thought he was only dealing with me.

"That's cool," I said, before hanging up the phone.

But my bosses flipped out.

"You're not going in there. There's no way we can cover you," said Jack Brison, my supervisor.

I knew he was right, but that wasn't going to stop me.

"And what are you going to do with the money?" Brison asked.

"Well, I'm going to have Tony be the money guy. They don't know about Tony. Let me go up and talk to them and I'll bring Taglia down. Have Tony pull up in the car. We'll let Taglia get in the front seat."

You always want the agent in the back seat. Basic stick-up-robbery prevention.

"Tony will flash the money. Then we'll have another car come up. When it does, Tony will immediately get out of my car, get in the other car, and go," I said.

Brison approved the plan, but Mullen was reluctant.

"We don't think you should do it at his apartment," he said.

"Why? We're the ones at risk," I said.

But Mullen wouldn't budge.

It looked like I'd have to postpone the meeting. I kept pleading with him, but evidently the US attorney's office had enough evidence already to make arrests. Mullen was hoping some of the Brothers would flip under interrogation. He could turn them against one another, and they'd start making deals to save their own hides.

But then, out of the blue, Taglia called me up. "Hey, my guy is coming up from Florida tonight. If you're still interested, you've got to bring the money over," he said.

So now I had to do it, and on the fly. We didn't know whether this guy was lying, if he knew anyone in Florida, if he had any cocaine at all. His telephone toll records showed no calls to or from Florida. We were still following him around, but he was hanging out with the same shitbags he was always with every day.

"OK. I'll be there," I told him.

I agreed to go, without checking first with my bosses. That pissed them off, but they didn't stop me. They knew this could be our last chance to get Born.

"You get in there, and get out," Brison warned.

We got the team together and I went over the plan one last time. Then John Lynch jumped into his Firebird and drove about twenty miles west of the DEA office to Taglia's condo.

I parked on the street and bounded out of the car with my "male clutch," a black leather handbag that a lot of dopers used to carry their money in. I walked to the front door, pressed the intercom, and Taglia buzzed me in. The elevator took forever to arrive. Once in, I pushed the button for the sixth floor. I took a few deep breaths to stay calm.

Off the elevator, first door on the right. I knocked, Taglia answered. "Come in," he said, all friendly. "Have a seat. Have a beer."

"No thanks, man," I said. Westerman was there, taking up most of the space in the living room. He stood up when I came in, set down his Budweiser.

Taglia looked at my bag. "Where's the money? I know you can't fit all that money in there."

"No, no, no. I got my cousin Tony. I want you to meet him. He's down-stairs with the money," I said.

Westerman grabbed my bag. He opened the zipper. There was a gun in there. I had purposely taken that old shitty-looking five-shot with me. If they saw my DEA gun they'd know I was a cop.

"He's got a fucking gun!" Westerman said. "He's a Fed."

I thought for just a second that I'd left my credentials in there. But no, thank God, I'd gone through my checklist before I left the office. You always do that when you're undercover: You got to leave your ID. You have to remove your handcuff key from your key chain. You can't let anybody see that. That's what they're looking for.

I had to think fast. "You gotta understand, I got stuck up last week. I got a lot of money on me..." I rambled, trying to persuade them I was carrying the gun for protection. I had thirty minutes inside the apartment building. After that, agents would knock down the door. I was approaching the twenty-minute mark. I was thinking about the big-ass fishing knife in Westerman's boot. He had showed it to me about twenty times during the last few months.

Finally, Taglia stopped me. "OK, Fucko. Let's go get the money."

Westerman jumped in, waving his beer. "He's a fucking rat. A rat motherfucker. We're all done," he said, shouting at me. "You got a wire on, motherfucker?"

I quickly pulled my shirt up. "See anything?" I said. "What about now?"

Taglia started to calm down, but time was running short. The cavalry was about to barge in. I didn't have a weapon, and was standing right where the crossfire would be.

"Wait here," Taglia said. He disappeared into his bedroom. He came back with his coat on.

"Let's go see the money," he said.

"Great, but he can't come," I said, pointing at Westerman.

"Oh, he won't come. He's been drinking." Taglia tossed me my bag. My gun was inside, but he'd taken out the bullets.

We stepped out the apartment door. Three scruffy-looking DEA agents were walking down the hallway toward us.

Goddamn, I cut that close, I thought.

But Taglia never noticed them. Into the elevator and down, out the doors and into the street. The moment we hit the curb, Tony pulled my car around.

"Over there," I said, pointing to my Firebird.

Taglia got in the car. Tony showed him the money—$300,000 in cash. He didn't want to count it. I think he was shocked that I came up with it.

"So, what do you want to do?" I asked him.

"I'm leaving now. I'll be in touch through Blessing," he said. We kept the bag with the money.

So Tony and I drove off back to the office. When we got back, all the older agents told us it was over, we'd been had.

"He's never going to call," one of them said.

But a couple of hours later, the phone rang. Nancy's Pizza. Be there at 8 p.m. So Tony and I drove back to Addison with Blessing, our informant. We got a table while our agents set up surveillance.

We'd just sat down when Taglia, Westerman, and three other gang members walked inside.

"Where's your guy?" I asked.

"He's coming," Taglia said.

We ordered pizza and sat there waiting for hours while the waitress kept bringing food and drinks. Tony was getting angry. "We're not paying for all these fucking guys," he whispered to me.

Finally, Taglia got up and went to the pay phone in the back. When came back to the table he had news, at last.

"The guy's here. It's in the blue car out front, in the trunk," he said.

I sent Blessing outside to make sure the stuff was there. He opened his trunk, and when he returned to the table he had fucking white powder all over his face. He nodded his head and grinned. "It's in there."

Things got dicey. The surveillance team and agents outside and inside with us were trying to figure out what we were doing. I got up to go to the bathroom, hoping an agent would follow me.

"I got to take a piss. I just drank like forty beers," I said to the gang members.

An agent was already outside the bathroom. I turned to him inside the door and said, "It's out there."

"Yeah, we got the car. We saw the informant."

My heart was racing. "Get ready. They've got people all over the place. Here's the deal: I'll keep Taglia and Westerman inside here. Tony can take one of the mutts to the trunk of my car to get the money. He'll signal."

The bust signal was Tony pulling his shirt up or taking his hat off. Well, I was watching, watching, watching as they walked out there, but Tony didn't even have the key to the trunk. It was in my pocket.

It was too late. Tony gave the signal, and the agents swooped in, shouting "DEA. DEA. DEA!"

The restaurant and the street outside erupted into a melee. Some of the gang members ran for the door, and others took swings at the agents. I grabbed Taglia and smashed his face into the floor. He kept yelling, "You fucking Fed." A gangster's gun came out. BOOM! But no one was hit. Out the window I glimpsed the agents pulling John Newell from a pickup truck parked just ahead of my car. Long red hair and a sawed-off shotgun—they'd set us up for a robbery for sure. Newell went down on his knees, then onto the ground, clutching his chest. No one had laid a hand on him. He was faking a heart attack.

Meanwhile, a couple of our toughest agents dragged Paul Born out of his custom-carpeted Chevy van, parked directly across from the pizzeria. Our surveillance had picked him up when he put the dope in the trunk of the car. They threw him to the ground, seized his Desert Eagle .357 Magnum, and searched the van. He had two kilos of coke in there.

That night, I tried to interrogate Born about his Florida connection. He wasn't talking. "Lock us up!" was all he wanted to say. That, and "Fuck you."

Born and his minions were each charged with conspiracy to possess with intent to distribute cocaine. It took a few years, but all the guys we arrested that night were convicted. Born got the most time: twenty-three years in a federal prison.

I didn't know it at the time, but the Brothers takedown was a pivotal case in my career. It showed me just how available and profitable Colombian cocaine was, and how many other criminal organizations like the Brothers were now involved. More importantly, it reinforced my belief that no matter what obstacles you faced—no matter what anyone said—you could never give up. You had to go after guys like Born, the leaders. It was something I'd remember years later during my hunt for a ruthless Mexican drug lord: El Chapo.

Five years in, and I was thinking about my future.

My friend Van Quarles—Little Wolf—had been in Washington for about a year, and he had just called to let me know there was an opening for a trainer in Quantico. He thought I'd be perfect for the job. They needed a real hands-on guy to show recruits the ropes, give them real-world experience, especially working undercover. It was a lateral move but I knew it could be an important one in my career.

I hung up the phone and exhaled. I wasn't sure I was ready to leave. On the surface, everything was perfect. Chicago was my home. Monica and I had both been raised here, we both loved the city. Tony was an incredible partner. My family and friends were here. My parents weren't getting any younger. So there was no reason to leave, right? But I knew I'd have to spend time in other agency offices, doing different jobs, if I wanted to get promoted. And after years of undercover work, I had finally come to the realization that I wanted to run my own office. I wanted to become a special agent in charge. Maybe even an SAC in Chicago.

Before I did anything, I talked to Monica.

She was happy in our little house and with our life in Chicago. We both wanted children. If I stayed in Chicago, I would only go so far. She was torn. On one hand, she was excited to move to a new place. It would be an adventure. But she liked her job and was worried that this would be the first of many moves.

Meanwhile, I reached out to Corcoran for advice. But he told me what I already knew: If I wanted a promotion, I had to go. I was lucky to be in Chicago for so long.

"Don't be afraid to try new things," Corcoran said.

Finally, I talked to Tony.

I told him I was thinking about applying for the position. But I tamped down expectations. "Even if I apply, I don't know if I'll get it. They're going to have a lot of applicants."

Tony was quiet. I tried to fill the silence. "Look, you know sooner or later they're going to break us up. We can't be a team forever, right?"

Tony knew I was right, but I could see the words still hurt. He said he wasn't angry.

"I'm probably never going to leave Chicago, because of my situation," he said, alluding to his family. He just had a son, and he and his wife wanted more children. "You're right. We were lucky we got to work together for five years. Go for it."

I decided to apply for the position, and within a week I got the news: I was selected. They wanted me out there as quickly as possible.

The rest of my time in Chicago was a blur. We had to get movers, say good-bye. Tony seemed distant. I knew he wanted the best for me. This transition would be hard for me, too. He was more than a partner. He was my best friend.

After my last day, my friends threw a good-bye party for me at Gleason's, a bar near the DEA office. We drank beer and told war stories. In the middle of the celebration, Tony pulled me aside. He wanted me to know that he was proud of me and wished me the best.

I smiled and I raised my bottle of Miller Lite to toast our friendship. After everything we had been through, we were friends for life. Nothing could ever change that.

CHAPTER 5

NO-NAME OFFICE

One of the lessons I learned in Chicago—especially in the Nedrick "Rick" Miller corruption case—is how big criminal drug trafficking networks are, and how deep. Street dealers worked under other, more powerful figures. Gangsters, organized crime networks, and international traffickers were in this business to make a stunning profit, and they didn't give a damn how much devastation their products wreaked on communities and families. I came to the stark realization that I was part of an important fight, with nothing short of the security of the nation at stake.

And I found that in order to dismantle a criminal enterprise, you had to learn everything about it, down to the smallest detail. You had to know its leaders, its hierarchy, and how it operated. My bosses knew that, too, and that's why I was here, in a colorless room with no windows, no comfy chairs, no pretty pictures on the white cinder-block walls. My office was as big as a closet, and the floor was concrete. The only furnishings were a desk, a phone, and a bank of computers.

Outside the building was just as bland, one of hundreds of nondescript warehouses that line both sides of Interstate-95 between Washington and Richmond, Virginia. No one would ever guess that inside the building, inside my office, was the heart of the DEA's campaign to bring down Escobar and the Medellín and Cali cartels.

I can't talk about my time in the room because the information is still classified. But I can tell you that this wasn't the job I applied for when I was in Chicago. I was supposed to be a trainer at Quantico. And for six months in 1990, that's what I was.

Monica and I moved into a family-friendly neighborhood just outside the city. Our neighbors worked for the DEA, the FBI, and other government agencies. I spent my days at the academy training recruits, teaching them about real-world situations they might encounter on the job. I preached what I'd learned from Corcoran: In the field, they needed to cooperate with other agencies. We all worked for the same team, and interagency cooperation was the best way to get the bad guys. I taught a class on surveillance. One day, I had my students try to follow me as I "fled" in my little red Mazda Miata. They couldn't keep up with me, so I drove home and parked in my driveway. I called my neighbor and we cracked open a few beers while we waited for the students to finally roll up.

That's what it was like: Our neighbors were always over at our house for cookouts and parties. Family and friends visited—including Tony and his wife. Monica and I showed them around Washington. Corcoran called now and then to see how I was doing, and we got together for beers. Life was good, but I couldn't see myself doing this for very long. I knew eventually I'd have to go back in the field.

Then everything changed. Several times each week I met up with Gary O'Hara, a former colleague from the Chicago office, to jog five or six miles. I liked O'Hara. We now worked together at Quantico.

Running with O'Hara was never just an ordinary run. In those days he was terribly addicted to nicotine and trying hard to stop smoking. He wore two nicotine patches on his arm and had packs of cigarettes hidden all along the tree-lined route, just in case. We were jogging along the usual path, when he stopped. I thought it was to catch his breath, but he said he needed to give me a heads-up. He said Corcoran asked him to talk to me about a "sensitive subject." Corcoran wanted me to be part of a classified project targeting the Colombian cartels. President George H. W. Bush wanted to crush Escobar and his minions before the 1992 presidential election. He said the Colombian cartels were still out of control and

Bush wanted to show he was "tough on drugs." O'Hara said Corcoran asked him to join and he said yes.

"Are you interested?" O'Hara said.

I didn't hesitate. "Of course."

He stopped me before I had a chance to ask questions. He said Corcoran would talk to me. Until then, I couldn't say a word. In fact, if I took the job, I would have to keep it secret. I couldn't tell anyone, not even Monica. I would become invisible. I wouldn't even be able to list it on my résumé.

At that point, I had a bunch of questions. Would I work undercover? Did they want me to infiltrate one of the cartels? Would I travel to Colombia?

I knew that when Bush took office as president in 1989, he shifted the focus of the drug war from intercepting boats at the border to attacking cocaine's roots in South America—including cartel bosses. I knew the United States had spent hundreds of millions of dollars trying to stop Escobar and the Colombian cartels. Still, in early 1991, cocaine continued to flow unimpeded into the United States.

Corcoran called, as promised. We decided to meet at DEA headquarters to talk about the post. He said he still couldn't tell me much, that I'd learn more on the job. The job involved investigating the Colombian cartels, but no undercover work, and no travel to South America. Still, Corcoran said, my new job would be critical to bringing down the cartels.

After all the years and dollars spent chasing Escobar, DEA still didn't know much about his operation. We knew Mexicans were somehow involved—they were helping the Colombians smuggle dope—but no one paid them much attention. No one knew the key Mexican players, their business arrangement with the Medellín cartel. Those were questions that my unit would try to answer.

My office would be in a room in a warehouse. Corcoran would be my direct supervisor for the project. But he said I'd report to Joe Keefe, the project's coordinator. Keefe would be, in effect, my handler. If I found out any information, I would tell Keefe, who would get it to the field. Corcoran said he had known Keefe for years and that I would love working for him. He also said my job, and the unit, were classified. No one except a handful of people would know about it. And Corcoran said he'd selected me because I was smart, tough, aggressive, and "got the big picture."

"Jack, I know you can do this job, and do it well," he said.

I was flattered and, from his sales pitch, I knew the job was important. I accepted the position. I really didn't know what I was going to tell Monica. When I got home, I told her I was no longer going to be an instructor, but instead I would be working for Corcoran. She asked if that meant we had to move. I told her no, and she was relieved. But I wouldn't be able to talk about my job, I said. Classified. Nada. Radio silence.

And she quickly discovered I wasn't kidding. My working life was shrouded in secrecy. I couldn't tell her what I did at work. I couldn't tell her *where* I worked. When my neighbors asked about my job, I changed the subject. I had to keep Tony and my other friends in the DEA in the dark. Nobody except my immediate supervisors knew that I was gathering critical information about the Colombians. Keefe was my main contact. And, fortunately, he was a smart, savvy guy who had my back.

We hit it off right away. In terms of style, Keefe was the antithesis of Corcoran. He was a shade over six feet tall, a soft-spoken, barrel-chested agent with broad shoulders. Keefe was a sharp dresser. Unlike Corcoran, Keefe wore custom-made suits, his shoes were always shiny, and his brown hair was perfectly coiffed. He looked like he had stepped off the pages of *GQ* magazine. Forget about junk food—Keefe was a workout fiend who loved raw broccoli and celery. When I asked him if he wanted to grab a cheeseburger, he would pass with a polite: "Not today."

We first met at a Washington restaurant, and spent much of the dinner talking about sports. Keefe was from Boston, he loved the Red Sox, the Patriots, and the Celtics. He had two sons and a daughter, and he coached his sons' basketball teams.

Then he talked about his professional philosophy. Keefe said he knew federal agencies didn't like to share information. They all wanted the credit for successful operations. But without sharing information— without targeting the leadership of criminal organizations—how could they be successful? The Colombians were depending on law enforcement not talking to each other, not connecting the dots. "That has to end," he said.

In the days before the internet exploded, it was important for DEA and FBI agents to pick up the phone and talk to each other. They had to co-ordinate investigations with federal prosecutors. A tiny piece of paper, a receipt, a nickname, a tattoo, a wiretap could yield valuable information. But what good was it if no one shared that information? What good was it if critical reports moldered in a police officer's desk drawer?

"We have to be smart," he said.

And forget about metrics. Who gives a shit about how many low-level drug dealers we bust or how much money we seize from a stash house? He said we should always be asking a simple question: How much did we damage the criminal organization? If the answer to that question was not much, what good was the bust?

I hung on every word. Ever since Corcoran took me under his wing, interagency cooperation had been my mantra. I told that to Keefe. He smiled and said he knew why Corcoran chose me for the job.

So I spent five years learning everything about the Colombian and the Mexican drug lords. Operations, logistics, smuggling routes, how they paid their bills, and how they paid off politicians. I learned techniques they used to plot hits on rivals and double-cross their friends, who was married to the daughter of which associate, which of the big boys had a pilot's license or an engineering degree or a fondness for big blondes. I became an expert on all the key players. And we shared the information with DEA, FBI, and other agents in the field.

I was in the unit when Escobar was jailed in Colombia, escaped, and died in a police shootout on December 2, 1993. I learned the names of the Colombians in the Cali cartel who leaped into the void after his death. And it was during my time in the unit that I first heard the name of a man I would hunt for the next two decades: Joaquín Guzmán Loera, "El Chapo."

My introduction to Chapo was a particularly lurid investigation that involved the mass execution of several gangsters by one of Escobar's rival drug runners, a vicious little brute from Sinaloa known as "El Chapo," or "Shorty." Three local policemen who happened to be nearby were rounded up as well, so Chapo had them beheaded. "He was sending a message," a fellow agent told me. The images were seared into my soul. I never forgot the brutality, or the name.

During my five years with the classified unit, I kept my job a secret, even when Monica and I became parents in 1992. After years of trying to have a baby, we decided to adopt a child. It was a long process and at times we thought it would never happen. We had to take weeks of classes. Adoption officials regularly visited our house and interviewed our friends. Monica and I had to write separate letters to prospective birth mothers who would ultimately decide which family would adopt their child. We expressed our deep love for family and friends. I wrote about my passion for sports and all things Notre Dame. We both said we loved music and that Christmas was our favorite time of year—that we started decorating our house and listening to Christmas music in October. When an agency called on December 10, 1992 and said they had a three-month-old boy ready for adoption, we jumped at the opportunity. We only had five days to get ready. Our friends helped us paint and decorate the nursery. We brought our boy home on December 15 and named him Kevin. A steady flow of friends, agents, and neighbors flooded our house all through the Christmas season. It was the beginning of our family.

I found myself wanting to spend more time at home, with family and friends. And my secret job was taking a toll. I talked to Tony all the time, and our families vacationed together every year. But he knew he couldn't press me about my work. My neighbors would ask at cookouts, but I'd shrug my shoulders and just say that I couldn't say. They understood. Still, I felt like I was living a double life, maybe everyone thought I was a spy or a secret hit man! Who knows what the hell they thought? Work is such an important part of life, it's depressing when you can't talk about how you spend so much of your time.

It didn't help that Corcoran left DC in 1994 to take a position in

Miami, and Keefe was about to move to North Carolina to become the ASAC at the DEA's Charlotte office. I had gotten close to them. Both were now urging me to think about moving on. I had spent enough time in the unit. They were right. But where would I go? I couldn't tell anyone what I'd been doing for nearly five years.

Before he left, Keefe had lunch with me in the DEA cafeteria in Washington. We made small talk, but he could tell I was anxious.

"Look, Jack, you need to get back in the field. Where would you like to go?" he asked.

I thought about it for a moment and then blurted out: "Chicago."

Keefe smiled, but didn't say another word about it. What I didn't know was that the DEA's career board was meeting the next morning. There was an opening in Chicago for a group supervisor, and Keefe lobbied the board for me to get the job. A few days after the meeting, I got a call out of the blue. Congratulations, you're headed to Chicago! I was stunned.

I could see Keefe's fingerprints all over it; Corcoran probably played a role, too.

I called and thanked them for their support, then I rushed home to tell Monica. Although we had made good friends in Quantico, she couldn't wait to get home, surrounded by her family and friends. "When do we leave?" she said, grinning from ear to ear.

"Not soon enough," I responded.

In the end, I learned a lot about the way the drug lords operated. I learned from Corcoran and Keefe about the power of sharing information. Now, I was taking everything I'd learned and bringing it home. Where I intended to put it to good use.

CHAPTER 6

BACK WITH A VENGEANCE

I was back in Chicago, my hometown. It was the spring of 1995, and I was now a group supervisor, responsible for fifteen agents. Jim Morgan was the SAC, in charge of the Chicago office, my boss. Chicago DEA hadn't changed much while I was away. The bashed-up furniture was still there, and that awful green carpet. And cocaine was still the biggest drug on the DEA's target list.

Cocaine trafficking didn't end with Escobar's death. The Cali cartel had stepped in without missing a beat. In the classified unit, I had studied the Mexican drug lords' business relationship with the Colombians. A loose group of Mexican traffickers, called the Federation, had been smuggling Colombian cocaine into the United States for decades. Once across the US border, the Colombians kept total control. They cut the cocaine and then sold it in bulk or in nickel and dime bags to anyone who had cash, from small-time street dealers to major distributors. The Colombian cartels viewed the Mexicans as nothing more than glorified mules.

Our intelligence reports, however, revealed that the Mexican drug lords had just started to rewrite the narrative. No longer content to just smuggle dope across the border, they were making bold business moves that would eventually gain them control not only of cocaine, but of the lion's share of all illegal drugs entering the United States. And I knew from my time in the classified unit that the Mexicans were as ruthless as the Colombians.

That's why I was so angry when I found out that my office had dropped the ball on a major drug trafficking investigation.

During my last months in the classified unit in Washington, we had developed information about a Colombian-Mexican cocaine trafficking ring. Los Angeles had long been the hub for both Mexican transportation cells and Colombian cartel operations. Once cocaine was smuggled across the border, it went to Los Angeles. From there, the Mexicans would transport cocaine to Colombian cells in New York and south Florida. But now, it looked like the Mexicans were delivering Colombian cocaine to a Mexican cell in Chicago. At the time, we didn't know why. But we knew it was a major development.

We passed our tip on to our Los Angeles office. Their agents got a court-ordered wiretap and intercepted an incriminating telephone call to a Chicago-based smuggler from one in Los Angeles. Our Los Angeles office shared the information with our Chicago office, but nobody in Chicago acted on the tip.

I didn't know about the fuckup until a few days before I left Washington. That's when my mentor, Keefe, approached me. "Jack, as soon as you get to Chicago, you have to get going on this thing. This is a major, major investigation."

I was stunned. The Chicago office I knew wouldn't drop a ball this big, and I wasn't going to let Keefe down. Within days of arriving in Chicago, I was cleaning up the mess. I told my SAC, Jim Morgan, that I was going to assign my agents to the investigation. I called my counterpart in Los Angeles, David Marzolow, to let him know we wanted to work with his agents.

Then I pulled my investigators into my office.

"Hey, boys, we got something to work on right now," I said.

I told them that some of the key players in a cocaine smuggling ring were in Chicago. We'd have to follow them, collect as much information on them as possible. But we wouldn't arrest them. Not yet. We wanted to see how many people were involved in the organization. And we'd coordinate every move with Los Angeles. We didn't want to do anything to jeopardize the investigation. I said I was going to send two agents to Los Angeles to meet with their investigators. "I want to make sure we have all the latest information and I want to make sure we're talking to them. They're our partners," I said.

Some of my agents grumbled. This was a new way of thinking. So I reemphasized the point: This was a joint operation. No rogue agents or operations. Every lead had to be investigated. Every arrest had to be coordinated.

And I made sure that happened. I stayed on top of everything. I spoke to Marzolow in LA at least once a day and kept my bosses in Washington updated.

Meanwhile, I kept pushing our agents.

It didn't take long for our investigation to start paying dividends. We quickly collected enough information to get a series of court-ordered wiretaps. We assembled an ever-clearer picture of the trafficking ring. We put together a map showing cocaine-smuggling routes northward to Chicago from Colombia and a reverse flow of millions of dollars in cash from drug sales. The investigation got so big that the FBI assigned several agents to the case. They answered to me.

Every day, new intelligence reports landed on my desk. As I talked to agents, reviewed transcripts and studied the documents, I saw a fundamental change in how the Colombians and the Mexicans were doing business. The Colombians had always paid Mexicans in cash to move their cocaine to US markets. But a certain Mexican crime boss named Joaquín "El Chapo" Guzmán Loera was being paid in drugs. Other Mexican drug lords followed suit. Now, Chapo and the other Mexican gangsters had their own supply of cocaine, and were effectively pushing the Colombians out of the US market.

And the Mexicans were taking other steps to boost their market share. Although cocaine entering the United States came from coca plants grown in Colombia, Bolivia, and Peru, Mexican drug lords had built clandestine laboratories to process the drug. They had already cornered the market on marijuana and were processing heroin, too. While the heroin market in the mid-1990s was small compared to that of other drugs, the future was wide open.

All the changes were reflected in the smuggling ring's operations. The Mexicans were stashing Cali cartel cocaine inside the trunks, wheel wells, and other crannies of hundreds of trucks and cars that crossed the US-Mexican border in California, Arizona, and Texas. The cocaine went to wholesale stash houses in Los Angeles, and later was distributed not only to Colombian drug dealers all over the country—but to Mexican ones as well. The Colombians were happy with the arrangement as long as they were making money. In fact, the new business model actually reduced the Colombians' criminal exposure. When the Mexicans expanded into new US markets, they were still selling Colombian cocaine. But now, the Mexicans were taking the risks, not the Colombians.

Sitting at my desk, I stared at that damn name: El Chapo. His payment-in-drugs idea was brilliant. So was this smuggling operation that involved the Cali and Sinaloa cartels. I knew his name from my time in the classified unit, but I still didn't know a lot about the man. DEA didn't think he was a major player. He'd been involved in the murder of the three police officers. He had been in a Mexican prison since 1993 for drug trafficking, murder, and kidnapping, and he was running his criminal empire from inside the joint. Other than that, he was a mystery. In time, I knew I'd learn more about him. But, right now, I had work to do.

The wiretaps revealed that a Chicago man they called the "lawyer," Tomas Gonzales, was the head of the cell, but we couldn't tail him because we didn't have his address. We didn't know where to find him, and we didn't know what he looked like. Our informants said Gonzales dressed and acted like a "respectable businessman." He was the antithesis of the flashy Colombians, who used mountains of cash to buy bright red Ferraris and upscale homes in gated communities. They said Gonzales drove a gray Ford Taurus and never slept in the same house more than two nights in a row.

We had heard his voice on dozens of incriminating calls, but we didn't have the technology in those days to track them to their source. But what we heard was disturbing. Gonzales had a bad temper and routinely threatened his men with violence. On one call, when a thug griped about guarding the stash house, Gonzales snapped: "If you don't stop complaining, I'll cut your fucking balls off and send them to your wife in Mexico."

The wiretaps revealed something else: El Chapo was in charge of the operation. Gonzales talked incessantly about keeping Guzmán happy, referring to him as the "boss on the mountain" or "the short one." Gonzales worried about being late with El Chapo's "money" because "the short one knew where every penny was."

We needed to find Gonzales and the stash house. The wiretaps revealed that he was moving massive amounts of cocaine from there, dope that was going to cities all over the country. We knew he had cash there. And, from my experience, I knew he'd probably have critical records there about the operation. We started putting together a "pattern-of-life analysis" on Gonzales. That was easier said than done. Nowadays, we use cell towers to track a suspect's movements. (The phone signals bounce off the towers, showing where—and at what time—a suspect was at a particular location.) But in 1995, a pattern-of-life analysis was a lot more labor-intensive. There were far fewer cell towers then, and no social media to track a person's movements, no Facebook, Snapchat, or Instagram. A lot of shoe leather was involved, walking around a particular area, asking everyday people who might have dealt with the suspect questions about him—waitresses, barbers, mechanics. We talked to anyone who might have contact with the suspect.

We finally got a break. On a wiretap, Gonzales said he was going to meet a buyer at a Mexican restaurant near Hazel Crest, a blue-collar suburb, about two miles from my childhood home. "I know that place," I told my team. I went along with them. We knew Gonzales drove a gray Taurus. And when we pulled into the parking lot, there it was. So we waited. When a man left the restaurant and jumped in the car, we made our move. He fit the description: The guy was about five-foot-nine, 170 pounds with short black hair and a bushy mustache. But we had to make sure it was him. So when he left the lot, I had one of my cars pull in front of him and slow down. When my car pulled alongside the Taurus, I dialed Gonzales's number. And when I saw him pick up the phone and say hello, we knew we had our guy. Now that we knew what he looked like, we backed off. We didn't want him to know we were tailing him.

After that night, Gonzales disappeared. We had no idea where he was staying. But we knew he was still in Chicago. We monitored his phone calls and shared information with our Los Angeles office. They did the same with us.

Months after we started the investigation, we moved into a new phase. We started picking off members of the ring. We'd have state and local police make the arrests to hide the fact that the Feds were involved. Those arrests helped, because they triggered frantic telephone calls between the traffickers. They all wanted to know what had happened, who was picked up, and where they were stopped. And they usually talked then about new people in the ring, which widened our investigation and helped us build a conspiracy case.

On one call, Gonzales reached out to a Los Angeles–based trafficker called the "doctor." Gonzales said he suspected that law enforcement knew about their operation. He said he was worried that a buyer had flipped and was now "working for the three letters," meaning the DEA. He warned the doctor that they had to be careful.

After that call, I knew it was just a matter of time before we wrapped up the investigation. But we still hadn't located that damn stash house. From the wiretaps, we knew it was somewhere in the Hazel Crest area. But where? I'd spent countless days and nights with my team searching the community.

"It's probably right in front of you," Tony said.

"Yeah, right. We searched everywhere," I said.

Tony wasn't on my team. When I returned to Chicago, I asked for him. But he was working on a case with our financial investigative unit. Still, I ran everything by him.

"Start from the beginning," he suggested. "Look at every house."

He was right. We went back to our informants. I reviewed the transcripts, the reports. It was tedious, painstaking work, but maybe I'd find a clue, something I had overlooked.

In the meantime, a wiretap revealed that one of Chapo's guys had ordered Gonzales to meet another buyer. The meeting would take place in the same Mexican restaurant. The buyer's name didn't ring a bell. So I called Marzolow. He didn't know the guy, either. So we came up with a plan. We'd sit on the place. If we could see who was sitting with Gonzales, we'd have a marked police car stop his vehicle, get his name, and let him go. I got my team together and went over the details.

But things didn't go as planned.

We got to the restaurant just as Gonzales was pulling out of the lot. He was alone. "Dammit," I muttered. The buyer was gone. I was in a car by myself while my team was in vehicles behind me. Instead of regrouping, I decided to tail Gonzales. Maybe he'd lead us to the stash house, I thought.

Gonzales was driving about forty miles an hour, but slowed down as he approached a set of railroad tracks. As I pulled up behind him, I saw flashing red lights and heard warning bells—all signals that a commuter train was coming around the bend. Then Gonzales did something that stunned me. As the crossing gates closed, he accelerated. And stupidly, I did the same. The back end of my car cleared the tracks just seconds before the train roared past. It was a dangerous move, but I didn't want to lose the jagoff. Now I was pissed. I knew the rest of my surveillance team would be stuck, waiting for the train to go by. So I was on my own— and from the wiretaps, we knew Gonzales was heavily armed. I followed Gonzales, who was driving about sixty miles an hour along the narrow two-lane roads. But what he did next was brilliant. Without warning, he screeched to a halt, bounded out of the Taurus, sprinted across the road, and jumped into a red Nissan.

Moments later, he sped by me in the opposite direction. Even though he probably knew I was tailing him, I didn't want him to see me so I ducked below the dashboard as he passed. The chase was over. *This guy is good,* I thought. What I would later learn is that paying attention to small details, such as planning in advance for quick getaways, was a Chapo trademark, something he preached to his lieutenants in the Sinaloa cartel. And that's why, years later, when Chapo was on the run, he always seemed to be a couple of steps ahead of law enforcement.

When I told Tony what happened, he shook his head. "What are you fucking crazy?" he said. I shrugged. "Hey, you would have done the same thing." Tony smiled. He knew I was right.

Meanwhile, we kept looking for the stash house. And a few days before Christmas, we found it through good old-fashioned police work. I had gone back over our wiretaps and interviews with informants. I had a hunch it had to be near that Mexican restaurant. So I decided to stake out the neighborhood near the joint. And one day, out of the blue, we spotted Gonzales in the neighborhood and we followed him until he pulled into a driveway. We had driven by that home a dozen times before. It looked like every other house on the street.

By now, we assumed the stash house was empty, because Mexican drug traffickers usually shut down for Christmas and head to Mexico for the holidays. But then we picked up a call from Gonzales to a man guarding the house. Gonzales told the man to get 250 kilos together. He was at the Mexican restaurant with a buyer.

Bingo! I headed out with my agents to the stash house. It was winter, and we were in Chicago. The roads were covered with ice, and snow had just begun to fall. We slalomed to the stash house in time to see a guy loading cardboard boxes into a white Dodge minivan. During one trip, a box ripped open and ten kilos of cocaine slid down the driveway. We laughed our asses off as the guy chased the dope.

While some of the agents stayed behind to watch the house, I went with another team to the Mexican restaurant where Gonzales was meeting with the buyer. When Gonzales left, we began following him.

Meantime, back at the stash house, the guy finished loading the van and pulled out of the driveway. He was driving along a busy Chicago street, probably on his way to meet his boss. We had the Chicago cops stop him. They pulled him from the minivan and threw him in a police car.

But what we didn't know was Gonzales was only a few cars behind the minivan and saw the stop. He knew something was up. We followed his Taurus to a bar, where he bolted inside with a bag under his arm. I sent in a DEA and an FBI agent. I wanted to know if he was meeting someone. They saw Gonzales hand the bag to an older Mexican guy. After the exchange, the guy left the bar and got into a new gold Cadillac. I got on the phone and had agents tail him. We had our surveillance plane up above to make sure we didn't lose him, but it was snowing so hard, the plane had to land. We lost the Cadillac.

I sent our whole team in to the bar to arrest Gonzales. It was time to end the nonsense. But when they went in, he wasn't there. He had disappeared. Then one of the FBI agents who reported to me asked if she could speak to me in private. She confessed that she had left one of our handheld radios in the bar the first time she went in, and Gonzales must have found it. Until the battery died, he could hear all our radio traffic. He was in the wind. *Are you fucking kidding me?* I thought. I was angry, but what could I do? The damage was already done.

I called Marzolow to let him know what had happened. I added, "I think it's time to we start arresting these dirtbags." He agreed. A few weeks later, we began rounding up key players in Los Angeles, Chicago, and other US cities, including the man Gonzales called the doctor: Jorge Valazquez, a Mexican physician and horse trader.

In Chicago, we got a search warrant for the stash house. We recovered ten guns, 125 kilos of cocaine, and $100,000 in cash. But the most important find: a ledger. The figures in the book were staggering. It showed that a thousand kilos of cocaine and $10 million in cash passed through that house every month.

We didn't publicly disclose the operation until May 1996 because it took months to arrest all the suspects. But when we did, President Bill Clinton praised our work. So did Attorney General Janet Reno. At a news conference, prosecutors and DEA officials, including Morgan, said they broke up a coast-to-coast Mexican-Colombian cocaine smuggling ring. Federal agents had arrested more than 150 people.

"This investigation has driven a stake through the heart of one of the largest, most sophisticated organizations bringing vast quantities of cocaine into the country," US Attorney James B. Burns said at a news conference.

And Burns lauded the way we handled the case. He said the investigation was a significant departure for law enforcement. Usually, they targeted "retail traffickers"—dealers who sold cocaine on street corners. This time, he said, federal, state, and local law enforcement all worked together to get the wholesalers—the big boys, the cartel guys, the folks who owned and transported the cocaine.

I was proud that Burns recognized the wisdom of my approach. I used everything I learned as a street agent, everything I gleaned from Corcoran and Keefe, and absorbed from the classified program in Washington, to help dismantle Chapo's operation. Agents in the office congratulated me. So did Corcoran and Keefe. They knew how hard I'd worked, and how I'd pushed for our office to work closely with Los Angeles and other DEA offices. They saw how I got the FBI and other federal and local agencies involved in the case.

"Another big one. Got any more tricks up your sleeve?" Tony asked.

For me, the most important part of the case wasn't the dope or the people we arrested. It was the information. We learned so much about how they operated in terms of the cells they had in different cities. We didn't know anything about them, and, all of a sudden, we had a big organizational chart on how people like El Chapo worked. We discovered that Gonzales was a new breed of trafficker—a ruthless, but disciplined professional who blended into the community and had deep ties to El Chapo. We never knew that before, but that would help us in the future.

And the investigation revealed that the Mexicans were beginning to dominate the US drug market and that Chicago was becoming a Mexican cartel hub. That's because Chicago itself was a major transportation hub for the United States, and the city had a large Mexican population, so cartel members like Gonzales could hide in plain sight. We uncovered details about the new business plan between the Mexican and Colombian cartels. And there was something else: I discovered that El Chapo—even though he was behind bars—was a powerful figure in the drug world. Back then, my assessment ran counter to most of our intelligence reports.

We later learned that the bag Gonzales had handed to the man in the bar had $1 million inside. Gonzales was never arrested. He managed to escape to Mexico, but not from the wrath of El Chapo, who had lost 250 kilos of cocaine. Gonzales disappeared. His body was never found.

After the big cocaine trafficking bust, my group launched several major operations. We made dozens of high-profile arrests. We kicked ass and I had agents asking to join my team.

But with success came opportunities. After two years in Chicago, I was offered a job as resident agent in charge of the DEA's Milwaukee office. It would be the first time running my own shop. Both Keefe and Corcoran recommended that I take the job because I needed office supervisory experience if I was going to move up in the DEA. So I accepted.

The hardest part was the administrative work. As a street agent I could go to my supervisors and get money for undercover drug deals. I didn't have to worry about anyone except myself. Now, I was *that* guy. I had to handle budgets, evaluations, and scheduling. Not very exciting. But to keep sane, I'd go out with my agents on undercover investigations.

Two years into the job, I got a call from Keefe. He was heading up a new DEA division, a unit that would develop critical information to help agents in the field. My name came up. I was due for a mandatory rotation to headquarters. Would I be interested? I said I needed time to think about it.

I knew the move would be difficult on my family. We had a good lifestyle. We would be leaving behind close friends. But the offer was too good to turn down, especially if I wanted to be a special agent in charge. So I said yes. What I didn't know was that my new job would be the beginning of my long and deadly fight to bring El Chapo to justice.

CHAPTER 7

GET SHORTY

When I arrived in Washington, Keefe briefed me on the elite group I would be joining: Born of the classified project where we'd both served in years past, SOD was built with agents from two dozen federal agencies, including the DEA, FBI, IRS, and ATF. The unit had several dozen employees, and was recruiting more. They worked in a building near Chantilly, Virginia, but they didn't want to publicly disclose the address.

My new job was eerily similar to my old one. Keefe was my boss. I worked for a special DEA unit, but this time in a supervisory role. My office was in a nondisclosed location. And, like my years with the classified project, there's not a lot I can divulge about my time with the DEA's Special Operations Division. The tools and methods we used are still classified.

Over the years, a few stories were told about SOD and the way it operated, suggesting we used illegal surveillance techniques to aid in criminal investigations. That's simply bullshit. I can say this: We legally collected and developed critical information that helped agents investigate Colombian and Mexican drug cartels—organizations that threatened America's security.

SOD agents funneled information legally from intercepts, wiretaps, informants, and a massive database of telephone records. Their findings were forwarded to other DEA offices and federal prosecutors, so we didn't waste resources going after the same bad guys in two or three different cities. What they found went to help authorities either launch or bolster ongoing criminal investigations of domestic and international drug traffickers. When SOD agents discovered connections to current investigations, they advised agents in the field, and field agents were encouraged to contact SOD when they needed more details. But SOD was new, and needed to do a better job promoting itself and building relationships with the field offices. "They should be using us as a resource," Keefe said.

The unit not only analyzed information, it provided money and manpower for big cases. In a multijurisdictional case, SOD agents would go to the field offices involved and sit down with intelligence analysts and agents, gather all the information they could, and feed it into their computers. With luck, they could then paint a picture of the organization and its links in other cities, Keefe said. "We can get an idea of the size and reach of a criminal gang," he said. When we busted Chapo's LA-Chicago smuggling ring in 1995, that case went a long way toward helping SOD map his multijurisdictional network. But the reality was, the true extent of Chapo's influence and operations was only now coming into focus. In the early 1990s, when Guzmán first popped up on the DEA radar, we considered him one of Mexico's most dangerous drug traffickers. But we really didn't know much about him.

During my time at SOD, I made a deep study of El Chapo, and discovered a marketing and logistical genius, a ruthless businessman, a born smuggler, and a truly evil bastard. I used all that information later on to help hunt his ass down.

It was clear to me from the start that Chapo was a much more influential figure than we were giving him credit for. I needed to know everything about Guzmán and his Sinaloa drug cartel. So I read intelligence reports, transcripts of wiretaps, and informant interviews. I turned to an agent in my unit, John "Steven" Comer, who had been following El Chapo's criminal career. I had to separate fact from the fiction. I knew the myth: Guzmán the folk hero, champion of the downtrodden, a rich man who gave poor boys opportunities, a noble peasant who used his fortune to help rural communities in Mexico build schools, hospitals, water systems.

It was all bullshit. Like Pablo Escobar before him, Guzmán was no Robin Hood. He was a criminal, but an enterprising, outside-the-box thinker, a master manipulator, a born businessman. He knew every inch of the border, every gate and ranch and tumbleweed, every old smuggling route through which tires, tequila, or fake-label blue jeans had found their way over the border since forever. He'd studied the maps, gamed the system, bribed the guards. He'd figured it out.

He knew how to tunnel. He knew how to work the lawless parts of Mexico. He moved amazing quantities of drugs over the border, despite our best efforts, and he had a sales network on the other side, too. El Chapo was the most business-savvy sonofabitch who ever ran a criminal organization.

Guzmán was supposedly barely literate, but he was schooled from an early age by some of the best teachers in the trade. His was not the standard curriculum.

He was born in 1957 in a mountain town in Sinaloa state, birthplace of most of Mexico's drug kingpins. His father raised cattle and opium poppies on a patch of poor soil, and in his spare time he beat the crap out of his family. Young Joaquín left home in his early teens. He hired on with a traveling undertaker, but soon tired of chipping gold teeth out of the mouths of the dead.

Other, more lucrative opportunities beckoned. Sinaloa state was a crucial drug trafficking area. For years, narcotics had flowed north through the district from South and Central America to coastal cities and into the United States. Young Chapo realized that he was *enchufado*, connected. His uncle, Pedro Avilés Pérez, was an aviation pioneer of sorts—he was the first smuggler to fly drugs into the United States. He hired his nephew to do odd jobs. Guzmán flew along on drug runs to the US border, soaking up bird's-eye knowledge of roads and checkpoints. He had a head for numbers. He noticed that the peasants up in the hills growing and processing the product were barely surviving. The smugglers made all the money.

Chapo's criminal career really took off when he took a job with Miguel

Ángel Félix Gallardo, known as El Padrino, the Godfather, founder of the Guadalajara cartel. El Padrino showed Chapo the drug trade from the top down. Like Chapo, he didn't have much formal education, but he was a master at moving illegal goods over the border.

And El Padrino was *enchufado*, too. He was a conduit for Pablo Escobar's Medellín cartel. Mexico didn't produce cocaine, but its overland highways gave Colombians an alternative to risky Caribbean routes.

El Padrino was a schmoozer, a former federal cop and bodyguard to the governor of Sinaloa. He attended *quinceañeras*, weddings, and baptisms. He paid off the federal police and backed politicians who looked the other way. He controlled much of the local press. El Padrino's business had three divisions: Production, Finance, and Corruption.

El Chapo moved up fast. In the 1970s he cut his teeth moving a lot of Gallardo's marijuana. It's a challenging job. Marijuana has a shelf life; it's bulky, heavy; and it smells. Guzmán got it over the border in light aircraft, or in tractor trailers with false bottoms. If you can smuggle a load like that, moving a kilo of heroin is a piece of cake.

Guzmán quickly learned the charm, the payoff, the threat of violence, and the violence, too. If you delivered late, he would kill you himself. He gained a reputation for calmly walking up behind his victims and shooting them in the head.

At the same time, El Padrino showed El Chapo the importance of keeping a low profile. When fate finally caught up to him, some of Gallardo's neighbors were shocked to learn he was a drug kingpin. They thought he was a tomato farmer. El Chapo was a low-key scumbag for a long time. He stayed off the radar.

But then everything changed in Mexico's drug world.

In 1985, El Padrino discovered that Enrique Camarena, one of his associates, was an undercover DEA agent. Camarena had burrowed deep into Gallardo's organization and exposed the connections between drug traffickers, Mexican law enforcement, and high-ranking government officials. Camarena and his pilot were soon abducted, tortured, and killed, their bodies thrown into a shallow grave north of Mexico City.

Camarena's murder brought the full fury of a DEA investigation to El Padrino's doorstep. He went into hiding, but his business continued unabated. The United States leaned hard on Mexican law enforcement to find El Padrino, so he decided to divide up his territory, just in case.

At a 1987 meeting with Mexico's top drug traffickers, El Padrino franchised his operation. He would still retain control of the national operation, but day-to-day business would be parceled out to territorial leaders. El Chapo took over the Pacific Coast operation.

Two years later, Gallardo was arrested and sentenced to nearly forty years in prison. By then, Guzmán had built his own syndicate: the Sinaloa cartel.

The Colombian drug cartels were waning in power, and Sinaloa stepped in to fill the void. Chapo took control of the cocaine pipeline between South America and the United States.

Still, that wasn't enough for El Chapo. He tried to grab control of rival cartels that had once been part of the Gallardo empire, triggering a bloody range war. Guzmán targeted the Tijuana cartel, which was led by the Arellano Félix brothers, Gallardo's nephews.

In February 1992, six of Guzmán's top lieutenants were found dead, dumped along a Tijuana highway. Guzmán sent gunmen to a Puerto Vallarta discotheque to kill the Félix brothers. Nineteen people died in the attack, including eight members of the Tijuana cartel. The Félix brothers escaped.

In May 1993, Tijuana cartel gunmen came for Guzmán in an airport parking lot. They killed seven people, including Cardinal Juan Jesús Posadas Ocampa, archbishop of Guadalajara, but Guzmán got away.

A few months later, Guatemalan authorities arrested El Chapo and extradited him to Mexico. He was convicted of murder and drug trafficking, and sentenced to twenty years in Puente Grande, a maximum-security prison.

But Guzmán hung onto his empire, even behind bars.

The first thing Keefe did when I arrived in Washington was put me on a team that tracked Mexican methamphetamine. I was a little disappointed. I wanted to go after the high-profile drugs, but Keefe knew what he was doing. He knew methamphetamine was the new wave rolling into the United States. And he knew Chapo was a player.

By now, Chapo and his Sinaloa cartel already controlled most of the cocaine, marijuana, and heroin being smuggled and sold in the United States. Now, he was investing heavily in methamphetamine.

So I learned everything I could about methamphetamine: how it was manufactured, shipped, and distributed, as well as the key players involved in meth trafficking. At the time, the highly addictive drug was mostly known as "hillbilly heroin," a Midwest drug made in mom-and-pop, stovetop operations. But that was changing, thanks to El Chapo.

By the time we had cracked the LA-Chicago smuggling ring, he had been expanding his drug empire from the safety of a Mexican prison for several years. His deputies bribed the guards and prison officials, so Chapo received conjugal visits, computer and telephone access, and catered meals. Prison protected him from the dangers of the outside world. He was safe. No one could get to him while he was in prison.

And now here I was, sitting at my desk, reading the latest intelligence reports, frustrated as hell. Chapo's name seemed to be on every page.

"Can you believe this guy?" I asked Comer, my staff coordinator.

"Who?"

"El Chapo."

"Whatever it is, I can believe it," he said.

A sharp, soft-spoken guy, Comer was tall and wiry, with thinning white hair and a matching white goatee. Like Keefe, he wore fashionable suits and neatly pressed shirts. Not a thread out of place. When we went out, he never took off his suit jacket. I'd bust his balls about that all the time. He was a foil for me. I was the hothead, and he was the gentleman. I never heard Comer raise his voice.

He had transferred into SOD from our Los Angeles office. He had witnessed Chapo's takeover and domination of the southern California methamphetamine market. He was sure it was only a matter of time before Chapo's business acumen, logistical skills, and highly disciplined criminal network succeeded in flooding the nation with crystal meth, ice, crank—whatever you want to call it.

"So how do we stop him?" I asked.

Comer said he had been thinking hard about that. He said we not only had to target the cartels and find their giant methamphetamine laboratories, we had to go after the chemical companies that produced the base ingredients. Hold them accountable.

Good idea, I said. I knew the antihistamine pseudoephedrine was a key ingredient in any homemade methamphetamine recipe. The DEA had asked retailers to keep any cold and flu medicine with the ingredient behind the drugstore counter, but that wasn't working. So why not target companies selling pseudoephedrine and the other chemicals used to produce methamphetamine? And why stop there? We could target companies that sold laboratory equipment needed to build and stock drug factories. Would it work? We didn't know. But it was worth a shot.

We ran the idea by Keefe. He gave us the green light and asked for updates. Sources said many of the big methamphetamine laboratories were in California. We just had to find them. People were buying chemicals in different parts of the country and somehow getting them to the clandestine locations. We didn't have the manpower to sit outside chemical companies and follow their trucks all over the country, so we began contacting chemical brokers, the middlemen who bought and sold chemicals for manufacturers.

I knew all the ingredients, and how they were used to "cook" methamphetamine. Ether, for example, is an important cooling agent, but it isn't added until the end of the process. So we started by looking for West Coast ether suppliers who shipped large quantities of the stuff. If we could find the suppliers, we could build enough probable-cause evidence to get a court-ordered wiretap for their phones. That could lead us to the people buying ether for the drug traffickers. And it could get us closer to locating the methamphetamine laboratories.

After some prodding, the brokers began turning over chemical company manifests. And we immediately saw suspicious activity. "What the fuck is this guy doing with ten barrels of ether in a week?" I said to Comer. "Let's start on that." Without the broker's help, we wouldn't have found that nugget. We would have been lost.

We reached out to federal prosecutors. We had to educate them about methamphetamine and what we were trying to do. This wasn't like targeting a guy on a dope-dealing case; the suspect was buying legal chemicals from a legitimate company. We had to explain the connection between the buyer and the drug traffickers, the long chain of transactions. It wasn't easy. We hit some roadblocks.

At one point I asked Keefe to intercede, and he called on his old buddy Robert Mueller. In the 1980s, long before he was FBI director and then appointed special counsel to investigate whether Russia interfered in the 2016 US presidential election, Mueller worked with Keefe in Boston, where Keefe was a DEA agent and Mueller a federal prosecutor. They stayed in touch, even when Mueller left twice to go into private practice. (He gave up the big money both times because he missed being a prosecutor.)

Keefe reached out on my behalf to Mueller, who was then the US attorney in northern California. I was coordinating a methamphetamine case involving a less-than-upright chemical company. We had taken down several methamphetamine labs, and the chemicals used in their processes all came from the same California business. We only had to read the name on the labels.

I told Keefe that DEA field agents and the SOD attorneys couldn't get Mueller's office to work with us. "Don't worry about it, I'll set up a meeting," Keefe said. The next thing I knew, Keefe called me into a meeting in Washington, and Mueller was sitting right there. I had no idea Mueller was coming.

I explained to Mueller what evidence we had. "Sir, we need to go after this company. They're supplying the chemicals for meth labs in California and beyond," I told him. He understood, and promised to take care of it right away.

About a week later, I got a call from one of his attorneys, asking if I'd be willing to work with them. "Of course," I said, and the next day, Comer and I were on our way to San Francisco. I saw Mueller briefly before the meeting with his attorneys. He shook my hand and said, "It's funny how things somehow work out, isn't it?" The relationship was a fruitful one.

It was a hectic time. I was so tied up with methamphetamine cases that I was working longer and longer hours. I was on the road more than ever. Monica was great. She didn't complain, but I could see that it was taking a toll on her. We bought a nice house in Fairfax Station, Virginia. But, as before, she had to make new friends and find a school for Kevin. The two of them didn't see much of me, and when I was home, my phone didn't stop ringing.

But the hard work was paying off. Through our dogged research, DEA offices launched more and more methamphetamine investigations. And in one high-profile case, called Operation Mountain Express, we smashed a major drug smuggling and distribution ring that sold common cold tablets for conversion to methamphetamine.

The smugglers, the majority of whom were from the Middle East, purchased barrels of pseudoephedrine pills in Canada and transported them to the United States, mainly through Detroit. From there the pills were sold to methamphetamine laboratories in California and Mexico. The distribution ring was headed by ten people whom I called the "Commission." They shipped their profits home to the Middle East—and possible terrorist organizations.

By the time the investigation was over, we had arrested 160 people, searched dozens of locations, and used civil and administrative enforcement actions to close down pseudoephedrine operations at eighteen companies.

I had spent nearly two years on Operation Mountain Express, as well as others involving Mexican methamphetamine. But just before we announced the arrests, Keefe told me I was headed to St. Louis, to become the assistant special agent in charge there. Corcoran would be my boss. It was a pleasant surprise. I looked forward to working with him again.

As I was saying my good-byes to Comer and other friends in the office,

I watched the DEA's news conference about the bust. And there was Keefe's mug on the TV screen.

"This was the first time that US law enforcement has been able to connect a major group of pseudoephedrine distributors directly to US-based, Mexican-controlled methamphetamine laboratory operators," Keefe said.

Attorney General Janet Reno echoed his words.

"The operation should have a significant impact on methamphetamine trafficking in the United States by limiting the availability of pseudoephedrine and deterring others who might be considering the illicit diversion of chemicals and pharmaceuticals," she said.

Reno was too optimistic.

What we didn't know then was that El Chapo, like a grandmaster chess player, was already thinking five moves ahead. He had studied the market, the product, and the supply chain. And in 2005, when the Combat Methamphetamine Epidemic Act took effect, he laughed all the way to the bank. American lawmakers ruled that any cold and flu medicine containing pseudoephedrine must be kept behind the drugstore counter and sold only to adults with ID. Buyers were registered in a computer system that tracked their consumption.

Chapo saw it coming. He bought up industrial quantities of pseudoephedrine from China, and set up his own chain of clandestine methamphetamine laboratories in Mexico. He controlled the product from start to finish—no crop cycles, no bulky, smelly packages, no Colombians. And a bottomless market. Brilliant.

While I was at SOD I focused on developing strategies and collecting intelligence to fight Mexican methamphetamine, to prevent it from taking hold in US cities. But little did I know that, in St. Louis, I'd confront the devastating impact the drug had on families in small towns and big cities across the Midwest. Those are images seared into my memory.

CHAPTER 8

ST. LOUIS BLUES, 2000

The methamphetamine crisis followed me to St. Louis. Corcoran and fellow agents there said it was unusual, as this new wave of drugs wasn't so much an urban phenomenon, but a rural one. I already knew why methamphetamine had become so popular in small towns and villages in Missouri. It yielded a cheap, intense high. You could find it in just about every flyspeck on the map. If you couldn't, it was easy to make. You could get most of the ingredients at local hardware and drugstores. It was the perfect drug for rural areas where the hard stuff—cocaine and heroin—was difficult to find. The only essential ingredient was pseudoephedrine, or its cousin, ephedrine, which were found in many cold medicines. And stovetop meth labs were easy to hide in the countryside. In 2000, on the prairies outside St. Louis, a great number of the mobile homes scattered on wide lots in rural townships were nothing more than do-it-yourself meth labs.

I knew methamphetamine wasn't a new drug. It had been around for a generation. During World War II, military leaders on both sides used it as a stimulant to enhance their soldiers' endurance and ward off fatigue on long campaigns. In the 1950s, it was prescribed as a diet aid. Easily available, methamphetamine was used by college students, truck drivers, and others. But with widespread use, abuse followed. In 1970, the US government made it illegal for most uses.

After that, motorcycle gangs controlled the vast majority of illegal methamphetamine production and distribution throughout the United States. Slowly, methamphetamine gained a foothold in rural communities in the Midwest and parts of the South and West, mainly because it was a cheap alternative to harder drugs that were often difficult to find and too costly in those remote areas.

Methamphetamine came in a white powder, or a solid, crystalline form that looked like shards of glass or clear-white rocks. It could be snorted, injected, or smoked. But smoking it quickly elevated methamphetamine levels in the brain, giving users a rapid, intense high, making it both more addictive and potentially more harmful.

By the early 1990s, it was the drug of choice in many rural communities. And that's when thousands of do-it-yourself meth labs began popping up to meet the growing demand, creating an army of addicts—and a new business venture for Chapo and the Mexican cartels.

"You're getting here at the right time," Corcoran told me. Missouri was an early epicenter of the methamphetamine epidemic that eventually reached all parts of the nation.

Corcoran had been in charge in St. Louis for nearly two years. When he took over, he said they didn't handle many methamphetamine cases. Now, methamphetamine had spread into all the old Bible belt towns where unemployment was high and social services and hospitals were overrun. Kids were dropping out of school, babies were born addicted. The fundamental social structures in these largely agricultural communities were unraveling. Agents were spending most of their time knocking down mom-and-pop meth labs in rural Missouri. And they were facing a new threat: El Chapo. He was beginning to flood the region with imported methamphetamine, exacerbating the crisis.

"Jack, this is bad," he said, shaking his head. "There are meth addicts in every corner of the state. It's an epidemic."

Corcoran had been my mentor for years. I knew him as a brash, confident guy. But I could tell he was frustrated. His reaction surprised me. If he was this concerned, it had to be bad.

"I'm going to jump on it," I said.

At first, it was a little bit of a juggling act. I had to make sure my family was settled. My sister Barbara lived in St. Louis, and so did one of Monica's college friends, Jill. We bought a house on a tree-lined street that was only a short distance from my office. We sent my son to Ste. Genevieve du Bois, a good Catholic school. He was into basketball and was getting pretty good at it. With everything in place, I threw myself into my job.

One of the first things I did was look for Joe Cronin, a young agent Corcoran wanted me to meet.

"He reminds me of a young Jack Riley," Corcoran said.

"I'm not that old! I'm only forty-two," I reminded him.

"Yeah, but he's a lot younger than that," he joked.

I found Cronin sitting at his desk, staring at his computer screen. He was a thin baby-faced guy with short brown hair, in his early thirties. Joe Average.

"You got a minute?" I asked.

He looked up. "Sure."

He followed me into my office and I closed the door. "Joe speaks highly of you. And if he feels that way, something tells me we're going to get along," I said. "Tell me about yourself."

Cronin came from the South Side of Chicago. He'd been a geologist before he joined the agency in 1996. He said he'd wanted a change, and boy did he get it! The DEA wasn't exactly what he thought it would be. Cronin was a numbers guy who wanted to bring down international criminal networks, narco-traffickers, money launderers, and drug smugglers. But here he was in rural Missouri, knocking down mom-and-pop meth labs.

I liked what I heard. Cronin was aggressive and articulate, but it seemed nobody had taken any particular interest in him. He needed a mentor. I told him the small operations were important if only for collecting information to build bigger cases. Otherwise, they were a waste of time and resources.

I told him the DEA was in the middle of a crisis. "I'm going to need your help," I said.

I relayed the same message to my other agents. I sensed that many of them were overwhelmed by the sheer number of cases on their desks. I needed to remind them why they'd joined the DEA in the first place. We had to do a better job of explaining our mission, and energizing the team by actually achieving it. We'd all have to work together, shake things up, if we were going to deal with methamphetamine, much less the other drugs plaguing the heartland.

I went to Corcoran. "We need to make some changes," I said. The building itself needed updating, to reflect the scope of our work and enable the free flow of information. We had only two computer stations in one closet-sized room. Our intercept rooms, where agents listened to recordings of wiretap conversations, were dank, airless booths. The DEA agents rarely mingled with people from the other federal agencies, much less state and local police. That had to change.

"We have to think big and act big if we're going to get a handle on this crisis," I said. That would send the right message not only to our agents, but to our federal law enforcement partners in the St. Louis field offices, which covered the entire state of Missouri and southern Illinois.

"How will you do that?" Corcoran asked.

"A task force," I said. "Let's bring together federal, state, and local law enforcement. We can get funding from the DEA's Organized Crime Drug Enforcement Task Force to identify all the major criminal groups operating in the area. With our own task force in place, we could use the OCDETF money to update our technology, expand those intercept rooms, and buy the communications devices we need to try to link together all these organizations and eventually bring them down."

Corcoran gave me the green light to start making changes. I began telling my agents that I didn't care about metrics. If we did our job, if we focused on the criminal syndicates, the statistics would follow. I took a hands-on approach, especially with the younger agents. I walked around the office, reviewed all their cases, read all their reports, and offered suggestions. I'd always say, "What about this?" or "Did we try that?" or "How about we do a wire on that?" I encouraged them to go undercover, signed off on funding for them. Undercover was the best way to cultivate confidential informants, the people who provide critical information on criminal enterprises.

I glad-handed, cajoled, and bullied the state and local law enforcement agencies into a task force. The St. Louis police were dealing with an increase in drug-related murders, so I brought them into the wire room so we could build cases together. If gang members were killing each other over drugs, I knew a cartel was likely involved, because El Chapo and the Sinaloa cartel were recruiting gangs all over the country to sell their dope.

Meanwhile, Cronin became my go-to guy. He followed me around, just as I had done with Corcoran back in Chicago. He was smart as a whip and understood how to use new technology to catch the bad guys.

It took a little time, but the entire division became energized. The change happened at a perfect time.

When I got there, the St. Louis DEA office had a celebration if they arrested a few dealers selling meth in a trailer park. We could do better than that, I told them. We started tracing the imported methamphetamine in St. Louis to its source back in Mexico and learned all the steps and stops in between. We started using our techniques to build cases. I had to make clear to the US attorney's office and several more agencies the scope and significance of this. If we wanted to take out the entire distribution network, we had to step back and take the thirty-thousand-foot view.

I went out with agents on undercover operations and raids. It's one thing to sit at a desk reading reports, passing on leads to agents in field offices. It's another to be out on the street. I saw the impact drugs had on communities in Chicago when I was an undercover street agent. I bought dope from everyone: Irish guys, black gang members, Italian organized-crime enforcers. I saw some bad shit. But it was nothing compared to the devastation I witnessed in down-home Missouri.

I went into homes where Granny and Grandpa were stoned out on the sofa, the baby crawling around on a chemical-soaked rug, while the kids were out back cooking up a new batch. Three generations, and everybody hooked, their lives and minds ruined. As Corcoran said, it was a mess.

And I was angry.

It would be easy to place all the blame on El Chapo and the cartels. They knew Americans had an insatiable appetite for the drug. So they exploited it. Yes, I hated Guzmán and his thugs. But a lot of my anger was directed at Washington—the policy makers and even some DEA officials. They didn't understand the devastating impact meth was having on so many communities. Maybe, it was because methamphetamine hadn't spread east of the Mississippi River. Maybe, it was because some senator's son wasn't hooked. Whatever the reason, Washington believed it was a local issue, best handled by the states with some assistance from the DEA. In essence, we were setting ourselves up to play whack-a-mole—hit a mom-and-pop meth lab here, hit a do-it-yourself meth lab there. I kept telling my bosses that we needed a bigger strategy because we were now dealing with Chapo and Sinaloa. It was a whole new ballgame. We weren't dealing with mom-and-pop dealers or scumbag bikers. We were dealing with a criminal mastermind.

Nothing illustrated that more than a case that came to us from Tucson, Arizona. An informant told our agents that an American horse breeder was going to pick up a trailer with a thousand pounds of marijuana in Tucson and drive it to St. Louis. (The informant was a high-ranking Sinaloa plaza boss—the guy who controls the shipments of dope smuggled across a section of the border.) When our agents stopped the horse breeder, he flipped. But he was worried. He had to be in St. Louis in a day and time was running out. If he wasn't there, he said the deal would be off—and his bosses would be suspicious. So I got the Arizona National Guard to fly his pickup truck and trailer to St. Louis in a C-130.

When we got to St. Louis, the guy was supposed to call the buyers to let them know where to pick up the trailer. I had him park on a downtown street, just in case my guys had to watch it all night. After he parked, he unhooked the trailer and drove to a nearby location where we were waiting. When he called, he said he couldn't reach anyone. I just had a bad feeling about the guy, like he was trying to scuttle the deal. We waited a day and no one showed up. Something didn't feel right and I didn't want to burn our informant in Tucson. So I had two St. Louis cops with a drug-sniffing dog walk by the abandoned trailer. They made the seizure so no one would know the Feds were involved. In fact, the cops called the media to let them know they had seized $500,000 worth of marijuana—just so Chapo would think the cops got lucky.

When we searched the load, we were stunned. We found about twelve pounds of pure methamphetamine hidden inside the bales. The weed was a cover. And we discovered something else: Our informants told us that Chapo was giving away the methamphetamine to grab a bigger share of the market. His goal was to get addicts to buy his dope—which was much stronger than the typical mom-and-pop shit—and to get new people hooked.

I told Washington what we were facing. I told them what I was hearing from the rural sheriffs. At meetings, the sheriffs said they were worried about the cartels. They'd say, "You know that car you stopped on the interstate that had fifteen pounds of meth in it? Do you know how long it would take these mom-and-pop operations to make fifteen pounds?" I understood. It would take months for stovetop operations to produce fifteen pounds. But Chapo? It might take one of his labs a few hours. The sheriffs knew what was coming. I knew what was coming, too. So with Washington turning a blind eye, I became more determined than ever to use every tool at my disposal to shut them down.

On January 19, 2001, the fight against Chapo and his cartel got that much harder. I couldn't believe it, but I shouldn't have been surprised. I strode into Corcoran's office and told him what he already knew: El Chapo had escaped from prison. I was pissed. "How the hell did that happen?" I asked.

He didn't know. Neither did Keefe or anyone else in the DEA. Guzmán escaped from a maximum-security prison in a laundry basket. *A laundry basket?* He had to have help from the guards, I told Corcoran. It's not like it was a real prison. Guzmán owned the guards. The warden. He owned everything. The only thing he couldn't do was leave. But that was OK. He brought the party to his cell—women, food, entertainment. He did it while building his empire, by killing his rivals and increasing his market share. Savvy guy.

His getaway was big news in Mexico, but it was barely mentioned in the United States. No one cared. The big news was that President Clinton avoided indictment in the Monica Lewinsky scandal, just as George W. Bush was ready to be inaugurated as the next president. That was the problem, in my view. No one outside of federal law enforcement knew the name *El Chapo.* Hell, most people in federal law enforcement didn't know it, either. I can't tell you how many colleagues had no clue who Guzmán was or what he did; that he was one of the biggest drug lords in the world; that he controlled much of the cocaine, heroin, marijuana, and methamphetamine flowing into the United States. Now he was free. There was so much damn corruption in Mexico that he might never get caught. If he could run his cartel from a jail cell, imagine what he could do on the outside.

I was in a bad mood. I called Tony. "Can you believe it?"

"Yeah. Did you really think he was going to stay in jail forever? He could see the handwriting on the wall," he said.

Tony was right. He was comfortable in prison as long as there was no threat of extradition to the United States, where he was charged with drug trafficking. Under intense pressure from the United States, Mexico was starting to bend. Chapo knew that. It was time to leave, so he climbed into the laundry cart and rode to freedom.

"There's going to be a range war down there," I told Tony. El Chapo on the loose would destabilize the narcotics economy. Chapo would probably seek revenge against his rivals, who would likewise be looking to settle old scores. I prayed I was wrong, but I didn't see any way to avoid bloodshed unless someone captured Guzmán right away. And that wasn't going to happen.

The sad fact was, as long as the violence stayed on the other side of the border, most Americans wouldn't give a damn. But once it spread to US soil, people would look for someone to blame. That's when El Chapo would become visible.

I was driving to work when my cell phone rang. It was Monica, in tears. My heart skipped a beat. I thought something had happened to Kevin.

"Did you see it?" she sobbed.

"What are you talking about?"

"The planes. They slammed into the World Trade Center. We're under attack."

I didn't know what she was talking about. I tried to calm her down. "Let me get to the office and find out what's going on," I said.

I turned on my car radio and there was live coverage on every station: Airplanes had slammed into the Twin Towers. Then another plane had crashed into the Pentagon. And then a fourth plane crashed in a remote Pennsylvania field. I couldn't believe what I was hearing.

In the office, it was worse than I'd imagined. The images were heartbreaking: Thick black smoke billowing from the Twin Towers. The Pentagon on fire. I was concerned, but I didn't want to scare Monica. I called her back and told her it was probably a terrorist attack, but we had the situation under control. "Make sure you and Kevin stay inside," I said, not knowing what was coming next.

Meanwhile, all air traffic was ordered to land. I sent our agents to airports in our division to help the FBI board the planes. Some of the small airports had several large craft sitting on runways. Washington ordered us to show a presence on the grounded aircraft, not only to look for possible terrorists, but to reassure passengers that law enforcement was on the job.

Corcoran was beside himself. The World Trade Center was in his city, his hometown. He kept in touch with his old friends there. He probably knew people inside the Twin Towers. Like so many other Americans that day, everyone in our office wanted to help. We wanted to do something. But what?

That afternoon we had a conference call with leadership and were given the latest news and direction.

I was stunned when I realized what was happening here: The agencies created to keep us safe were not sharing intelligence, not connecting the dots. Later, investigators confirmed that federal agencies had information that could have prevented the terrorist attacks, but they didn't pass it on to those who could act on it. I promised myself I was never going to let that happen in DEA. Not if I could help it.

I also knew this was a wake-up call. We relied too much on electronic surveillance. We had to get back to the street, developing informants and doing undercover work to figure out how these criminal organizations operated from the ground up. I knew Chapo was probably watching. He and the terrorists knew that cops don't always talk to cops, and the holes in our security network were big enough to fly a jumbo jet through. We had to do better.

We had more than enough drug cases to keep us busy, terror attacks notwithstanding. But methamphetamine was never off our radar. And no matter how many methamphetamine laboratories we dismantled or drug traffickers we arrested or criminal organizations we busted, nothing seemed to stop the drug from spreading into more and more communities.

"Is there anything we're missing, anything we're not doing?" I asked Cronin. He shook his head no. We were in overdrive. Imagine what this place would be like if we weren't being aggressive, Cronin said. El Chapo had an endless supply and overwhelming demand for his product. It was the perfect storm.

In September 2004, I was awakened in the middle of the night by a Missouri Highway Patrol trooper who had heard me speak at a town hall meeting in Franklin County. He had just been called to what remained of a little roadside motel just outside Kirksville. The place had literally exploded, and two bodies were found inside a rented room, severely burned in the explosion. The trooper thought that it might have been a makeshift meth laboratory. The chemicals used to make the drug are extremely combustible.

I sent agents to the scene, and they found that the trooper was right. The hotel room was an active methamphetamine laboratory, with ether canisters a hundred yards from the hotel, and drug-cooking equipment in the kitchenette. We were lucky. The explosion could have killed people in other rooms or at a gas station nearby. But what scared me the most was that the cooks were undocumented Mexicans. My first thought was that perhaps Chapo was moving some of his laboratories to Missouri.

We kept the case from the press and found that the two dead guys had been setting up labs in motel rooms in other rural towns. Was this a trial run for Chapo? Was cooking meth right in the heart of addiction country a way of getting his product closer to consumers? I hoped not. But with El Chapo you didn't know. We were always a step behind.

Rural Missouri's high addiction rates garnered national attention, and the media began parachuting in. In 2005, I got a request from *Good Morning America*, saying that correspondent Chris Cuomo wanted to do a piece on methamphetamine in the heartland. Cronin said we should bring Cuomo along when we busted a local methamphetamine laboratory. We could show him up close what we do and how the drug quickly turns people into addicts. I agreed to take the reporter for a ride-along. We had been planning to take down another laboratory in a mobile home, so the timing was good.

I briefed Cuomo on the operation and the dangers. I told him he'd have to wear a Kevlar vest, just in case. As we drove through the rural landscape, I explained how methamphetamine had destroyed hundreds of families here, and that El Chapo was responsible for most of the drugs coming into the area.

As our cars pulled up to the house, I told Cuomo to stay down. There might be a family in the house, or guns, or explosives. Anything could happen. When our main entry team bounded out of their cars and breached the front door, the "cook" left his wife, parents, and two young children in the front room, bolted to the bedroom, and barricaded the door. Something bad was about to happen.

I glimpsed at Cuomo. "Stay here," I warned him, before jumping out of the car and walking toward the house. As I approached an open bedroom window, I saw the cook holding a gun. Luckily, he was facing the door, not the window. I pulled out my weapon, stuck it through the opening, and pointed it at him. "If you don't drop the fucking gun and turn around with your hands up, I'm going to put a couple of rounds through your head," I said calmly.

The guy dropped his weapon and turned to face me just as three big-ass DEA agents knocked the door down. The door, along with the agents, landed on top of the guy, who literally shit in his pants. It was a scene straight from a cop show. I was just glad I didn't have to take him to jail in my car.

On the way back to the office, I explained to Cuomo the significance of a bust like this one. We would gather information from the scene that could help with ongoing drug trafficking investigations.

And while this mom-and-pop operation wasn't connected to Chapo, it was helping his business, I said. That's because this little house created new addicts. And those people would now turn to Guzmán for dope. The Combat Methamphetamine Epidemic Act had just taken effect, and now any cold and flu medicine containing pseudoephedrine would be kept behind the drugstore counter and sold only to adults with ID. Buyers were registered in a computer system that tracked their consumption.

Mom-and-pop operations were about to go out of business, but we knew Chapo had already bought up industrial quantities of pseudoephedrine from China. He had been building methamphetamine laboratories in Mexico for years.

"Now Chapo is really going to corner the meth market," I told Cuomo.

As far as the raid, my agents found twenty guns in the house, as well as explosives. The two children were removed to the care of the state. They tested positive for methamphetamine. Meanwhile, the house was condemned and torn down.

* * *

I knew that, sooner or later, I might get the call. It came in the spring of 2007. My boss in Washington, Michele Leonhart, said she was "strongly suggesting" that I consider an important post: SAC of El Paso. After twenty years, I'd be running my own territory, a border office—one of the largest in the DEA. I'd worked so hard for this. So why did I feel like shit?

Both personally and professionally, just about everything in my life was going smoothly. Federal, state, and local police routinely worked together with us to bring down big drug traffickers. We were still trying to get a handle on methamphetamine. The epidemic had spread all over the nation and, with more education and law enforcement awareness, we were seeing fewer laboratories in rural areas. But no matter what we did, we were always a step behind Chapo. Fewer mom-and-pop meth labs meant more customers for him. He now controlled 80 percent of the methamphetamine market in the United States. But it looked like he was branching out again. We were seeing more and more high-grade heroin on the streets and I suspected that Chapo was behind it. If that was true, Chapo was capable of creating a new generation of heroin addicts. How many more lives would be ruined before he was caught? It kept me up at night.

Cronin was still my right-hand man, making suggestions about new initiatives to go after the bad guys. Corcoran retired, and we gave him a big send-off. Just about every agent who ever worked for him showed up for the party. Keefe had stepped down, too. They were my mentors, but both of them had put enough years into the agency. They wanted to try to enjoy their lives. I didn't know how you could do that, not with everything we saw on the job. At times, we encountered the worst of humanity. Fieldwork and wiretaps exposed the dark side—with corruption and executions. How do you forget that?

At home, my relationships with Monica and Kevin were the focal point of my life. Kevin had become a good shooting guard. He loved basketball. A few years earlier, I had coached his fifth-grade basketball team to the city championship, and he was the MVP. The team's success was a big deal for Kevin's little Catholic school. The stands were packed with cheering fans.

I was worried how Monica and Kevin would react to the El Paso news. My family had lived in St. Louis longer than anywhere else. We finally had stability. Now, I was going to uproot them to go to El Paso? I knew it was a dark, violent place.

In the years since his escape, El Chapo had consolidated his grip on the drugs being smuggled into the United States. And, as I predicted, he did it with violence. The cartels were engaged in a bloody range war, opening fire on one another with no regard for anyone standing nearby. Tens of thousands of people had been murdered in Mexico since then, many of them innocents. My office would be right across the Rio Grande from Ciudad Juárez—the deadliest city in Mexico.

Leonhart didn't say I had to take the post. But I know I really didn't have a say. She said they needed someone like me in El Paso, someone with SOD experience, someone who had been on the front lines in the methamphetamine wars. A consensus builder. "You'd be perfect," she said.

Right, I thought. *But my family will kill me.*

I dreaded telling Monica, and her response was just what I'd expected. She fought back tears. She reminded me how Kevin was thriving. He'd made a lot of friends, and so had we—our lively social life revolved around our little church, the school, and Kevin's sports.

Kevin had just graduated from eighth grade and was looking forward to starting high school in the fall. He had great friends, even a nice girlfriend.

Monica was devastated. She didn't want to leave St. Louis. And then there was Kevin.

Our boy had been too young to really remember the earlier moves, but this would be the first to make a real impact on him personally.

Monica paused for a moment.

And then she reluctantly said she'd go. I could see her pain and I felt miserable. I didn't know how I would ever be able to make it up to her. We told Kevin, and his crestfallen response just about killed me. I thought about leaving the two of them in St. Louis while I worked in El Paso. I'd just commute, go home once or twice a month. But we nixed that idea. Our family needed to stay together.

I talked to Corcoran, Keefe, and Comer. They all agreed that an SAC position on the border would be a great career move, but they'd understand if I didn't take it.

Tony's take was a little different. The DEA wanted him to transfer to Washington. But he was going to retire rather than uproot his family. "I can't do that, Jack. I've got twenty years in. I won't do that to my kids. I'll find something else to do," he told me. Tony understood how much I loved my work. He knew I didn't want to leave the DEA. Not yet. I still had too much work to do.

I wanted to get El Chapo. He had become my white whale. No, I couldn't stop now. I was selected for the job. It was one of the most difficult decisions in my life. I had made many wonderful friends in St. Louis, and accomplished just about everything I could there. I had fought El Chapo from afar. Now, I was going after him at ground zero, the border. This was going to get personal.

CHAPTER 9

NEW SHERIFF IN TOWN, 2007

As El Chapo eliminated his rivals and consolidated his power after his 2001 prison break, the violence got worse. The Mexican government tried to rein it in. In 2004, the army learned that Chapo was throwing a big party in La Tuna, his hometown. Helicopters swooped down on the ranch where Chapo was hiding out, but he managed to escape through the hills. The same year, two hundred soldiers raided a ranch nearby, and Guzmán got away with a few minutes to spare. President Felipe Calderón in 2006 even moved the military into Ciudad Juárez, to try to stabilize it, but it didn't work. He had a few heroes on hand: General Rolando Hidalgo Eddy seized dozens of planes and vast quantities of opium and marijuana. Chapo answered by dumping the body of an informant outside Eddy's headquarters. The note attached warned Eddy to back off.

Now, in the summer of 2007, Chapo had been free for six years, and the law was still chasing him around Mexico.

He emerged a week before I arrived in El Paso, when he married an eighteen-year-old beauty queen, Emma Coronel Aispuro. He invited all the local police chiefs and magistrates to the wedding. The Mexican military arrived with helicopters and troops, but once again, Guzmán was gone.

Informants said he was holed up on the Sierra Madre of Sinaloa, but exactly where, no one could say. He was always one step ahead of the law. He seemed to enjoy this cat-and-mouse, Billy the Kid shit.

At one time, Guzmán was more like his mentor, El Padrino, content to live in a shack deep in the mountains, shunning the flashy narco lifestyle. Nightclubs and discos? No. Chapo was rarely seen in public. But now he was taking more risks. Maybe he felt safe, now that he had an army of his own, and all that money, and a young bride to keep happy. *Forbes* magazine said Chapo was a billionaire. But what good was being a billionaire if you couldn't go out and spend your money? As I prepared for my new job, I knew we had to find him soon. I was worried about what he would do next.

It was my first day on the job, so I "dressed to impress." I jammed my feet into a pair of brand-new cowboy boots, too shiny and a half-size too small, a gag gift from a couple of cops I had worked with in St. Louis. They'd thought it was funny as hell, a gringo from the Midwest going down to run the border office. I was going to have blisters by the end of the day, but everybody in Texas wears cowboy boots, right?

It was July 7, 2007, my first day as the SAC in El Paso. I wanted to show my agents that I was willing to fit in. And these weren't ordinary cowboy boots. These were handmade, mahogany-tone Ropers.

Boss boots. Serious shit-kickers.

I tucked a white button down into my Levis and knotted my green tie. I slipped my brown belt with the engraved Notre Dame buckle through the loops of my pants and ran my fingers through my hair.

I was ready.

Monica was standing in the kitchen with Rudi, our old Bernese Mountain dog, staring out the back window over miles of scrub, sand, and cactus. No trees. Nothing green to be seen.

"I think we landed on the moon," she said.

She was still depressed about leaving St. Louis, and the new landscape only reminded her of what we had left behind. There, we'd lived on a tree-lined street with a big, grassy yard like a moat around the house. Now we had a desert in the back, and a scabby little tree and a gravel garden out front. Our four-bedroom house was new, but it looked just like the others on our cul-de-sac: one-story, low-slung, beige adobe, engineered to disappear into the background.

"I have to go," I said.

My wife and son and dog walked me to the door.

"Be careful. Use your head. Don't forget to treat people right," Monica said.

Kevin was more of a wiseass: "Catch a bandit for me."

They watched me clomp down the driveway to my old red Honda Accord. It was my ride until I got a government car. "Damn boots," I mumbled.

I thought about what I always did on the way to work: El Chapo. I'd come to El Paso with a mandate: Take down Chapo's operation. But before I could tackle that, I had to try to turn around the culture in the El Paso office. The office was responsible for half of West Texas and all of New Mexico, an area that encompassed nearly a third of the United States border with Mexico.

After I was appointed, I started hearing from agents I knew in El Paso. Morale was low, they said. Leadership was lacking, and field agents felt like they had no voice. I had new agents, hotshots hired from Los Angeles, New York, Chicago, and their first port of duty? El fucking Paso. They had no experience. Their families were ready to leave them. They were ready to quit.

I couldn't blame them.

With all the killings in nearby Ciudad Juárez, living here was dangerous. Hundreds of innocent people in Ciudad Juárez were being caught in the crossfire, whacked for just walking down the street. Our analysts told us there were hits every night in Ciudad Juárez, only a few miles south of El Paso. And the violence was spilling over, more and more, into the United States.

I was replacing an SAC who hadn't brought his family south because he probably didn't want to run the risk of having them living so close to

Ciudad Juárez, the murder capital of the world. More than ten thousand murders had been committed over there in the previous few years, bloodshed fueled by Chapo's struggle to take over the Juárez cartel.

That's why bringing my family down with me had been so important, I told myself. It was a sign of solidarity with my agents, a show of commitment.

I looked at the scenery I was passing and wondered if I had made the right decision. Industrial slaughterhouses loomed along both sides of the interstate, with forlorn horses and cows penned outside, waiting for the inevitable. The temperature was in triple digits already, and the wind was blowing.

It smelled like death.

I rolled off the interstate and found my way to the redbrick DEA office. It looked like a fortress in a war zone. The three-story building was surrounded by a ten-foot-high fence, festooned with razor wire. The DEA occupied the first floor and half of the second; the Federal Bureau of Investigation had part of the second and the entire third floor.

I parked the car and headed for the door. The heat rolled down like a window blind, and I felt my shirt plastered onto my back. There was a half-gallon of water in the crack of my ass. When I finally stepped onto the second floor, a roomful of men in cowboy boots, badges, and guns turned and looked at me like I was from Mars. The tie, I thought. The pressed shirt.

A tech guy smirked at my feet.

"Pretty boots. Did you polish them this morning?" he joked.

"I just took them out of the box," I said.

My office was bare, but the window offered a wide view over the Rio Grande and Ciudad Juárez on the opposite bank. I summoned my three assistant special agents in charge inside.

"We're going to be aggressive," I told them. "I came here to make Guzmán's life miserable. We're going to take him down."

They didn't look impressed. They told me about the morale problem, about the agents chafing to move on, the understaffing. No one wanted to serve on the border any longer than he had to, and some good agents were overdue for reassignment. My two predecessors were hardly ever in the office, they said. There was no plan. The agents on the ground had no direction. I already knew all that, but I gave them my full attention. When they finished, I waited a moment or two before starting in.

I'm a team guy. I learned that playing basketball, and I preached that throughout my career. If you want to reach a goal, everyone must work together. If my team is not behind me, we're not going to win.

"It looks like it's time for some changes," I said. "First, we're going to build a team. We're going to take care of our people. And we're going to win."

We walked together into the middle of the main office. I asked for everyone's attention.

"Boys, I just had a meeting with the supervisors. They brought me up to speed on what's going on here. So know this. I'm going to do right by you. And this is what's really important: The people who have done their time, I'm going to get you out of here," I said.

I heard a collective sigh, then a release.

I told my agents I was going to bring together all the agencies, from the FBI down to the local sheriffs' departments, to create a special task force to fight El Chapo. Then I took off my tie and looked down at my boots.

"I came to work in these today, but I'm going to go back to wearing topsiders," I said.

Everybody laughed.

"Look, you guys are my heroes," I said. "So, if you go out there to work every day for me and you communicate, if you share information with me and among yourselves, I will get you anywhere you want to go. Otherwise, it's not going to work."

The agents applauded. This felt like a good day, a good start.

A day or two later, one of my deputies said the local newspaper wanted to interview me, the new agent in charge of the El Paso office. I'm a media guy. I believe the press is the best way to get out your message. So, a few days later a reporter came to meet me. The guy was a tired old hack; he'd seen it all. I was just another gringo who didn't understand the border. His first question: Why was I here?

"I'm not here to understand the border, whatever the hell that means," I said. "I'm here for one reason. I'm here to get El Chapo Guzmán under control. I know who El Chapo is. He probably knows who I am. I'm here to destroy his organization, on both sides of the border."

That was the most dumb-ass thing I could have said. My bosses didn't want me to antagonize Chapo. But I said it, and I meant it.

My quote appeared in the newspaper about a week later. Then I got a call from a Mexican intelligence official. Someone had hung a huge banner from an overpass at the international border crossing, with my name on it.

I asked him for a picture. "Welcome Jack Reilly," it said.

El Chapo had misspelled my name.

My biggest fear was that the newspaper might print it, and my wife would see it. She would freak out.

Well, damn, I thought. I was in trouble already.

For the first few weeks, it seemed like I was always on the road. I'd been having meet-ups with local law enforcement, police chiefs, sheriff's deputies, the guys on the ground. Mike, an old buddy from SOD who was now a supervisor in my Las Cruces field office, had let me know what to expect.

Some of these local cops were great guys, gung-ho. Some of them didn't give a damn about drug enforcement: They were put on earth to run speed traps or bust heads in tavern brawls. Worse were the ones who couldn't be trusted. The entire border was utterly corrupt, he said.

"You need to see for yourself," he said. Mike was a lot like Comer—a quiet but confident, hard-charging agent. He lived near me and had been coming over to help me get acclimated. He had been divorced a few times, but had recently remarried. (Over beers, he told me over and over again, "I'm not going to screw this one up.")

So I took Mike's advice. I drove slowly along the border, paying visits, shaking hands, feeling them out, seeing if my agents were right. I had to figure out who I could trust, and get them onboard. I introduced myself, explained my philosophy: Guzmán depended on US law enforcement officials not talking to each other. If we started sharing information and working together, we could take him down.

I was setting up a task force made up of federal and local law enforcement. If they sent their best guys to join the force, I'd train and deputize them, even pay for their overtime. We'd target Guzmán's operations and build cases with the federal prosecutor's office. In return, any money we got in asset forfeiture, we'd split with their departments. "This way, we all win," I'd say.

Over and over again, I made my spiel. Most of the chiefs were receptive to the task force concept, but I knew that for my ideas to take hold I'd need to get the county sheriffs onboard. They wielded the real power in these desolate, wide-open plains.

Their biggest problem, of course, was the fear of violence spilling into the United States from Guzmán's range war.

If I could get everyone on the same page, if everyone shared what he knew, we had a good chance of stopping Guzmán. So I decided to attend a Texas border sheriffs' meeting in Alpine, Texas, about three hours southwest of El Paso. But when I walked into the room at the Brewster County Courthouse, I knew I was in trouble.

The meeting had just started, and the sheriffs stared at me. No one smiled. I was one of the few gringos there. A few moments later, they took a short break. And when they resumed, the chairman asked me to speak. I stood up, introduced myself. Then I told them I would do anything I could to help them. But today, I was just there to listen. They nodded, I sat down.

They turned their attention back to the agenda. And with the next item of business, they started speaking in Spanish.

Really? I thought. They're doing this to mess with me.

They continued in Spanish, as if I weren't there.

I snapped. I picked up my notebook and threw it against the wall.

"Look, you fucks. You're right. I'm not from here and I can't speak a lick of Spanish," I said angrily as I peered at everyone in the room. "But we're either going to work together, or the cartels are going keep kicking our asses."

The room went silent, but most of the sheriffs shook their heads in agreement.

"I want you all to know something: I'm not going away. You hear me? I'm not going away."

I'd said my piece.

Then a strange thing happened. One of the sheriffs got up, walked over to me and shook my hand. Two or three more came over and did the same. And when the meeting started again, it was conducted in English.

I had made my point.

On the drive back to El Paso, I thought about what I had done, and what I was doing. *What the hell have I gotten myself into?* I thought. Everybody out here operated in their own little silo, minded his own patch, walled off from everyone else. That's exactly what El Chapo wanted. We were divided, and as good as conquered.

This was like the Wild West, crooked, arrogant, and apathetic, even with all hell breaking loose a couple of miles away. I was up against it here. I was going to have to use everything I'd ever learned in my career, everything I'd learned in my life, even, to push law enforcement and my own agents to simply do their damn jobs.

Sure, I can do this. Piece of cake, right?

Clearly, my career up to this point had been in preparation for El Paso. I'd been studying Guzmán from afar for years, I'd seen up close the effects the cartels had on the streets of US cities. Finally, I'd made it up to the front lines, up close and personal.

The sheriffs down here might not like me, but I wasn't here to make friends. I knew how to form a working law enforcement organization. I knew how to take my time, gather the intel, join up the lines, file the briefs. I bust drug dealers for a living, from the lowest lowlife schoolyard nickelbagger to the jet-set millionaire *jefes*.

My days of watching and waiting for El Chapo had come to an end.
It was time to act.

When I got back to the office, I created a war room. I had the storage room cleared out, and we squeezed a conference table and several uncomfortable chairs into it. I put in a bank of computers along one wall, a pull-down screen, and an array of maps, tacked up and studded with pins to indicate suspected stash-house locations along the southern edge of the Rio Grande—warehouses, gas stations, garages, and family homes used to store drugs after shipments were smuggled over the border.

On my end of the long table was an overhead projector, a relic of a bygone age. The DEA had moved on to PowerPoint years before, but I was old school. The projector was easy to use. I could switch between maps and charts and text without fumbling with a keyboard. If an agent said we had the wrong location for a stash house, I could make the fix right on the plastic sheet.

When I called people in there to talk, they knew I meant business.

Now, here I was, standing by the projector, waiting as the thirty-something members of the new multiagency task force filed into the room for our first meeting.

It was a standing-room-only crowd, each one invited personally. Not just my DEA guys, but reps from an alphabet-soup of law enforcement agencies, intel, police, border patrol. I'd told them we were going to kick El Chapo's ass, but now I intended to show them how we'd get it done.

I'd spent weeks reviewing reports, maps, interviews with informants, wiretap transcripts. I studied all the ongoing investigations, arrests, dope seizures, and court cases filed by federal prosecutors in this territory. I made notes. I outlined. I was ready. I lowered the lights and switched on the overhead projector.

"I wanted to get everybody together to make sure we understand what our objective is," I said. "Let's not keep doing the same things over and over because that's the way we've always done them. If it's not working, we got to either stop it or fix it."

First stop? Metrics, I said.

"Let's start at the top and work down. I'm not here to criticize my predecessors. They did what they could. But look, most DEA offices are still using an old metric system, an old way of measuring success. They judged themselves by how much dope and money the office seized in a year. The suits in Washington supposedly use those numbers when they put together a new budget or send new staff."

I paused for a second.

"My predecessor was a metrics guy. He didn't care who went to jail, just how many. You all just had to make enough easy busts to boost statistics. People, it's time to throw that shit out the window."

I showed them a few photos of El Chapo.

"Washington wants Guzmán locked up. So do I. He's not the only bad guy we're after, but when we damage him, we're damaging them all. I mean, the guy's been on the lam for years and his operation is still growing. We gotta take him down. So what do we do first? We're going down to the other end of the scale, down to the operational people, the day-to-day, front-line drug movers."

I put photos of houses up on the screen.

"Who rents the stash houses? Who pays the truckers and pilots and bikers who take the dope north from the border? Those are the people who get busted. Those are the guys we're going after first."

"We have to get little before we can get big," I said. "This is where we start with the communications thing. The clerk at the 7-Eleven. The mechanic. The delivery guy. The code enforcement officer. The meter maid. These guys know this place from the ground up. They see things going on. They talk. We listen."

My guys knew what I was talking about. I saw some heads nod in agreement. I was warmed up now, feeling like a revival preacher laying down the Gospel message.

"Nothing is too small if we can connect the dots. Now if we don't connect the dots, we're going to continue to stumble. We're going to have these small hits but we're not going to hurt the organization. Guzmán is strategic. We have to be strategic. We need to employ a different way of thinking."

I explained that Chapo's organization in the United States is predicated on the fact that cops don't talk to cops.

"Take a seizure at a truck stop in southern Kentucky. Ten kilos of heroin, two guns, $30,000. It's a slam-dunk reelection for that county sheriff. You can bet he didn't call DEA or FBI with the telephone numbers he found in the cell phone, or the hotel or car-rental receipts. He's had his news conference, he's told the world. His work is over and done.

"But I'd say . . . " I paused. "*We'd* say, 'Sheriff, that's great. But that dope was never intended for your county. So, please, did the bad guy have any pocket trash on him? Was there a beeper number, an address? Did he tell you where he was going? Did you even ask him?' He's probably going to say nobody asked. Nobody looked. Nobody did anything. And Guzmán knows that. Most of the people who get arrested driving an eighteen-wheeler or a motor home or a car with a hidden compartment have no idea who the boss is."

I was hitting my stride now. School was in session and I was making sure every one of my agents understood the threat. Understood what we were up against.

"And this where Chapo is brilliant. One of his guys on the ground, from the trucking company, will get a receipt from the sheriff, an inventory of everything seized in the bust. Then Chapo dispatches attorneys who find out if the sheriff's department followed proper forfeiture procedures. He gets a synopsis of the traffic stop. He is studying, analyzing, connecting the dots. If the border patrol is looking for certain hidden compartments in Toyota Camrys, or troopers in Georgia are stopping M2 Freightliner refrigerated trucks, he sees that. He changes his delivery systems in response. That's how involved he is."

I told them that when I started in the 1980s, I'd drive around Chicago all day with my partner, Tony, and our surveillance team. We'd see a guy on the corner and buy a nickel bag and stick our guns in his mouth and throw him in jail. We didn't care where the dope came from.

"We duplicated each other's cases, wasted a ton of taxpayer money. It was all posturing, turf battles, ego shit. We lose, because we don't communicate, we don't integrate. If we want to win, law enforcement's gotta start integrating."

I had made these presentations before because I'd formed these task forces before. I re-used a few overhead projector transparencies from years back:

A DEA-funded task force. Federal, state, and local law enforcement members. A "force multiplier." We train and deputize local law enforcement. They see and hear things we cannot. Build a consistent network of information. But everyone had to be in the same office, commingling. They had to talk to each other. Otherwise it wouldn't work.

"I already told all you guys this. I don't care what kind of badge you got, everybody in this room is a cop as far as I'm concerned. But the DEA guy has to report to an FBI guy. The FBI has to talk to the DEA guy. The Internal Revenue Service guy and the ATF guy need to know what you got, and they're going to give you plenty, too. It's the only way this is going to fly. And if we don't have state and federal prosecutors onboard, we're spinning our wheels."

I emphasized the last point.

"This is teamwork. It's strategy. Border patrol. You stop a guy. He's got four or five interesting telephone numbers. A couple are for phones in El Paso, a couple are in Chicago. Doesn't look like much. But you turn them over to us. We put the numbers into our computer, and watch if those numbers match up anywhere and see if they come up in other investigations across the nation. Bingo! Now we have a lead on where all the pot is coming from and where it's going. It's critical. It works."

I got nods from around the room. My message was resonating.

"Here on the border it's even more important. Half of these people don't even know who their boss is. Some of them have thirty-five different names and bullshit IDs. So if a suspect has a personal nickname or tattoo or a limp, you can put that in there, too, and connect him up to a case outside of El Paso, way up North into the United States and even Canada.

Like here's a guy who drives a car. We figure out he's making five or six trips a year, and he's known as Flacco. A wiretap in Boston turns up a Flacco. Now, we have the link between him and an organization out East."

I slipped into the nitty-gritty details of my slide presentation, mostly maps and photos of warehouses. "We need to pinpoint where the dope crosses the border and where it's being stored locally," I said.

I told them how, two weeks before, I'd done a ride-along with some El Paso police officers. This is what I discovered: Nothing stays in El Paso. Everything moves north. Standing tall and shiny a short mile from the Mexican border is a line of brand-new aluminum warehouses.

"What are they here for?" I asked the local policemen.

"Oh, they're customs transit zones," one guy said, "part of the free trade agreement with Mexico. No-go zone for us."

"Bullshit," I said. "El Paso is one big drug warehouse. That's all you are. You're like a rental building. It comes in and it leaves."

And he said, "Yeah, but if they're not selling it here, it's not El Paso's problem."

"Really? It comes through right here! It's everybody's problem. And that's why you've got to start working with us," I said. "We need you guys."

Two weeks earlier the police had looked at me like I was speaking Chinese. But now I was getting my point across to everyone in the room.

"We're going to turn up the heat. We're going to start chipping away at El Chapo's organization from the bottom up. We start with the stash houses. That'll hamstring him right away."

I told the agents to take a long-term view of every case they work: How do we handle this suspect, this evidence, this prosecution in a way that gives us long-term benefits? Simple. Just pass along good information, often details that would normally end up in a file because it didn't have anything to do with El Paso or any local police department statistic.

I used my name as an example of what I was trying to do.

"If the biggest asshole in El Paso is Jack Riley, and he's moving the most dope and he's having the biggest impact not only in Texas but in the rest of the country, then my position is shut the office down and put everybody to work on tracking down Jack and getting him locked up and his empire dismantled. If we don't take that approach, we're not going to hurt Chapo's operation," I said.

"It's time to push our informants and recruit some new ones in the real estate industry, maybe place somebody undercover as a renter of a warehouse."

More new warehouses were going up along the border. If the owners or managers were dirty, I wanted my agents to show them we were watching, and we were not going to let up. If we couldn't get inside a warehouse, I wanted our guys to run a drug dog sniff along the vehicles parked near the building. I wanted word to travel that we'd use every legal means to kick the transporters' asses.

My throat was drying out from all the talk. It was time to wind it up.

"Listen up for just another minute. This is important. If you have an idea, out with it. Some of you've been sitting out in the desert for years, figuring out what doesn't work, and what might. I'm not afraid to try something different. If it's legal, let's try it."

People started shifting in their seats.

"Let's go have some fun," I said. "Let's turn up the heat out there. And when you hit the stash houses, I'd better get an invitation. It's been an awful long time since I kicked down a door, but I still know how."

Not long after the war room meeting, we began focusing on Chapo's "foot soldiers," a gang that did a lot of his dirty work on both sides of the border: the Barrios Aztecas. I'd use them to send a message to Guzmán: The heat was on.

Most people from outside El Paso, and maybe the Southwest, had never heard of them. The gang started in 1986 when five inmates from El Paso organized a Hispanic protection racket inside the local prison. The Aztecas were mostly bilingual Mexican-Americans. By the 1990s, the gang had spread to other jails and prisons, and, as founding members were released, they took their loyalties and criminal contacts with them to the streets of El Paso.

When Guzmán first approached them with a deal, the Barrios Aztecas put their ex-con army at his disposal. It was a sweet deal for both sides. They could move large amounts of Chapo's narcotics northward via El Paso, and likewise carry large amounts of cash and weapons south again to Ciudad Juárez. They were El Chapo's army on the ground, moving legally and relatively easily across the US-Mexican border.

They were violent assholes, too.

El Chapo hired them to carry out hits and take the rap if they were caught. They were fond of exceptionally brutal robberies and home invasions, where any kind of resistance meant instant death. They were vicious, and sloppy. Members of the Aztecas spent a lot of time in police custody. They thought they were major players in the cartel, but they were grunts. If things went wrong, Chapo didn't care what happened to them.

Like a US company that moves its factories to Mexico and China because of lower labor and manufacturing costs, Chapo used the Barrios Aztecas as an endless source of cheap, expendable labor—his transnational longshoremen and goon squad.

Ever the savvy businessman, Chapo was paying the Barrios Aztecas in drugs instead of cash. Depending on the job, the gang would get a kilo or two of raw cocaine, chop it up, and put it on the streets of El Paso, Ciudad Juárez, and other cities and towns all along their stretch of the border, thus becoming Chapo's retail sales team as well.

I began working the phones, pressing my task force guys to watch each traffic stop and parole violation for possible confidential informants who knew anything about the Barrios Aztecas and their operations. I pushed them to get gang members to roll on their leaders.

We soon gathered enough information from our informants and surveillance to get court-ordered wiretaps. And those wiretaps were helping federal prosecutors build a case. It took a few weeks, but reports were promising: We'd infiltrated the gang. We were ready to move on to the next level.

While the Barrios Aztecas weren't key players, they were part of my grander scheme. By taking on the Aztecas, we were once again harassing Chapo. My message to him was simple: We're going after the people you deal with every day. We'll shut them down, and we'll shut you down.

The investigation was big enough to qualify as a Racketeer Influenced and Corrupt Organizations (RICO) case. I wanted to start arresting these pricks for drug trafficking, distribution, extortion, money laundering, and murder. But I knew we still needed more evidence. I just had to be patient.

Meanwhile, evidence that drug trafficking was well-established in American border towns was hard to miss. My next road trip was to Columbus, New Mexico, a sleepy, scruffy town of two thousand souls. It stood in a patch of desert three miles north of Puerto Palomas, Mexico, a straight shot west of El Paso.

In the fall of 2007, you didn't have to be a genius to notice there was something odd going on there. Median income was $15,000 a year. People lived humbly in simple frame houses or prefab double-wides. But real estate was turning over in Columbus. Houses were selling, sometimes for cash. New homes were going up, too, larger and more luxurious. And parked along the residential streets were brand-new Lincoln Navigators and Cadillac Escalades with flashy wheel-rims.

Where did all this sudden wealth come from?

"Let's investigate the real estate deals, maybe even have one of our agents go undercover," I told Dan. "Let's push our informants."

This much money in a poor community smelled like corruption. The town only had a handful of cops, and several of them had resigned in the past few years, caught up in scandals. The Luna County sheriff's deputies weren't helpful, either.

This was the back end of New Mexico, miles of windswept desert, nothing to distinguish north from south. The border guys said no one could really be sure where the United States ended and Mexico began.

We started out of town at midafternoon. Out in the distance stood something strange. It looked like the tall lifeguard chair at a swimming pool, way out to the south. The horizon was wavy, but I knew that wasn't a mirage.

"Is that on our side?" I asked.

"About fifty yards into Mexico," the border patrol agent said.

I asked Dan to drive up closer, as close as we could go. Once there, I got out of the car and started walking.

"Jack, you have to be careful," Dan called after me. "We can't just waltz into Mexico."

"We can't? Watch me," I said.

I was feeling full of myself. Things were going well since I had started a few months before. In and around El Paso we'd hit stash houses, including some of the new warehouses. We found drugs, we arrested people, and we sent the information we collected out to aid investigations in other parts of the country. We launched a major investigation into a brutal street gang with strong ties to Chapo.

Informants were talking, and task force members were clearing out the receipts and phone numbers in their desks and notebooks. We were running to keep up with all the leads.

And for analog guys like me, I made sure there were charts and paperwork hung on the walls and easels in the war room. I felt better with the paper in my hand, rather than seeing images blinking on a computer screen. To me, the big picture is much more visible that way.

I had fun. I went out a few times with my surveillance teams. I was by my agents' sides when they busted some of the stash houses. We were aggressive as hell. We made it seem like we had agents all over the place. We weren't just hurting El Chapo in El Paso, but all over the United States. We were sending a message to Guzmán, and to all the cartels: It was no longer business as usual in El Paso.

My bosses in Washington praised our approach. In just few months' time, we'd produced more leads for law enforcement agencies around the country than any other DEA territory. Now we were spreading out, taking the message on the road. That's why I went to Columbus, New Mexico.

A great deal of cocaine, marijuana, and methamphetamine came through this little corridor.

I bounded out of the car and started walking toward the structure, followed by Dan and several border patrol agents. As I got closer, I saw it was a crude tower, made of wood and steel, about thirty feet high. A ladder led up to a deck at the top. It was like a kids' treehouse, but without any trees.

"They send somebody up there at night with a radio," one of the border patrol agents said. "When the coast is clear, they tell their bosses. And then..."

He didn't have to finish.

"What the hell?" I said.

These guys felt so secure here that they could build a damn watchtower in plain sight. I was surprised they weren't flying a flag, too.

"So why is it still here?" I asked.

"It's in Mexico."

"So what? Knock it down."

"Huh?"

"Knock it down. It won't take five minutes. When it gets dark, knock this fucking tower down!"

So that night, agents did that. They left their business cards in the rubble. The traffickers rebuilt the tower the next day. This went on for another two days—we tore it down, and they rebuilt it. Finally, the traffickers gave up.

I knew that tearing down the tower wouldn't stop the flow of drugs into the United States. That wasn't the point. I wanted to send a message to the cartels. We know who you are. We know what you're doing.

We're going to make it hard for you.

But as I would soon find out, they were going to make it hard for me, too.

In the darkness outside my office window, the lights of Ciudad Juárez shone on the Rio Grande. I hung up the phone and tried to calm my nerves. The latest stack of intelligence reports waited on my desk, but I couldn't focus. I wondered if anyone over there could see me up here, silhouetted in the window. I thought about crosshairs and high-powered rifles, then told myself to get a grip. I thought about the people on the ground in that densely packed town, and wondered how many of their fellow Mexicans, the *narcotraficantes*, would end up killed tonight.

The turf war between Sinaloa and the other cartels showed no signs of letting up in Mexico. And that was especially true in Ciudad Juárez, the lucrative smuggling corridor into the United States. The city's mortuary was filled with dozens of unclaimed and unidentified bodies.

The reality was that El Chapo and Sinaloa had been profiting rather than suffering as a result of the drug war. He had perfected the strategy of "bribes over bullets," corrupting Mexican authorities instead of fighting them into submission. Government officials on all levels, including law enforcement, were on his payroll. So Chapo knew in advance what the government planned to do, and El Chapo played the authorities' every move to his advantage.

When the Mexican army took down his longtime rivals, the Arellano Félix cartel, which controlled Tijuana, El Chapo was ready to roll. He took over Tijuana, one of the cartels' primary transportation plazas for billions of dollars of illegal drugs smuggled annually into the United States. And when President Calderón started cracking down on drug trafficking through Ciudad Juárez, El Chapo seized the opportunity to destroy the Juárez cartel.

The stars had aligned perfectly for Guzmán. He controlled most of the drugs coming into the United States: marijuana, cocaine, and methamphetamine. Now, he was shifting his attention to heroin—just as I had suspected before I left St. Louis. He knew heroin had the potential to become his most profitable drug yet because of America's growing appetite for opioids. Heroin is extracted from the opium poppy, the same plant that gives us morphine, opium, codeine, Percocet, and OxyContin, some of the most powerful pain medicines on the market. Guzmán did his homework, put together a business plan. He knew that more and more Americans were becoming addicted to pain pills every day, and he believed that, at some point, the US government would make it harder for people to get them. If that happened, heroin could easily fill the void—and Chapo would reap the benefits.

Our agents reported that Guzmán had been pushing Mexican farmers to grow more opium poppies. Now, there were so many opium poppy fields in the mountains that Mexico was poised to become the second-largest region of poppy cultivation in the world, just behind Afghanistan. But there was a major difference. Afghanistan's heroin went to Europe, Asia, and Africa. And those profits were used by drug lords there to bankroll the Taliban and other terrorist groups. (In fact, some of the drug lords were Taliban leaders.) Mexico's heroin went to the United States. Those profits went into Chapo's pockets. So once again, Chapo planned ahead while we were stuck in gear. That's why we had to shut down the border, make it harder for him to get his drugs into the United States. With every stash house we hit, every truckload of drugs we took off the road, we slowed down his push into the United States.

Maybe that's why he'd put a bounty on my head.

I had just gotten off the phone with one of my DEA intelligence agents. His Mexican counterparts had tapped the telephones of several of Chapo's deputies, and chatter was lively today. A guy wanted to hire hit men in Ciudad Juárez to whack me. He was willing to pay them $100,000 to cut my head off.

"The boss wants it done," Chapo's deputy said.

I was pissed at that price. I'm only worth a hundred thousand bucks! I tried to laugh it off, but this was serious. The phone rang again. It was Mike. He'd heard.

"We have to tell Washington," he said.

"It's all bullshit," I said.

"Jack, you have to report this," he said. "You got a family down here. We can't have this. I mean, you want to stay and take such a risk?"

"Yeah," I said. "I got work to do. I love it. If you tell headquarters, they'll probably throw me in a van and have me out of here tomorrow.

And you know what? If that happens, El Paso is back to business as usual. And Chapo wins."

"Jack! Listen, man," he said. "It's not that simple!"

The guy really cared, but I cut him off. "Just remember this. The US ambassador to Mexico didn't want us to inflame him. He said: 'Don't make Chapo mad.' And I said, 'No. I'm going to stick my fucking needle in him.' Now, I'm getting to the guy to the point that *he* has a problem. I'm getting to him. We are getting to him. This is not the time to run away."

Mike agreed not to tell Washington. After hanging up, I returned to the window. Chapo wasn't bullshitting. The threat was real. But I wasn't going to stop. I wasn't ready to leave. Not yet. Not when we were on a roll.

CHAPTER 10

THE STARK TRUTH

Only a few short weeks later, I found myself waiting in the dark, crouched behind my car with my Glock in my hand, knowing there was no way out.

The Ford F-150 pickup truck and a Ford Explorer had been following me since I got onto the highway in El Paso. I thought I had lost them when I jumped off an exit and pulled into a school parking lot. But I was wrong. The pickup truck sped by the school. But the Ford Explorer pulled in, screeched to a halt about fifty feet from my car, and then killed its headlights.

Now I was staring at the SUV, trying to see who was inside. I couldn't make out much. Maybe the shadow of two men.

At that moment, I thought about Tony. Even though he wasn't there, his spirit was. He taught me that if you're in trouble, go down swinging. God, I wish he were with me now. I thought about my wife and son—what would happen if I died in a shootout. Although we never talked about it, I knew if anything bad happened to me, Tony would take care of Monica and Kevin. And he'd hunt down the bastards who did me in. And how would Monica and Kevin react to the news? Fuck, I had to stop thinking about shit like that. I had to focus, stay ready.

Come on, you bastards. Make a move, I thought.

It all happened so fast. Just an hour earlier, I was in my office, poring over intelligence reports. A conference call had just ended and I was about to take another when my phone rang. It was Monica. She wanted to know when I'd be home. I checked my watch. It was nearly 7:30 p.m.

As usual, the job was taking precedence over my family. I'd sworn I'd spend more time at home, and I kept the promise as best I could. But I was busier than ever, and it was getting more difficult trying to make time for my family. I hung up the phone, said good-night to a few agents still at their desks, and headed home.

Now, I was trying to figure out my next move. I had been in danger before. Bad guys shot at me. Drug dealers jumped me in dark alleys. But nothing like this. El Chapo was a stone-cold killer. He thought nothing about whacking cops. So squatting there, Glock in my hand, I did the battlefield calculus: I could wait for them to make a move, or I could rush them, firing my weapon. That might be the only way I'd have a chance.

"It's showtime," I said.

But just as I was about to sprint toward the Explorer, the driver turned his headlights back on, spun around, and bolted out of the lot. Moments later, the pickup sped down the same road, following the SUV, their tail-lights receding into the night.

"Holy fucking shit," I said out loud. "You motherfuckers."

I climbed back into my car and picked up my BlackBerry. I called Mike and told him I was OK, and headed home. But first, I'd stop by his house to talk. I called Tony and filled him in.

I got back on the highway and drove straight to Mike's house. He was standing outside, waiting for me. He didn't give me a chance to talk.

"This is no joke, Jack. These guys aren't fucking around. You have to tell someone this time," he said.

"If they wanted to kill me, they would have killed me," I said, trying to downplay the incident.

I didn't want to tell him what I really thought. They were trying to get me to a secluded area where they could whack me. But something happened at the last second, something that stopped them from taking the next step.

"With all due respect, you're being an asshole. You're not taking this seriously," Mike said. He said he was so worried he sent two deputies on the task force to look for me. They were headed southbound on Interstate-10, but they missed me because I had already left the highway.

"Trust me, I'm taking this seriously," I said. "Just do me a favor. Don't tell anyone—especially my wife."

Mike shook his head in disbelief. "I don't know..."

"Just do me that favor."

He frowned and reluctantly agreed to keep it a secret.

As I stood outside Mike's house, I knew this Irish gringo had become such a pain in the ass that Chapo and the other drug lords were looking to kill me.

Now I was really pissed.

"This is war on these fuckers," I said to Mike. "We're not backing off from these people. We have to talk tough and act tough."

I got back in my car and drove home. I got out of my car and took a deep breath. I didn't want Monica to know. But when I got inside, she could tell I was rattled. Hell, she could probably smell it on me.

"Are you OK?" she asked.

"Yeah," I said. "I'm just a little upset. Notre Dame basketball lost tonight. Nothing to worry about. Nothing at all."

The next morning, I got to the office energized. If El Chapo wanted a fight, we'd bring it to him. The drivers on my tail had to be his henchmen. They were the most likely suspects. I wanted an update on the Barrios Aztecas investigation. I checked with my agents, task force members, federal prosecutors.

My agents told me they were still getting good information about the gang from informants and surveillance. And prosecutors told me it was just a matter of time before they started presenting evidence to a federal grand jury.

But that wasn't enough.

I pressed my agents to do more: "Turn up the heat," I said. I slammed down my phone. I wanted to send a message to Chapo: If he thought I was going to back off, he was mistaken. I took a deep breath. When you're pissed off, you don't think clearly.

Mike called and said he was trying to find out information about the vehicles. I thanked him, then turned my attention back to work. But for weeks after the chase, I watched every step. And every time I left the office, I made sure I was hyperaware of my surroundings. I never wanted to be caught off guard again.

I never told Monica about the chase because I knew it would only stress her more. No one in Washington found out, either. If they did, they probably would have pulled my ass out of El Paso in a hurry. No, I managed to keep both of those threats a secret.

Still, Monica knew how dangerous it was in the field. Every day, the news was filled with stories of violence on both sides of the border. Drug-related murders in Ciudad Juárez continued unabated, and now the cartels were taking down people in the United States.

Heavily armed gang members were hitting stash houses not just in the Southwest, but in other parts of the United States, too. Phoenix alone was seeing hundreds of kidnappings, most of them connected to the narcotics trade. The victim often paid someone's drug debt with his life.

We were working just a stone's throw from Ciudad Juárez, which in 2007 was one of the most dangerous places in the world as the fight between rival cartels intensified. Ciudad Juárez had 1.5 million people—and they faced death or injury every time they ventured outside. Hundreds of people a month were being killed in the city. DEA had agents working over there, trying to gather as much intelligence as possible. They answered to the regional director in Mexico City, but I talked to them all the time. I made a habit of sneaking over now and then, to encourage them and see what they were up against. It was one thing to look at the city from the comfort of my office, another to get a street-level view.

This time they were talking with a possible informant, a woman who worked in real estate. She might be helpful in identifying the true owners of the warehouses that were popping up along the border. If things went well, she could tell us who was buying buildings to use as stash houses.

"You don't have to do this," one of my agents said.

"Yeah. But I want to," I responded.

I stood outside headquarters until two agents pulled up in a black armored Chevy Suburban. I jumped inside. They knew the exact route into Mexico without any fanfare. Minutes later we crossed into Ciudad Juárez. I knew I should have followed the proper protocol, making sure the State Department and the US Consulate knew I'd crossed into Mexico. But that was a pain in the ass. The bounty made it more risky. But I wasn't going to be here for long. And there was something wonderful about being back in the field.

Ciudad Juárez reminded me of the images I saw on TV of Beirut in the late-1970s. The only thing moving on the desolate streets was the occasional skinny dog. Most of the businesses were boarded up. Once in a while, I'd see a cluster of people, but I knew by the way they dressed—and the cars they drove—they were cartel. Had to be. And they were heavily armed. Some carried semiautomatic AK-47 and AR-15 rifles. The city was a powder keg. At any moment, you could find yourself in the middle of a firefight between rival cartels, or the cartels and the military.

At one time the city had a thriving business district, fueled by American tourists. But no one went to the city anymore unless they had to, and, sometimes, they went and didn't come back. The missing person reports came to us.

"It's a combat zone," one of the agents said.

We pulled into a lot. A woman got into the car.

She was wrong from the start. The jewelry, heavy gold necklaces, and bangles. Why would she be draped in gold, in a city plagued by street crime?

We drove around the city while the agents asked her questions, trying to get a feel for her background. I sat back and listened.

She spoke in broken English, saying she wanted to help us stop the narcos. She was keenly interested in what part of the border she'd be working on. She must have asked ten times which town, which county, what we were working on. That struck me as wrong. And she didn't ask for money, or even ask how she'd be paid. Very strange. She fidgeted, picked at her long fingernails and the clasp of her handbag.

She had the biggest handbag I've ever seen, which made me uneasy. Plenty big enough for a gun, if not a rocket launcher.

We drove. I kept looking to see if we were being followed. We weren't. We finally decided to drop her off. She was too suspicious, too nervous. Asked too many questions. We suspected she might be working for Chapo. Guzmán and his people were always trying to figure out what we were doing. Using a plant would be a good way to do that, but this lady was not up to the job.

We headed back to the checkpoint. The scrubby desert landscape outside the windows was depressing. Whenever a member of Congress or a congressional staffer visited my office, I encouraged them to come to the border. Unless you saw the proximity for yourself, you didn't realize how close El Paso is to Mexico.

Or how dangerous it is.

The riverbank on the El Paso side was a great wall of bulletproof glass shields. Border patrol often parked their cars behind the glass and watched for movement on the other side. Those shields protected them from bullets and rocks.

That's how it was, day to day, down by the river in El Paso.

Some people in my office lived in fear of the cartels finding out where they lived, and kidnapping or killing them or their family members. A supervisory agent phoned me late one night to tell me a clerk in our office was panicking, thinking someone had followed her home. She'd heard all the stories about El Chapo and the cartels targeting people in the United States.

"Call the El Paso police," I said. But then I quickly changed my mind. "Forget that. Tell all the supervisors I want them in my office. Now."

"But it's almost midnight," he said.

"I don't give a fuck," I snapped.

I made sure a couple of agents went to the clerk's house. She was safe. Then I got in my car and drove to El Paso. A couple of guys were already waiting when I arrived.

"We're not going to let these pricks intimidate our employees," I said. "I'm not going to wait for the El Paso cops. We're going to start our own special response team. I'm calling in the guys who are trained to kick some asses. We're going to be responsible, and keep our people safe. If anything happens, we'll get them out of trouble."

The supervisors agreed, so the next day I called Washington and started the process. Within a week, I got the green light for a rapid-response team made up of the "biggest and baddest" DEA agents. That went a long way toward changing the dynamics of the office. It showed everyone that I cared for their safety. The team went through extensive training and I began using them when executing high-risk warrants and making arrests. The local cops began asking for their help, too. As for the clerk, we covered her house around the clock for several days. And I gave her a week off with pay. I wanted to show the office that we were family. It was tempting to say we were overreacting, but with all the violence, and the goons in the SUV and the pickup truck, I just didn't know what would happen next. I had to take steps.

Meantime, I tried to stay upbeat, tried to live a normal life. But I was so consumed by my work that I didn't realize we were heading into the Christmas season. Without any snow, ice, or even cold, it didn't feel like December to this Chicago guy. Seventy degrees and pristine blue skies. I mean, you can't put Christmas lights on a cactus, can you?

My sisters had flown in for Thanksgiving. We'd had a blast, but Christmas on our own loomed over us all the time. Monica was still struggling. We both felt guilty about uprooting Kevin. He was a quiet kid, and had a tight-knit group of friends back in St. Louis. He was heartbroken about the move. Monica and I had shopped around, found the school with the best basketball team in Las Cruces, and signed him up. We dropped him off the first day of his freshman year and watched him bravely stride into the building.

"Did we do the right thing?" I said softly, trying to hold back tears. "The house still hasn't sold. We still can move back if this doesn't work." Monica made a sound in her throat, and I realized that she was crying, too. We sat there in the parking lot and held hands. We cried for our son, and for ourselves.

But when we picked him up at the end of the day, Kevin was smiling. He'd made a couple of friends, and a few weeks later he tried out for the basketball team. He started on junior varsity and then made his way up to the varsity team. That was quite an accomplishment for a freshman.

Now the high school basketball season was about to start, and, for the first time ever, I wasn't coaching Kevin. And I felt horrible that Monica was having such a hard time adjusting to this latest move. She'd put up with all my crap over the years—the late nights, the long weeks, the guns, and the secrets.

Monica was a lot like my mom, outgoing and sociable. But here, it was like living on an island. Our new house was spacious and pretty, but the neighbors kept to themselves. The yards were wide and deep, and there were no sidewalks. If you wanted to go anywhere, you had to drive. Monica felt isolated and lonely. When our family and friends came down to see our new setup, we dreaded their good-byes.

I was torn. While I felt really bad for my family, I was beginning to see concrete progress in the office. We were doing great things with the FBI and our state and local counterparts. That year my best Christmas gift was knowing I was pissing off my man Chapo.

But if it was up to my wife and son, we'd leave tomorrow.

A few days into 2008 I got a call from the US attorney's office. It was time to start arresting leaders of the Barrios Aztecas.

A federal grand jury had handed up indictments against five key members of the gang. Charges included racketeering, murder, extortion, money laundering, and trafficking in marijuana, cocaine, and heroin.

But I knew the investigation was still ongoing and that more gang leaders and members were likely to face charges. There were plenty of Aztecas to choose from. The gang had about three thousand members in the Southwest and in Mexico, both in prison and on the streets.

This was just the beginning.

Law enforcement had known about these pricks for years, and had tried before to dismantle the organization. But I was well aware that it was our office, and our multijurisdictional team that made this case work.

The drug lords in Mexico were going to be very pissed.

Our investigation laid bare the inner workings of the gang, where they stashed drugs and money, how they got them across the border, the deals they made with Chapo and other drug lords—information already helping us in other investigations across the country.

Our gang members–turned–informants told us the Barrios Aztecas felt like they owned El Paso—they could get away with anything. Now, as we picked off their leaders, they were turning on each other like scared rats.

Informants and tapped telephones also gave us an inside look at the bloody narco-war between the Sinaloa, Gulf, Tijuana, and Juárez cartels over control of lucrative smuggling routes along the border. This range war rained down mayhem, from drive-by shootings and gruesome "message" killings—where bodies were beheaded and mutilated—to slick assassinations and military-scale firefights.

Much of the bloodshed was going on right here, within sight of the US border. About half the killings happened in and around Ciudad Juárez, literally steps from El Paso. The Barrios Aztecas gang was right in the middle of the violence.

Shortly after we began arresting the gang members, I was offered a little break south of the border, a trip to Mexico courtesy of the Mexican attorney general. Several DEA officials, including my boss, Michele Leonhart, and I, were offered a firsthand look at Culiacán, the birthplace and spiritual heart of the drug-lord culture.

The Mexicans wanted to show us how hard they were working to battle the cartels. Our intelligence told us the federal police were too corrupt to take any meaningful action. That's why the military was leading the fight, but they hadn't made a dent.

I told Monica about the opportunity, but she didn't like the idea. I assured her I'd be safe. But I was just a little uneasy, too. With Chapo running the show down there, anything was possible.

Culiacán is the capital of and the largest city in the state of Sinaloa, the cradle of the Sinaloa cartel. We were scheduled to meet up first in the resort town of Cabo San Lucas to discuss mutual cooperation between Mexico and the United States. Then, if we wanted to, we could jump in a helicopter and fly to Culiacán, to see the government's antidrug program at work.

I talked to a few buddies before I left. I knew violence in Sinaloa was out of control because of Chapo's war with the Beltrán Leyva brothers, a rival cartel. We would be prime targets, right in the heart of their home territory. Mike wasn't sure it was a good idea. Tony didn't like it, either. But I felt that I should go and get a firsthand look at the area.

Mexican soldiers met us as soon as our plane touched down in Cabo, and escorted us every step of the way. We convened at a resort conference room filled with Mexican and US leaders.

The main speaker was Eduardo Mora, the Mexican attorney general. He insisted his government was going full tilt after Chapo and all the cartels. "They are on the run," he said.

Really? I thought. Our intelligence didn't bear that out.

Cabo was lovely, but outside the war between Sinaloa and the Beltrán Leyva brothers was escalating. The four Beltrán Leyva brothers had been Guzmán intimates since the 1980s. Alfredo, Arturo, Carlos, and Hector grew up poor in the same district as Guzmán, and broke into the drug-running business, first as small-time poppy growers, then as hit men and distributors for the Guadalajara cartel.

When Chapo was jailed in 1993, the brothers brought him suitcases of cash. In 2001, they helped him escape. A year later, when Guzmán brought together twenty-five of the biggest regional drug-trafficking factions to create the Federation, the brothers were there by his side. It seemed like a good idea—a mutual aid association for narcos interested in driving out the Gulf cartel to the east.

The Federation began to fracture as the Juárez cartel arose in 2004, and fissures emerged in late 2007, when rumors swirled that the Beltrán Leyvas were aligning with Los Zetas, the armed wing of the Gulf cartel. Soon the cartels began forming private armies.

The breaking point came in January 2008, when one of the Beltrán Leyva brothers was arrested. The brothers blamed Guzmán, and retaliated by killing Chapo's twenty-two-year-old son outside a Culiacán shopping mall. The violence quickly escalated, with shootouts in the streets, abductions, murders, and plenty of innocent bloodshed.

So sitting there in Cabo San Lucas, I knew that most of Mora's assertions were total bullshit.

Yes, we had some good counterparts in Mexico, but so many were on the cartels' payrolls, you didn't know whom to trust.

On the morning conference calls I could hear the frustration in other SACs' voices. We shared some great intel with our Mexican partners, but they never seemed to move on it.

After the meeting, Mora asked who wanted to go into the field outside Culiacán and see some secret military action.

What the hell, I figured. I volunteered to go along with a few of my agents.

We got to the airport and pulled up to a rickety old DC-10 with benches running along both sides of the inner fuselage. Damn, this is what we're going to take! Not a good sign. The pilot took off as if he were flying a fighter jet. There were only ten of us on the plane, and we were bouncing and sliding all over the benches.

When we descended over Culiacán, I gazed down at the houses, mostly ramshackle, adobe-colored homes that blended into the landscape. I saw the runway. It was really small, better suited for a Cessna than a DC-10. Were we going to make it?

We did. Before we got a chance to gather our wits, we were escorted to two Russian Mil Mi-7 helicopters that looked like they had seen better days. One was leaking oil.

As we boarded the helicopters, the soldiers handed us each a bulletproof vest—not to wear, but to sit on. They were concerned that traffickers were going to shoot up at the helicopters from the ground.

"You got to be kidding me," I said to one of my agents. "What the hell did we agree to do?" I thought about Leonhart, what she'd say about this, but she'd stayed behind. She was the smart one.

The helicopters lifted off. We flew over a big marijuana field just outside the city, then landed at the edge of the plantation. A general greeted us. He told us his troops went out for ninety days at a time, cutting down and burning every marijuana field they could find.

As he was talking, I glanced around as soldiers with automatic weapons spread out and set up a perimeter to protect us. They were ready if the traffickers made a run at us. I stood there in the middle of that field and realized that this was the most screwed-up piece of theater I'd ever seen in my life.

These government officials were spending all this time and money burning acres of ditch-weed marijuana that Chapo probably couldn't give away. I shook my head in disgust. Chapo probably planted these fields, put them here so the military could come in and burn them. He was giving them busywork, making them feel as if they were doing something. A secret military operation. Hell, at that moment Chapo was probably watching us and laughing his ass off. He saw the helicopters coming from miles away. The soldiers were nowhere near his real operation. It was absolutely surreal. We stayed in the area for hours, but after a few minutes I had seen enough. I got the picture.

We took the helicopter from the marijuana field back to the Culiacán airport, and then boarded the DC-10. As we flew back to Cabo, everything became clear. Government officials arranged these visits to prove they were doing something, to keep our dollars coming in. They must have known, as well as I did, that Chapo couldn't care less about a few acres of poor-quality weed. The simple fact was, at this point, Chapo was untouchable. The tentacles of his corruption reached too far into the government.

The stark truth was this: Nothing was simple in Mexico.

Not long after the Mexico trip, I got a telephone call from my boss, DEA Administrator Michele Leonhart. She didn't want to talk about investigations. She wanted me to consider a newly created position.

"I'd like you to interview for a Washington job," she said. "The Fusion Center is looking for someone to run the agency."

The Fusion Center brought together elements of the DEA, FBI, CIA, ATF, and the Departments of Justice and Defense, all under one command. Leonhart told me I'd be a perfect candidate.

I hesitated for a moment. I loved running my own office—a border office. In just a year, office morale had turned around. Federal, state, and local law enforcement agencies were sharing critical information with other offices across the country. We'd arrested the leaders of a ruthless gang, launched high-level corruption investigations, and harassed the shit out of El Chapo and the rival cartels. And despite the early success, we needed to do a lot more. I knew that the ongoing pressure would eventually lead the drug lords to make critical mistakes. And those just might take us to Chapo's front door. This was no time to leave town.

"I'm not sure..." I said.

"Call Stuart Nash," Leonhart said. "He's the Justice Department attorney doing the interviews."

I respected Leonhart and knew that when she suggested something, I should do it. So I said I would.

The Fusion Center, designed to bring all federal agencies into one room, was created after the 9/11 terrorist attacks on the World Trade Center and the Pentagon. An investigation showed that federal agencies had information about the terrorists' activities before the attacks, but they didn't share it among themselves. If they had, things might've turned out very differently.

At the Fusion Center, intelligence was shared across all agencies. International drug trading was treated as a threat to the safety and security of the nation, on the same footing as terrorism or organized crime.

The Fusion Center was supposed to be the tool to disseminate intelligence to field commands and police agencies across the nation. If the DEA had a case against Joe Blow, we could plug his name into the Fusion Center database and learn everything anyone knew about him. If he was already on another agency's radar, we could combine our facts and forces.

When I called Nash, he asked if I could come to Washington. I told him how busy things were in El Paso, and asked him to meet me halfway— I had already booked a trip to Chicago. Could he meet me there? He agreed.

I told Monica about the interview and saw her eyes light up. Kevin was all smiles. If we were going to move, it had to be before the start of the new school year.

"I don't know if I'll get the job," I warned them. "I don't know if I want it. I still have a load of things to do here."

As I flew into Chicago, I was of two minds about the position. I wanted to stay in El Paso with my agents. I was only going to the interview because my boss told me to. But...

I had met Nash before, and I liked him. We were opposites—he was a quirky, Harvard-educated intellectual, and I was more of a streets-of-Chicago guy, but we got along.

We met at a Smith & Wollensky steakhouse on the Chicago River. It was a warm June night with a cool breeze blowing. We sat outside drinking beers, bullshitting. Nash asked me why I wanted the job.

"Most people who run their own offices don't want to go back to Washington," he said.

I couldn't tell him "My boss made me do it." So I told him it was a good opportunity—a way to "spread my message."

But while I was talking, in the back of my mind, I kept thinking, *I don't want this job. How would I be able to leave my agents? We'd just gotten rolling in El Paso. What would happen to all that hard work?*

Nash smiled and told me he shared my philosophy of interagency cooperation. But the Fusion Center hadn't been operating that way.

"We need someone to come in and take charge," he said.

A few days later, Leonhart called again. "How did it go?"

"I think I did OK," I said nonchalantly.

She called again a week later with the news.

"Apparently, you did more than OK. He wants to hire you."

Damn, I thought.

"I don't have to accept it, do I?"

She didn't say I had to take it, but I knew she was looking out for me. I felt like crap. I knew why Nash wanted me. I had SOD experience. I was a street agent. I ran my own office. And it wasn't just any office; it was on the US-Mexican border. You can't get much better than that in terms of seeing the real world: Guzmán, the cartels. The whole deal.

I knew the move would do a world of good for my family, but I just hated leaving my guys. They had bought into my philosophy. Now I felt like I was jumping ship. I called Nash and accepted the post.

Now I'd have to tell my agents.

I phoned Mike, who congratulated me. "It's a good move. I'm really worried about your safety here," he said. Then I called everyone in to an office-wide meeting, so they'd know before the DEA sent out the official announcement. I felt nauseated. I could see the stunned look in some of the agents' eyes. I had to brush back a few tears. But after the initial silence, they came up and slapped me on the back or shook my hand. A few asked me not to forget about them when I left. I promised I wouldn't.

It was hard going into the office for the next few weeks, but I wanted to make it a smooth transition for the new SAC. I'd have to bring him up to speed on our investigations and I'd encourage him to continue our aggressive tactics—to throw metrics out the window, to follow every lead, and to treat agents with respect. If they work hard, they should be rewarded—they should be promoted, not held back.

On my last day, it felt strange, walking into the building. I would only be there for a little while, just time enough to carry out the last few boxes. I arrived with such promise, and I really had accomplished a lot in a short period of time.

I stood at my desk, turned, and stared out the window at Ciudad Juárez. El Chapo was still over there somewhere. I promised myself that just because I was leaving El Paso, I wouldn't stop dogging him. No, on the contrary. I wouldn't stop until we got him. I wouldn't stop until we crippled his organization. I was just moving the fight to another front.

CHAPTER 11

HOMEWARD BOUND

I had shifted quickly from the front lines in El Paso to an anonymous office in Washington. But the bland surroundings disguised what would be an important job. I was fighting El Chapo and the Mexican cartels, just as the violence reached a fever pitch.

When I started in the summer of 2008, the situation in Mexico was out of control. More brutal slayings as Sinaloa continued to fight the Beltrán Leyva brothers and just about every other cartel.

Hundreds of *narcotraficantes* in Culiacán and other places were killed every month. Victims were found shot dead in parked cars, decapitated, burned, rolled up in bloody blankets and dumped on the roadside.

Matters got so bad that we heard a state official trekked up to a ranch in the state of Durango, deep in the eastern Sierra Madre, and tried to broker a truce between Guzmán and one of the cartels. It didn't work.

President Calderón's push against the cartels only made the violence worse. The major traffickers weren't being killed—only police officers, soldiers, and innocent bystanders.

But all that violence did nothing to disrupt the flow of drugs across the border.

The Fusion Center was designed to go after bad guys like Chapo. I had a hundred agents from the DEA, FBI, ATF, ICE, and IRS, all of us working together to develop leads to stop the scourge of illegal drugs. And I made sure we got the information to agents in the field.

Every day at 8:30 a.m., I'd meet with my section chiefs to go over the Consolidated Priority Organization Targets, a list of the top 100 drug traffickers in the world. There were Afghans and Colombians on the list, but most of the gangsters were Mexican.

I'd ask my chiefs what they were doing to catch the drug lords, and what they were seeing in the field. But, inevitably, the conversation would turn to El Chapo. I explained that he was our biggest threat. Guzmán and his Sinaloa cartel controlled most of the drugs being smuggled into the United States.

"He's as dangerous as Osama bin Laden," I'd say. I pushed our agents and intelligence people to be aggressive in cracking down on his cartel's operations.

I threw myself into tracking Chapo, talking to informants, reading reports, trying to anticipate his next move. I was working so many long hours that, a year into the job, Monica thought it would be a good idea if she and Kevin moved back to St. Louis. "That's the only place he's ever felt at home," she said. I agreed. We bought a place there and got him into a good Catholic high school. On weekends, I flew home to be with my family.

After two years at the Fusion Center, I felt the urge to get back in the field. That's where I was at my best. So when I heard that the SAC in Chicago was about to retire, I talked to my boss, Leonhart, about the position. To my surprise, I got the job. I was headed home.

I called Monica right away and she was thrilled. We decided that she and Kevin would stay in St. Louis until he graduated from high school. Uprooting him again was out of the question. Meanwhile, I'd get an apartment near the Chicago office, and make a fresh start in my old stomping grounds. I couldn't wait to get there.

I picked a tough moment to arrive in Chicago. It was the summer of 2010, and the violence there, too, was out of control. City dwellers were awakened at night by gunfire and sirens. Every morning the newspapers reported gang-related shootings, robberies, thefts, and assaults.

I knew the gangs were fighting over territory—more neighborhoods meant more customers, and more cash. Intelligence told us that one man was responsible for supplying most of the drugs for sale: El Chapo.

Chicago had become Sinaloa's northern US franchise. Street gangs were their retail sales force. Chapo sent them the dope—heroin, cocaine, methamphetamine, and marijuana—and an assortment of local gangsters cut, packaged, and distributed it in clubs, schools, workplaces, and on streets and playgrounds all over the Midwest.

The big boys in Mexico didn't care about murderous fights over retail sales territories, or innocent people caught in the crossfire, as long as the cash kept rolling in.

When I got to the city, it was in the middle of a heroin crisis. Heroin seizures and heroin-related emergency room visits in Chicago were running at more than three times the national average. Heroin was everywhere, in easy-to-use forms that didn't have to be injected.

The drug had changed a lot since the 1960s and '70s, when desperate junkies shot up in dark alleys. The heroin for sale in Chicago today was much purer and much easier to use. It came in powdered and smokable forms, so users didn't need so much to get high, and didn't risk contracting AIDS or hepatitis by reusing needles. Heroin was now the drug of choice in many neighborhoods, including the highly prized suburban markets.

But it was more than that. Guzmán had Chicago in a stranglehold. He controlled up to 80 percent of the drug flow into the city. Chicago had become the hub of an international drug distribution network stretching throughout the Midwest and north into Canada. I knew drug dealers looked at the city in much the same way that logistics businesses and trucking companies did. Chicago was in the center of the country, connected to ports and shipping centers all around the United States. Local gangs and criminal syndicates offered a willing pool of cheap labor. And there was a great demand, too, for the product itself.

After I started, I began meeting with my agents and supervisors, one on one, and in groups. It was important to explain my strategy, my vision. I didn't have to tell them that Chicago had gone to shit. They already knew that.

I told them we weren't going to find El Chapo in Chicago. This wasn't a manhunt. Instead, we were going to ferret out his cells.

Chapo ran Chicago like a terrorist group, or a spy ring.

One cell oversaw the wholesale movement of narcotics. The other moved money, massive amounts of cash. Both cells worked for the same person, but they knew nothing about one another. So if we hit the money, we couldn't get the dope. And if we hit the dope, the dealers couldn't give up the money.

But I knew that, for all the cartel's ingenuity, their sales network had a potentially fatal weakness. They needed street gangs to get their product to the consumer. We could get to the gangsters. They were Chapo's "choke point," the most vulnerable link in the chain.

"So that's our focus," I'd tell my agents.

I explained that our new choke-point strategy would allow us to work our investigations from the middle outward. "We can take down the guys in the street, while at the same time connecting that dot to other dots, working it upward toward the cartel level," I said.

I sensed that everyone in the office was enthusiastic about my vision. Agents who'd been busting small-potatoes pushers were excited to be working on cases with an international reach, and the young guys were fired up, happy to know their boss wanted them to kick ass.

I knew it would take more resources to tackle my ambitious agenda. That's why I wanted to create a special unit, a strike force: federal, state, and local law enforcement all working together to get the bad guys. They would help us keep the drugs from flowing into Chicago and quell the gang violence.

First, I had to get the federal prosecutor onboard. And that's why I was here with two of my agents, at 9:30 a.m., in a waiting area outside his office. As the new SAC in Chicago, I wanted to remind Pat Fitzgerald what interagency cooperation could do to fight street gangs that had turned America's third-largest city into a war zone. I tapped my foot and glimpsed around the room. I was getting impatient.

Finally, the door opened, and Fitzgerald invited us inside.

"Jack, good to see you," he said, reaching out to shake my hand. I had met Fitzgerald a few months earlier when I visited Chicago to promote the Fusion Center.

My agents followed me in. We sat down at a conference table. First assistant federal prosecutor Gary Shapiro was already there.

Fitzgerald was a no-nonsense guy. Appointed in 2001 by then-President George W. Bush, Fitzgerald led high-profile prosecutions, including corruption convictions of two successive Illinois governors: George Ryan and Rod Blagojevich.

Fitzgerald had been an assistant federal prosecutor in New York, where he tried the terrorist who orchestrated the 1993 World Trade Center bombing. He'd handled numerous drug trafficking and organized crime cases, but I wasn't sure he was up-to-date on the growth of *narcotraficante* empires in the United States, with his attention so taken up with home-grown American corruption.

I didn't waste any time.

"Pat, I want to tell you what's going on at the border," I said. "Sinaloa runs its drug wholesale business direct from there to here, Chicago. Our local gangbangers are the retailers. It's there we need to hit them. All the violence? That's the gangs spreading out," I said.

"Easy won't do it. We can't settle for quick hits. The federal agencies need to work together," I said.

And to do that, we need a strike force. A cooperative, specialized unit.

Fitzgerald listened with a poker face.

"You know, Jack, we talked about a strike force before. But your guy shot it down," he said.

He was talking about my predecessor.

"He's retired. He's gone now. This is what I truly believe. This is my mantra," I said. "I've been preaching this gospel for years."

I sat back in my chair. Silence fell for a moment.

"Jack, the DEA is going to have to lead the way on this. So it's going to be up to you to make this happen," Fitzgerald said.

Just the words I wanted to hear. I let myself smile.

"Pat, I will do that," I promised.

We talked a little bit longer, but soon it was time to go. Everyone in the room got up and shook hands. And as I walked out of his office, I was optimistic. He gets it, I thought. Fitzgerald understood what I was trying to do. Now I just had to make it work.

The one thing I didn't expect was pushback from Leonhart, my boss, about the strike force. These units were usually funded by the federal forfeiture program, using money seized in drug busts. But Leonhart said she was afraid my unit would drain money from other important DEA projects.

I understood her concerns. I'd proposed a new office, with new equipment. I didn't want the interagency strike force to meet in the DEA office. That had worked in El Paso, but we couldn't do that in Chicago, where we had to save more face and massage more egos. We needed an independent place so the police chief didn't think this was "just DEA," and the FBI didn't assume DEA was calling all the shots. It all went back to my mantra: We can't work in silos. We have to commingle, compare notes, build trust, and just shoot the breeze, too. A new building, a clean, dignified place where guys had the best equipment, the best prosecutors— the best federal agents and cops would aspire to get onto the strike force. That's what I wanted.

I had Fitzpatrick onboard, as well as the local FBI chief, Robert Grant. Jody Weis, the Chicago police superintendent, supported the idea, and so did Mayor Richard Daley. Leonhart wasn't convinced, but I told her I was going to move forward with it anyway. I wasn't going to let a little thing like funding stop me.

Every day had been hectic since I got word I was headed home. I had been running around like a crazy man for weeks, finding a place to live, moving my belongings from Virginia, and getting up to speed on my sprawling DEA territory. I was responsible for nearly three hundred agents in thirteen offices in Illinois, Wisconsin, Indiana, Minnesota, and North Dakota.

Chicago was my hometown, so I was able to find a good apartment quickly. It was on the fourteenth floor, with a sweeping view of Lake Michigan, and a balcony where I could breathe the air and grill my dinner when I wanted to. It was a bachelor pad of sorts, with Monica and Kevin still living in St. Louis. I commuted on weekends, or they could come up to the city.

The apartment quickly morphed into a war room. Intelligence reports and papers were spread out on the kitchen table, and my phone rang non-stop with calls from Tony and other old friends and colleagues. Some were retired, but others still worked in the DEA or the Chicago Police Department or other law enforcement agencies. They updated me on everything going on in the city and beyond.

I wanted to make sure I was up-to-date on all our new cases and our old ones—especially an investigation that involved the twins. Over the years, I had been briefed about Margarito and Pedro Flores, twin brothers who were only five-foot-four and weighed maybe 140 pounds each. They were little guys, but they became the biggest drug dealers in Chicago history, and one of our strongest links to El Chapo.

They were groomed from childhood for a life in the drug trade, but they kept a low profile, and avoided senseless violence. And in 2008, at the height of their careers, the twins quietly turned themselves in. They'd been working undercover since then, helping the government bring down the Sinaloa cartel.

Their rise from Chicago's Little Village, a working-class neighborhood, to secret meetings in Mexico with El Chapo, was something out of a movie.

Born in 1981, Margarito and Pedro were shy, polite kids who helped with their father's marijuana business. When they were seven, they fished bricks of marijuana out of gas tanks. When they turned eight, they were translating drug deals from English into Spanish for their father. They rode along with Dad from Mexico to Chicago in a vehicle packed with marijuana.

When the Flores boys were ten, Chicago police raided their parents' home and found $195,000 worth of marijuana packed in feed bags. When they turned twelve, their father split for Mexico.

Meantime, the boys seemed to be growing up straight. As teenagers they worked part-time at McDonald's. Their older brother Armando took over their father's marijuana business, and paid the boys extra to keep them out of the Latin Kings, the neighborhood gang. They went to school at Farragut Career Academy, just a few blocks from home. Friends and neighbors said they were well-dressed, quiet kids.

When Armando was arrested in 1999 and sentenced to five years in prison for narcotics trafficking, the Flores twins stepped in to keep the family business going.

At first, they bought their marijuana, cocaine, and heroin, fifteen to twenty kilos at a time, from Saul Rodriguez, a local supplier. But their father lived in Mexico, and through him the boys had a direct link to the Mexican cartels. So they cut out the middleman. Their shipments of marijuana, cocaine, and heroin soon dwarfed anything Rodriguez had ever handled.

By their twenty-fifth birthday, the brothers handled the Sinaloa cartel's distribution throughout the Midwest, moving an estimated $1.8 billion in drugs through Chicago.

Their near-monopoly of the city's drug supply brought the usual riches and toys: Custom motorcycles, Bentleys, and their own real-estate empire.

In 2005, Chapo was deep into his Mexican range war when he heard about "Los Flores," a pair of Chicago brothers with the best broker network in America.

For years, they'd been buying in bulk from the Beltrán Leyva brothers, a cartel aligned with Chapo. One of the four Beltrán Leyva brothers told El Chapo the twins were smart, discreet, and always paid on time.

Chapo was intrigued. He invited them to Mexico for the rarest of honors: a face-to-face meeting at his compound. They impressed the big man because they were all about business, not bravado. Chapo and his principal partners, El Mayo and the Beltrán Leyva brothers, came to an agreement. They'd front as much dope as the twins could handle, and give them a break on the price. They would also allow them to buy on terms instead of demanding cash on delivery.

For the twins, it was like hitting the Powerball jackpot.

By the summer of 2005, Chicago was swimming in powerful Mexican heroin. Almost immediately, the city's hospitals were packed with junkies who abruptly stopped breathing after snorting or spiking the product. The lethal batch ended up killing a thousand users in less than a year.

The Chicago DEA went on a wartime footing, scrambling to get the poisonous drug off the street and track it down to its source. It came from a lab near Mexico City. Chapo had brought in chemists to make it extra-strong by adding fentanyl, a synthetic narcotic that looks and cooks like heroin. In May 2006, authorities raided the lab and arrested five employees. One of them had been busted previously in California for manufacturing fentanyl.

Chapo shrugged off the takedown. He had Chicago in a vise, as well as Milwaukee, Detroit, Cincinnati, Columbus, and Cleveland. From 2005 to 2008, the Flores brothers moved $2 billion worth of Sinaloa product. The arrangement worked beautifully for the cartel, with Sinaloa supplying half the coke and heroin in America. Chapo had partners in West Coast cities, was moving heavily into Europe, and was planting new cells in South America.

With cash pouring in from every port, he was paying millions a year in bribes to Mexican officials, and getting white-glove service in return. Guzmán trusted the twins. In May 2008, he called them to a summit at his compound in La Tuna. Pedro couldn't make it, but Margarito went, taking the five-hour car ride up the mountain.

There was trouble at the top.

Guzmán and the Beltrán Leyva brothers had declared war on one another, and Flores was given an ultimatum: Stop buying Beltrán Leyvas' dope or else. Margarito had to pick a team. Right now. If he said no,

Chapo would kill him, even though he'd made billions for the druglord. Margarito agreed, and was allowed to go free.

The next time the Beltrán Leyva brothers called, their cartel gave the twins a similar ultimatum. If they ever bought from Chapo again, bad things would happen to them. The twins were in a fix, stuck in the middle of two warring cartels. They could see only one way out. They had their attorney call the DEA. The twins would give them Chapo and the Beltrán Leyvas in exchange for protection.

In June 2008, DEA agents flew to Mexico, where the Flores twins met them with stacks of logbooks listing every drug shipment, dozens of mobile phones with texts and voice mails saved from Chapo's lieutenants, and flowcharts of brokers in the United States who regularly bought hundreds of kilos apiece.

It was a huge cache of information. I knew the Chicago DEA could not comprehend the scale of what they had. They were focused on Chicago stash houses, not the tangled webs of cartels in Mexico.

The twins agreed to stay in Mexico for several months and record their every phone call as they played both sides. They promised to tip the DEA to each major shipment going north. In exchange, they'd receive reduced sentences, and lifelong enrollment in the witness-protection program.

They kept their promises.

Over the next few months the DEA raided stash houses and stopped tractor-trailer deliveries. They seized three tons of cocaine and heroin and $22 million in cash. Sixty-eight people were arrested in Chicago alone, many of them brokers and gang chiefs.

By November 2008, the twins' connections took us higher up the cartel food chain.

Jesús Vicente Zambada Niebla, the son of Chapo's top lieutenant and a high-ranking Sinaloa operative, was arrested in Mexico in March 2009 and extradited to the United States. Five months after Zambada's capture, a federal grand jury in Chicago indicted him and forty-five others for operating a Sinaloa-led drug ring in the city. Zambada was the highest-ranking cartel leader ever to be prosecuted in the United States. He was the tip of the iceberg. The brothers had given us more clues than we could process at once, evidence that directly implicated Chapo himself—we now had two audio recordings of Chapo and Pedro Flores discussing a twenty-kilo order of heroin on the telephone.

Zambada was in jail, and I intended to pay him a visit. Yes, I knew he had already been interrogated, but I'd read and studied Chapo and his crew so deeply for so long that I wanted the chance to sit across the table from one of his intimates and ask him some questions. I didn't expect a lot of dialogue, but, at the very least, I'd let him know he was a scumbag, and we had his organization in our crosshairs.

Months passed, the year wound up, but I didn't give up on the strike force. A group of about twenty DEA and FBI agents and cops occasionally met in our office, talking and exchanging information. I kept pushing Washington to fund a proper office.

We kept busting drug dealers, kept listening in on telephones, kept our ears to the ground and our intel flowing, talking, uploading, comparing notes. We were leaning hard on the cartels, and the pressure was taking its toll. It was only a matter of time until El Chapo made a wrong turn—as he did with the "weed train."

It looked like any freight train headed north—except this one was loaded with marijuana, courtesy of Guzmán.

Like any good case, it started with a tip. We asked for help from SOD and agents in other DEA offices. Derek Maltz was my main point of contact at SOD, but Cronin was about to be transferred there from St. Louis. It was a good move for him. Comer had just taken over as associate special agent in charge in Atlanta. Again, a good move because Chapo was eyeing Atlanta as another hub, and Comer was aggressive as hell. Although Keefe and Corcoran were retired, I still ran ideas by them all the time. And, of course, Tony was my sounding board. I can't tell you how many times we talked to each other during the week.

My main office was in Chicago, but I was responsible for a big territory. And I made it a point to visit the field offices, to meet face-to-face with the ASACs and agents. I'd let them know about the change in philosophy: Forget about the little stuff. We were going after the big fish—and the biggest one was Sinaloa.

Although cocaine, heroin, and meth were Chapo's biggest money-makers, marijuana still held a special place in his heart—that's how he learned his chops. That's how, long ago, he'd proved to his bosses he could smuggle shit across the border.

SOD had concluded that Sinaloa was shipping pot to Chicago on freight trains.

"Really?" I said to Maltz. "Illinois Central? The Wabash Cannonball?"

"I'm not busting your balls," he said.

"OK. We gotta jump on this."

"I'm already on it," he said.

For months, we gathered information about how the marijuana came across the border and was loaded onto the trains. We examined all the possible freight routes to Chicago. There were dozens, so many it made my head spin. I had no idea trains were still so important.

Patterns emerged. We focused on a Chicago warehouse where we thought a crew was handling the dope.

When I talked to SOD, I'd ask for updates on the weed train.

Then we got a break. An informant told us the marijuana was coming in big sacks listed on the manifests as "Titanium Pigments," an element used to make paint and sunscreen. When we drilled deeper, we found the bags were coming from a business called Comercializadora de Minerales, in Jalisco, Mexico. The product was supposedly being imported by a company called Earth Minerals Corp., in Rockdale, Illinois, just south of Joliet.

It's brilliant, I thought. *Who the hell would suspect that?*

This is where SOD and interagency cooperation paid off. We told DEA, FBI, and other federal agents, and state and local law enforcement along the border, to be on the lookout for the shipment.

We didn't know how the dope would move across the border. We didn't know when the next shipment was coming in, or where the dope would be loaded onto the freight trains.

Then, in November 2010, we got another break. ICE agents found six cars of a Union Pacific train loaded with 340 "super sacks"—three thousand pounds apiece—from Comercializadora de Minerales.

With the help of a drug-sniffing dog, agents found bundles of marijuana encrusted in a thick layer of fine, rust-colored dust. When we looked at the shipping documents, everything lined up.

In the past, we'd have unloaded the train cars and held a news conference to announce that we'd seized a shitload of marijuana.

But that was then.

Instead, we placed the bags back into the railcars, sealed the doors, and let the train roll north. Our agencies, led by ICE, followed the train to its final destination, gathering more information about the operation along the way.

The sheer size of the operation suggested Sinaloa. Each one of the sacks had to be moved with hydraulic equipment, and carefully placed to balance out the load. They weren't just pitched over someone's shoulder into a freight car.

Dozens of phone calls, monitored by federal agents, revealed that unloading all that marijuana was no small logistical challenge, either. Several of the men involved were heard scrambling to ensure they had enough forklifts and sifter machines to separate the pot from its packaging.

One of the men was heard saying, "Save your energy and then go celebrate for two, three days, because you have lots to celebrate."

The bad guys had another thing coming.

A month after the discovery, when the train rolled into Chicago Heights, DEA agents were waiting, listening, and watching as the sacks of marijuana were unloaded and put into a warehouse.

When the last one was set in place, my guys swooped in and arrested seven people. Fitzgerald's office charged them with conspiracy to distribute marijuana. At a news conference, I told reporters we seized eleven tons of marijuana with a street value of $22 million.

"This is a great day for the good guys. Having served time on the border, this is the way it's supposed to work," I said.

Fitzgerald noted that it was an "intense, long investigation."

And I was quick to add, "Suffice it to say this is not the end of the investigation. Obviously, we're rolling from here."

Owen Putnam, my public information officer, would later chide me for the pun. But I didn't care. We'd worked together, and derailed Chapo's weed train.

CHAPTER 12

BORDER TOWN

When I got to Chicago, the most lucrative drug was heroin. Now, it was spreading all over the country—and Chapo was doing everything to make sure Americans got their fix.

Guzmán, ever the businessman, realized how dependent Americans had become on prescription opioid pain pills, and how similar they were to plain old heroin—they were practically interchangeable. He started shipping more heroin into the United States to capitalize on the demand.

Heroin has a long history in America. In 1898, the pharmaceutical giant Bayer began promoting heroin as a painkiller and cough medicine for children. Within twenty years, heroin was pulled from the open market because it was so addictive. Only doctors could prescribe it, and the family of new and improved opioid painkillers evolved over the years.

In the 1970s and 1980s, urged by pharmaceutical companies, doctors started giving opioids to patients with chronic pain syndrome, as well as postsurgical and dental pain, part of a cynical, industrywide push to "aggressively combat suffering." In 1996, Purdue Pharma introduced OxyContin and marketed it aggressively to doctors and patients as "a miracle pill that relieves severe pain for ten to twelve hours at a time."

But the relief didn't last that long. Withdrawal began almost immediately—the medicines turned out to be terrifically habit-forming, despite Purdue's claims.

By 2004, 2.4 million people were using prescription painkillers for nonmedical reasons. More and more people—regular folks—became addicted to the pills their doctors or dentists prescribed for them. More and more deaths were attributed to opioids. Public health and drug control officials stepped up their efforts to treat the addiction and curb the abuse.

Methadone clinics reopened, and opiate-addiction programs began enrolling abusers. Prosecutors began cracking down on doctors and pharmacies running "pill mills." But those much-needed reforms merely opened the door for drug cartels. And here comes Chapo, now moving heroin into the United States in bulk shipments. Heroin and prescription painkillers are similar enough that addicts who run out of one can substitute the other.

Soon heroin became the cheaper alternative. Our intelligence reports showed that Chapo had slowed down cocaine shipments to better flood the market with heroin. I talked to Cronin, who was now at SOD, and agents and intel guys from all over the country. He's brilliant, I told Cronin. He studied the market—then exploited it. Now we were facing a crisis that was destroying families.

By 2011, we were seeing more heroin than ever in Chicago. Users didn't have to use a needle to shoot up, so the face of heroin addiction was different, too—a lot of white, suburban, middle-class people, including older adults seeking pain relief and teens looking for a high. For me, it was like being back in St. Louis at the beginning of the methamphetamine epidemic—the overdoses, the deaths, the grieving families.

We started seizing record quantities of heroin, fifty and sixty kilos, sometimes up to a hundred kilos, all of it 90 percent pure. That was unheard of. After one particularly big bust, an agent said to me, "What a great case! We really put a dent in it, didn't we?"

"I don't think so," I told him. "This scares the crap out of me. There's just so much dope on the streets, it's unbelievable."

I made sure every state representative in my five-state DEA region understood that even though this thing was based in Chicago, it affected everyone in the country. And I knew it would only get worse when I discovered that members of one of the most ruthless gangs in Mexico were moving north.

Los Zetas were the new guys in the cartel world. They kidnapped and beheaded rival gang members and posted disgusting videos on the internet. They tortured innocent civilians just to make a point.

And now, the Zetas were here, in Chicago. With the heroin market exploding, they weren't about to stand on the sidelines when there was so much money to be made. They didn't trust local gangbangers to sell their dope for them. The DEA office in Laredo tipped us that the Zetas were sending some of their most trusted agents to live and work in Chicago and the Midwest.

That was a disturbing development. Leaders of Mexican drug cartels rarely ventured beyond the US border, but now it appeared they were sending up some key players to run their drug-distribution network out of middle-class suburbs, in nonborder states.

Putting their own guys on the ground gave them a tighter grip on the world's most lucrative narcotics market, and it maximized profits by cutting out unstable gangbanger middlemen. It was probably the most serious organized crime threat the nation had ever faced.

There were more than seventy street gangs in Chicago, and between 70,000 and 125,000 people belonged to one or another of them. I likened them to 100,000 Amway salesmen, each of them looking to expand his own drug-sales network.

Now, here we were, adding a cell of Los Zetas to the list.

The Zetas were sadistic. The gang was founded in the late 1990s by a group of Mexican army commandoes hired to guard the Gulf cartel. By 2010 they broke from their employers and formed their own criminal organization. They were best known for torture, beheadings, and indiscriminate slaughter. Unlike Chapo, they preferred brutality over bribery.

If they were coming to town, we'd be there to meet them.

My strike team jumped on the case. Informants tipped us on how the Zetas were bringing the dope into Chicago. Wiretaps started turning up more leads. Soon we had what we needed to arrest twenty people, including five members of Los Zetas.

I told Putnam it was time to hold a news conference touting the operation and to get the word out about these dirtbags. With Los Zetas on our streets, it was only a matter of time before the violence got worse.

At the briefing, I told reporters that the DEA and the FBI had worked together, and 250 kilograms of cocaine were seized from locations around Chicago.

I'd worked on the border, I said, and had been tracking El Chapo for almost my entire career. The big lesson was, no one was safe. The Mexican cartels were bringing their dope and guns to our neighborhoods now, and daily turf battles were turning parts of Chicago into a Mexican border town.

"One of the things that we've stressed since I've been up here is this: Even though we are two thousand miles away from Mexico, we have to operate as if we are on the border," I said.

I meant that. If we were ever going to make a difference, that's the way we had to think and act.

"Hey, boss, I want to run something by you," my agent David Lorino said to me. "It's Zambada. I think we're going to be done with the guy in a couple of days. Do you still want to talk to him?"

Jesús Vicente Zambada Niebla had been shuttling between a federal cell in Michigan and a Chicago jail since being extradited to the United States in 2009. Lorino had been the point man ever since, interrogating him and helping DEA agents from all over the United States get needed information from Zambada.

Zambada was the son of Ismael "El Mayo" Zambada—Chapo's right-hand man. "El Mayito," or the "Little Mayo," was a major trafficker in his own right. He was awaiting trial in a US federal court in Chicago on cocaine and heroin trafficking charges. Mayito was one of a slick new generation of Mexican traffickers, dubbed "narco juniors."

The Justice Department said his extradition was one of the most significant in years.

El Chapo was Zambada's godfather. So Zambada had been biding his time in jail. He said he'd talk, but first he had to speak to his father. It took a while to set that up. We had to give Zambada a cell phone, then give his phone number to his Mexican attorneys who somehow got it to El Mayo. Then we had to wait for the call.

Late one night, after most of our agents had gone home, Mayo called the number. We recorded it. "My son, my son, how are you?" he asked.

They chatted briefly. "I want you to know you have my authority to begin to cooperate, to get your life back," Mayo said.

That was it. The call lasted two minutes. It looked like Mayo was double-crossing Chapo. That's how I read it. But there was another fact in play: Mayo knew that enough time had elapsed now, that they'd changed their systems enough that anything the son said couldn't really hurt the father or the godfather.

So after two years of delays, Zambada Jr. started talking. And so far, the stuff he gave us was too old to use. That just angered the hell out of me. He was playing us.

Despite his uselessness, Lorino kept pressing Zambada. He'd often stop by my office and update me, because he knew that I'd been tracking him and the cartels for two decades.

"You should sit in," Lorino would say.

"Dave, I'd just be a distraction. You guys don't need me hanging over your shoulders."

But now the judge had set a trial date. I might not get another chance. This might be the closest I ever got to Chapo, so the hell with it. "You know what? Let's go see him now," I said to Lorino.

He flashed a wide smile. "That's what I thought."

I called the US Marshals who were guarding Zambada in an off-site Chicago safe house and told them I was coming for a visit. Lorino and I walked there. On the way I thought of the questions I'd ask. Lorino and several others had already interrogated him. This was for me. For my own sake. I just wanted to look him in the eyes, and see how reality stacked up to my expectations.

Once there, the Marshals led us into a small, dimly lit room, sunless as a basement apartment but bristling with surveillance cameras. I sat down at a tiny table with a DEA translator.

A few minutes later a door opened and a tall, gaunt man walked into the room. He was dressed in a purple velour tracksuit with gold chains dangling from his neck. He looked like a New York pimp from the 1980s.

I stared for a moment. This was Zambada? He looked nothing like El Vicentillo, Pretty Boy Vicente, handsome drug capo, son of the powerful Sinaloa cartel. *Really, this is the guy? You gotta be kidding!* I thought. *This is the son of Mayo, partner of Chapo, killer of innocents and destroyer of lives? This is it?*

He walked to the table and reached out his hand to shake mine. I did not respond. I kept my hands folded on the tabletop. I wanted to grab him by his neck, but I didn't do it. I was going to be professional, dammit.

He was a little taken aback, but he sat down. When he did, I stared straight into his eyes. He looked away. He was meek. A wimp. Without his guns and bodyguards, he was nothing.

The translator told Zambada who I was. I said I wasn't going to take much of his time.

"I just got a couple of questions for you," I said, waiting for her to translate.

"How are you being treated?" I asked.

The Marshals and agents treated him well, he said. Pleasantries out of the way, I cut to my real thoughts.

"I gotta know something: Did you know I was in El Paso?" I asked. He smiled and nodded his head yes.

Just what I thought. "Well, could you explain to me how you could justify the violence and murders that you, your father, and Chapo are responsible for?"

I had thought about that question for a long time, and I wanted to see his response. But there was none. He showed no emotion, made absolutely no movement in his body. He was normal, neutral, unfazed.

And then, through the translator, he said, "We were at war. We were at war for our families. We were at war for our territory. Sometimes there are casualties in war."

There was an awkward silence.

I felt myself flush red. I couldn't believe it. All those lives—they meant absolutely nothing to this scumbag. I wanted to reach across the table and cold-cock the bastard. I didn't do it. No, everybody was looking at me.

I regained my composure. I asked him, "How close and how often did you meet with Chapo?"

"Well, I've been around him off and on my whole life," he bragged. Chapo was like family, his mentor, a surrogate father.

I knew Chapo trusted Vicente more than his own kids. If Vicente hadn't been so careless, the Mexicans would never have arrested him. He was driving a nice car and going to nightclubs. Even though the Mexican cops were all being bribed, Zambada was so cocky and flashy with his money they thought they had to make a move.

But sitting there in the safe house in Illinois, his arrogance and cluelessness really shocked the shit out of me. It was one of those moments when you sit back and think, *Now I get it. I understand the way these people think. Criminals are animals. They're ruining their own country and they're ruining ours, and they tell each other, tell themselves, they're in a war. As if they had no choice.*

Maybe Zambada never pulled the trigger himself. He may never have dirtied his hands like that. But that didn't matter to me. It was the orders he gave. His father brought him up in the business, and he knew exactly what he was doing.

To hell with this guy, I thought. I've had enough. I wasn't going to dignify him with my presence any longer. I got up from my chair, turned around, and left.

I was pissed off, and disappointed, too: Is this what I worked my whole career for, to sit down and look into the face of this turd?

Lorino asked me on the way out what I was thinking.

I didn't know what to say. I just shrugged my shoulders. "Let's just get outta here. There's nothing here."

My office had embraced my strategy. We were opening dozens of new cases, exchanging information with offices and agencies all over the country and the world. We were walking the walk. Kicking ass, taking names.

We were doing a decent job, but Chicago itself was changing. The political landscape that underpinned my little sphere in the law enforcement world was shifting all the time.

Richard Daley had been mayor for nearly twenty years. He'd been a big supporter of the strike force. He asked for frequent updates on our progress, and I was glad to show him some solid results. Despite our cramped quarters at the DEA office and our informal status, we had more than twenty team members and were conducting several ongoing investigations.

I didn't know for sure, but I suspected that Mayor Daley was behind cutting through piles of federal agency crap and finding us $890,000 in Organized Crime Drug Enforcement Task Force funds, with a promise of $1.2 million more.

The money would help pay for expenses, like overtime for participating police officers, but it wasn't enough to move off-site. It was a good start, though, and I was grateful. I went to thank him. But during that meeting, he dropped a bomb: He wasn't going to run for reelection in 2011.

I was stunned. There'd been Daleys in Chicago City Hall since I was a kid. His father had been mayor from 1955 until he died in 1976.

"You have to promise me something," the mayor said to me. I nodded. "Whoever the next mayor is, you get in here and you explain as quickly as you can what you're doing," Daley said.

He announced his retirement. Rahm Emanuel, President Barack Obama's former chief of staff, jumped into the race.

He'd want to appoint his own police chief, which meant good-bye to Jody Weis, a strike force supporter. I could only hope we could get both the new mayor and the new chief to buy into the program.

It was just as I'd feared. Emanuel was elected mayor on February 22, 2011. And, sure enough, he fired Weis and named Garry McCarthy to the post.

McCarthy was a New York City police officer who worked his way up through the ranks. He became deputy commissioner of operations in 2000, and was in the middle of ground zero right after the 9/11 attacks, working closely with then-Mayor Rudy Giuliani to operate an emergency response command post. From there he became police chief in Newark, New Jersey—as tough a town as anywhere in America.

I did some homework on McCarthy; I called up everybody I knew in New York. Results were mixed. Obviously, he was bright and politically savvy, but a friend told me he had one of the biggest egos on earth. But beyond that, he was a really good cop.

We first met at a gathering of the top ten, a Chicago tradition where the top brass of federal law enforcement and the Chicago Police Department get together every two weeks to discuss the ten most dangerous criminals in the area. The meeting was usually held at the DEA office. We'd catch up on interdepartmental news, and talk about what we were doing to nab the bad guys.

When McCarthy showed up for his first meeting, I asked him to stick around afterward. We adjourned to my office, and sat down while he told me about his background. I liked the guy. He was a genuine, no-nonsense policeman.

I told him about the strike force, and how Chicago police were key players. He just listened. "I need to keep your guys on the strike force," I said. "I hope this is something you can get behind."

McCarthy said he had no intention of pulling out, that he liked the interagency cooperation angle. That's all I could get out of him. We shook hands, said good-bye, got back to work.

Over the next few weeks, McCarthy called me a couple of times, asking for DEA help after a series of neighborhood shootings. He clearly had no idea how many people were working for me, or that we already had ten to fifteen full-time guys at police headquarters. We knew most of the

Jack Riley sits on the porch with his father, Ralph Riley Jr., in the 1960s at their home in Homewood, Illinois. *Courtesy of the author*

Young Jack Riley gives his best Popeye the Sailor scowl as a kid in Homewood, Illinois, in the 1960s. *Courtesy of the author*

Jack Riley's grandfather Ralph Riley was a commander for the Chicago Police Department. He was known as Big Hands, because he was famous for putting his fists on criminals. *Courtesy of the author*

Jack Riley and his wife, Monica, outside their home in 1991 in Virginia, where he worked in the DEA's classified program. *Courtesy of the author*

A Chicago police officer, Nedrick Miller was also a drug trafficker. Riley helped investigate Miller's organization, and the DEA busted Miller and others in 1989. Here Miller is pictured with a fighting rooster he seized during a cockfight in his role as a police officer. *Courtesy of the author*

Jack Riley clowns with DEA agents Sherod Jones and Van Quarles in the late 1980s when they worked undercover in Chicago. *Courtesy of the author*

Jack Riley on the National Mall in Washington, DC, in December 1984. He was going through DEA training at the federal facility in Quantico, Virginia. *Courtesy of the author*

Jack Riley visits his son Kevin's school in the St. Louis area during the DEA's Red Ribbon Week in 2003. Red Ribbon Week began after DEA Special Agent Enrique "Kiki" Camarena was tortured and killed by drug traffickers he was investigating in Mexico in 1985. *Courtesy of the author*

Art Bilek, executive vice president of the Chicago Crime Commission, announces Joaquín "El Chapo" Guzmán is Chicago's Public Enemy No. 1. Riley is standing at right, next to the poster. *Courtesy of the author*

Jack Riley speaks at a 2013 news conference on Chicago gun violence as Chicago Police Superintendent Garry McCarthy (far left), Chicago Mayor Rahm Emanuel (right), and U.S. Rep. Bobby Rush (D-Illinois, far right) look on. Riley and McCarthy differed sharply in their strategies for combatting drug trafficking. *Courtesy of the author*

A DEA wanted poster for Tomas Gonzales, a Chicago-based drug trafficker who worked for El Chapo in the mid-1990s. *US Drug Enforcement Administration*

Margarito Flores, U.S. Marshals Service wanted poster. Margarito Flores and his identical twin, Pedro, were El Chapo's top customers in the United States. The Chicago brothers became key witnesses against Chapo and his organization, leading to the indictment and extradition of the drug lord to the United States in January 2017. *Courtesy of the author*

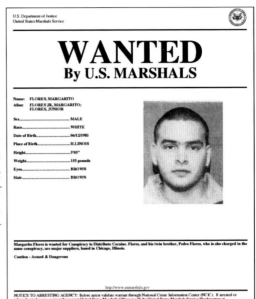

U.S. Department of Justice
United States Marshals Service

WANTED
By U.S. MARSHALS

Name: FLORES, MARGARITO
Alias: FLORES JR, MARGARITO;
FLORES, JUNIOR

Sex: MALE
Race: WHITE
Date of Birth: 06/12/1981
Place of Birth: ILLINOIS
Height: 5'05"
Weight: 155 pounds
Eyes: BROWN
Hair: BROWN

Margarito Flores is wanted for Conspiracy to Distribute Cocaine. Flores, and his twin brother, Pedro Flores, who is also charged in the same conspiracy, are major suppliers, based in Chicago, Illinois.

Caution - Armed & Dangerous

http://www.usmarshals.gov

NOTICE TO ARRESTING AGENCY: Before arrest validate warrant through National Crime Information Center (NCIC). If arrested or whereabouts known, contact the nearest United States Marshal's Office or call the United States Marshals Service Headquarters at

Jack Riley, the special agent in charge of the DEA in Chicago, stands in the interagency Strike Force office in 2013, where he points out Mexican drug cartel operations in the Chicago area. *Courtesy of the author*

Jack Riley meets with Enrique Galindo, head of the Mexican federal police, in March 2015. In a private meeting, Riley warned Galindo that El Chapo might break out of prison through a tunnel. He did so on July 11, 2015. *Courtesy of the author*

Jack Riley in a helicopter in Afghanistan during a February 2015 fact-finding trip after he was named the DEA's Chief of Operations. *Courtesy of the author*

Drug kingpin Joaquín "El Chapo" Guzmán is captured in Los Mochis, Mexico, on January 8, 2016, after trying to escape through a sewer. *Courtesy of the author*

Guzmán, head of the Sinaloa cartel and the No. 1 most wanted criminal in the United States, is extradited from Mexico on January 19, 2017. *Courtesy of the author*

El Chapo mugshot after he is captured in January 2016. *Courtesy of the author*

El Chapo built tunnels under his safe houses so he could escape if police raided his home. *Courtesy of the author*

El Chapo always planned his escapes in advance. So when police raided his home in Culiacán in 2014, he activated an escape hatch underneath his bathtub that led to a tunnel. *Courtesy of the author*

Jack Riley appears before the House Judiciary Committee on July 28, 2015, to discuss the U.S. heroin epidemic. *Courtesy of the author*

Jack Riley aims his gun at a suspect hiding in a house during a 2005 raid on a mom-and-pop methamphetamine operation in rural Missouri. The suspect had barricaded himself behind a bedroom door, and Jack's quick action stopped a potential shootout. *Courtesy of the author*

Jack Riley and his former assistant Jon DeLena share a drink at Riley's retirement party in January 2017. When Riley took over as the DEA's Chief of Operations in 2015, DeLena accompanied Riley on several trips, including one to Afghanistan. DeLena was later selected to head the DEA's office in Manchester, New Hampshire. *Courtesy of the author*

shootings stemmed from gangs fighting over drugs and territory. When the strike force made successful arrests, McCarthy seldom showed up for all the news conferences.

He brought with him the "broken window" theory of policing. The theory was simple: A single broken window left unrepaired would soon give rise to a dozen more broken windows, and graffiti, and then young thugs on a downward slide. Police could make cities safer by cracking down early on minor crimes like vandalism. The city should focus on small, quality-of-life issues like broken windows and cracked sidewalks. A clean, well-kept town makes for clean, well-kept citizens who don't tolerate or generate violence or other, more serious kinds of crime. McCarthy liked to say that approach changed New York City's streets in the 1990s for the better. He didn't get what we were doing, or how entrenched the gangs were in Chicago. I told him we needed to focus on the big targets—the cartels and the gangsters. But he was happy simply picking up the dime-bag dealer on the corner. "Jack, we're not chasing the kilo fairies around here," he told me, maybe a dozen times.

"Garry, this isn't New York. New York doesn't have the kind of street gangs we do," I snapped. "They don't do business with Chapo."

The physical makeup of Chicago is vastly different from that of New York, I said. These gangs are second, third generation; some of them never venture outside a five-block area. That's where the shootings are happening.

That's where the dope is being sold. It's heroin. The hard stuff. It's coming here straight from Sinaloa. Here in Chicago, if we figure out some badass gangbanger is moving dope, the police go get the guy right now. Get him off the street. But he's just one player in a much bigger organization. These guys work in threes. One with a pistol, one with the ounce of heroin, and the other guy watching for the cops. You need to take all three of them out. If we really want to do something for the community, that's what we need to do. We flip all three guys, and we work our way up from there.

"We've got to have a multipronged attack," I said. "That's the role I see for the strike force. That's why that whole choke-point concept is so important: It gives every agency something only they can do. We work together. We're not just picking the low-hanging fruit; we're going for the root of the tree."

But McCarthy said no.

"I'm not worried about international cartels. I'm worried about the kid walking to school who has to walk by the corner where they're selling. We need to just take those people off the corner."

"No, you have to take out all three guys. Narcotics doesn't work that way. That's doing exactly what Chapo wants you to do. He'll have a new seller out there tomorrow," I said, "and you're tying up all your resources just swatting flies."

He couldn't seem to grasp the urgency of the situation.

"Our undercover guys are seizing heroin laced with fentanyl," I said. "It's a completely different animal. It can kill twenty different ways, but that's kind of what Chapo wants. He wants people to get addicted. Garry, I don't know why you can't see that. These gangs don't support themselves stealing cars and mugging kids on the way to school. They're selling narcotics," I said. "And where do you think the stuff comes from? Do you think it's made here?"

All I wanted was cooperation, information we could follow up or use to make a case. And the way to do that was by building a strike force, where people felt empowered.

But McCarthy didn't get it, or he didn't want to.

It was so frustrated I decided to go on the offensive. I told Putnam to set up some meetings with reporters. I had to get my message out. I mean, the Chicago cops and federal agencies knew what I was trying to do. We weren't official, but we were effective. We were cooperating with each other, attacking the cartels and the street gangs. The public needed to know that. Then maybe McCarthy would feel the pressure and start to support us.

I told the news guys how we were focusing on the shadowy spots along the drug chain, where street gangs come into contact with Mexican drug traffickers. More than forty DEA agents, along with the FBI, the IRS, the ATF, and ICE, now worked alongside Chicago cops, sharing information, making arrests, building solid cases.

"In the past, there was distrust and we didn't share information with each other," I said, noting that prosecutors were reviewing each of the strike force's cases to decide which to take to the federal level. "We can leverage the strength of the county system and the federal system to do the most damage to the organizations we're going after," I said.

I wasn't sure where Mayor Emanuel stood on the issue—or on anything. I took former Mayor Daley's advice and immediately reached out to Emanuel. But he didn't return any of my phone calls. Then one day, when I was on the city's South Side at a community meeting about drugs, McCarthy, who was seated next to me, leaned over and whispered, "The mayor's outside and wants to meet you."

"Now?"

"Yeah."

So we got up and walked out of the building. And there he was, the new mayor, in a motorcade. He shook my hand. "I hear you're a Chicago guy," Emanuel said.

I nodded yes, and then McCarthy interjected, "He's not like the other Feds. He's more like the real police."

I took that as a compliment. Emanuel said we should talk—and a few weeks later we did.

Sitting in his office, I told him about the strike force. He listened. Emanuel didn't ask many questions, which was strange. In every other city I've worked in, a new police chief or mayor was briefed early on by the federal agencies working in that city. The new leaders learned what federal officials believed were the biggest issues facing the city, and what resources were available to deal with them.

Emanuel never scheduled any briefings. He never asked me how many agents I had or how much territory we covered. He had his own ideas about crime and policing in Chicago, so I'm not sure why we met that day. He said almost nothing to me.

The differences in philosophy were never clearer than when Garry and I were invited to speak about guns and drugs to a group of business executives at a downtown hotel.

It was like a tale of two cities.

McCarthy went first. He touted how the Chicago police force was using the broken windows theory to improve the quality of life in neighborhoods. Crime was local, he said, and his department would soon have the street gangs under control, much like former New York City mayor Rudy Giuliani did in the 1990s.

He gave them sunshine. I went dark on their asses.

I lowered the lights and put on a PowerPoint presentation, showing how the cartels had turned Chicago into a major distribution hub. With our local strike force, Fusion Center, SOD, and all the intelligence from wiretaps and informants, we had connected the dots between Chapo and Chicago street gangs.

"We can never take our city back until we attack Chapo, until we aggressively take down the drug gangs that run our streets," I warned.

The executives sat there with their mouths open. They didn't have a clue what was going on around them, but by the end of my presentation, they had the lowdown. The whole city knew. I finally had everyone I needed onboard.

CHAPTER 13

PUBLIC ENEMY
NUMBER ONE

The summer of 2011 was a bright new beginning for my family. Kevin enrolled at the University of Missouri, and Monica moved to Chicago.

Kevin amazed us both. We'd moved countless times in his short life, but he'd grown into a well-adjusted, outgoing young man nevertheless. He was never a whiner, even though he never had any sibling to lean on when he started a new school. No, Kevin stood on his own two feet. Sports helped him make friends, but I suspect that even at a school without a sports program he'd have been OK. I couldn't have asked for a better son.

It was great having my wife back again! Even though we saw each other just about every weekend, it was just not right living apart. I'd missed Monica terribly and I still felt guilty about everything I had put her through. It wasn't easy picking up and leaving after you'd set down roots in a community. We spent long hours on the phone, and often just the sound of her voice would turn around a bad day. I told her she was my soul mate, my moral compass. We'd been married more than twenty-five years, and our love was still strong. She was my rock, the love of my life, and I made sure I told her that every day, and every night before I went to sleep.

My lonely bachelor apartment turned into a home, a place filled with comfort, color, and the laughter of family and friends. We arranged our lounge chairs on the balcony and often sat there with a glass of wine, watching the sun set over Lake Michigan.

It all was the best kind of therapy after what my workdays had become.

Street gangs, drug crimes, and violence dominated the local news, and Putnam was working day and night coordinating journalists' insatiable desire for interviews and information.

I spent a lot of time talking into microphones and cameras. I had a good rapport with the media. They needed us to give them stories and facts, and we needed them if we wanted to get our message out. The city and region needed to see and hear and know that drugs, gangs, cartels, and violence were synonymous.

In late February 2012, Fitzgerald called and said the brass was coming to town: Attorney General Eric Holder was scheduled for a routine visit.

When a US attorney general visits a city, he usually makes some kind of announcement, maybe discloses a new crime-fighting initiative. But sometimes he just wants to check in with administrative leaders of federal law enforcement to see how things are going, what kind of help or resources they might need.

Holder's visit was a little of both. He spoke in the morning at Northwestern University Law School. He greeted the students with a speech about the war on terror. He made no mention of drugs, crime, or cartels. To me, drugs were the biggest threat facing the United States. Don't get me wrong: Terrorism was still a major problem, and our country was always on alert for the next attack. But how do you think terrorist groups fund their operations? Drugs, that's how.

Mexican cartels didn't use their profits to fund terrorists. Their drug money went to fuel their lavish lifestyles. But that wasn't the case in Afghanistan, where most of the world's heroin was grown. Afghan heroin went to the European, African, and Russian markets. The profits bankrolled the Taliban, Al Qaeda, and other terrorist groups.

I knew that because DEA had a small group of elite agents in Afghanistan working with Special Forces to destroy drug operations. In fact, the DEA had five Foreign-deployed Advisory and Support Teams, known as FAST. One worked in Afghanistan; the others in Central and South America. Not only did FAST conduct direct action, counterterrorism, and counter-narcotics missions, it engaged the enemy in combat.

I knew why Holder was addressing terrorism. It was in the news. But today Holder was in Chicago, ground zero in a war bigger than the terrorist threat. Couldn't he see what was going on in Chicago, in President Obama's hometown? Didn't he see how the city was being flooded with high-grade heroin?

Chapo was driving down the price of heroin, making it cheaper for people addicted to pain pills to switch to his product. I had been making the case to everyone I could find in the DEA and the Justice Department that the opioid epidemic was fueling the national heroin crisis. But no one seemed to hear me.

The meeting with Holder in Fitzgerald's office only confirmed my suspicions, no matter how I carried on about a crisis that was destroying American cities and towns, a catastrophe that cut across socioeconomic, ethnic, and racial lines. I felt like some horrible old prophet of doom, preaching to a crowd that had moved on to a newer, more appealing crisis.

When the attorney general got to Fitzgerald's office, we all filed into the conference room. Just about all the heads of the local federal agencies were there, including Robert Grant, the supervisor in charge of Chicago's FBI office.

I had a good working relationship with Grant. He had provided a number of agents for the strike force. He didn't give me much input, but that was fine. He seemed to understand what I was trying to do. At least I thought he did.

As was usual in these meetings, Holder went around the room and asked each director: "What are you up against? What are your problems?"

Grant told Holder about public corruption cases. I used my time to talk about the collaboration between the Mexican cartels and the street gangs. After everyone got a chance to express their concerns, Holder asked us if there was anything else on our minds. That's usually a chance to go off script, to talk about issues that are really bothering you.

Grant spoke up, but quietly.

"Mr. Holder, I have to talk to you about something," Grant said, his voice almost in a whisper. He had a pained look on his face that said he was ready to spill some burden he'd been carrying for a long time.

"With all due respect to Jack, I think the war on drugs is a complete bust, a complete waste of money," Grant said softly.

What? Am I hearing this guy right? I thought.

Before I had a chance to respond, Fitzgerald's chair pivoted to me, his eyes were popping out, the look on his face said, *Please don't say anything stupid.* He knew what could happen if I got mad.

Meanwhile, Grant continued, oblivious to the people in the room. He told Holder that, despite all the money we spent, we hadn't made a dent in the drug problem. We should use the resources someplace else, he said. He droned on and on. And Holder didn't stop him.

When Grant finished, Holder didn't respond. He didn't say a word. But that told me everything I needed to know. He tacitly agreed with Grant.

There was a ringing in my ears, but I knew I had to hold my temper. I had to keep my emotions in check. I clenched my jaw, I took a deep breath. I couldn't believe it. After working together for nearly two years, this man showed his true colors. He pissed on everything we'd been trying to do to stop the violence, to stop drugs from flowing in and destroying lives. He may have been the FBI director in Chicago, but Grant didn't know the streets like I did. He never saw the weeping parents or the hollow-eyed, desperate addicts.

The meeting adjourned a few minutes later. I stood up and told everyone, "I'm outta here." I turned and left the office, but someone followed me into the hallway. I turned around. It was Fitzgerald.

"Do you feel the same way?" I snapped.

"No. Look, Rob was out of line. He says stuff he shouldn't say. That was a personal thing, and he shouldn't have brought that up," said Fitzgerald.

I was having none of that bullshit. "Pat, I've buried agents and cops.

What would Rob say to their widows and families? He's the head of the damn FBI here. How dare he do that? How dare he do that!"

Fitzgerald let me vent. I don't know how long I was there, but I let loose. "We're trying to make a difference. We have a new animal on the street now—heroin laced with fentanyl. We have people dying all around us, from drugs and the drug trade, and trying to stop that is a waste of money? I'm disgusted," I said. "What Grant said is just disgusting."

I left the building, jumped into my car, and headed for Springfield, Illinois. I had a meeting with our agents there, and I wasn't going to miss it. I drove with the music turned up loud. I breathed deep, unclenched my jaw, flexed my fingers. Every few minutes my phone rang. It was Grant. I ignored the call. Old school FBI mentality. How could this guy, supposedly our ally, our partner, say something like that? How could he be so reckless?

When I told Tony about it, I got the usual response: "What do you expect? Those guys are assholes."

And you know what, he was right.

Fitzgerald understood what we were trying to do. He saw the big picture, the strategic approach. He supported me every time I asked for help. But Grant? What the hell happened?

Grant rang and rang, he must have tried another thirty-five times during that two-hour drive to Springfield. I never picked up the phone.

I never spoke to Grant again.

About two months after the Holder meeting, Grant left the FBI to join Walt Disney Company's Global Security Team. Shortly after that, Fitzgerald said he, too, was stepping down, going into private practice. I called him up when I heard the news. "Pat, you can't do this to me!" I said, joking.

"I have to. It's time," he said.

I understood. He had a young family and wanted to earn some money. He had done so much good in Chicago. I'd be losing a partner, someone who embraced the concept of interagency cooperation. Someone who—unlike Grant—truly believed we should be going after the bad guys. I just hoped Fitzgerald's replacement would be half as good as he was. Despite all the politics at the top, we still had some good momentum going on the ground.

After years of lobbying, I finally had the funding for a new headquarters for the strike force. Leonhart continually said Justice Department didn't have the money, but I kept pushing. I managed to cobble together funding from the city, state, and other sources to keep us going day to day.

And, finally, Leonhart came through. Our new building was a first-of-its-kind headquarters for seventy federal agents, police, and prosecutors to work side by side, year-round to fight drug traffickers. It was a setup meant to end the idiotic interagency rivalry and miscommunication that had hamstrung investigations for decades.

The Chicago Strike Force building opened in a city where Mexican cartels now supplied more than 90 percent of the narcotics, where street gangs killed each other and bystanders at an appalling rate.

I showed the journalists around the new building, giving my old sermons about interagency and interdepartmental cooperation, how occasional meetings and temporary joint task forces for specific investigations just weren't cutting it.

Staff included city and suburban police, as well as agents from the DEA, FBI, ICE, the IRS, and a half-dozen other agencies. In another rarity, federal and state prosecutors also worked alongside one another.

Sure, there were some skeptics. A few people said it looked great on paper, but getting federal agencies to act in unison would be like herding cats. It's true: Over the years competition had created situations where agencies unknowingly targeted the same traffickers and inadvertently foiled each other's investigations.

I knew there would be some hiccups, but I believed that our place and time had arrived. I had seen it work, firsthand.

A major focus of the investigations would be the point of contact between major traffickers and local gangsters, their street-level salesmen. Traffickers were especially vulnerable there, because they weren't familiar with the city. Gangbangers often used phones that could be easily tapped.

I told reporters that the ultimate goal was to arrest suspects, squeeze them to cooperate, and move from there up the cartel's chain of command to indict everyone from the street dealer right up to the kingpins in Mexico—the kind of investigation that led in 2009 to the extradition of Vicente Zambada.

As soon as the building opened, federal agents and local and state law enforcement lined up to join the strike force. It was exactly what I had hoped would happen.

And it wasn't long after the opening that a strike force tip led to a police corruption case.

A member of the unit said three suburban cops were forcing a low-level dirtbag to sell drugs on their behalf. As I listened, I jotted down notes along with questions: If three cops were involved, were there others? How high up the food chain did it go?

The policeman on the other end of the phone didn't know. He had just gotten the information from a man he had arrested with a couple of ounces of cocaine. He figured I'd want to know right away.

Corruption cases are usually handled by the FBI. Fitzgerald was gone by then, so I called Gary Shapiro, the acting federal prosecutor. He suggested I lead the investigation with DuPage County prosecutors, but if I discovered that corruption went any higher in the department, I had to call in the FBI. Kevin Powers, the DEA Chicago counsel, agreed with Shapiro. "You have to see this through," he said.

You can't blow off a tip—not when you encourage everyone on the strike force to track down every lead, he said.

He was right. So I looked into the allegations. I discovered that the case really began when the strike force policeman who called me heard from a cop in Schaumburg, a Chicago suburb. The Schaumburg cop said a guy was going into local bars, selling dope. Our strike force guy put the dealer under surveillance, bought cocaine from him, and then brought him in. During questioning, the dealer blurted out: "I knew you guys were coming, and I got three coppers that I deal with all the time. They're my get-out-of-jail-free card."

The dealer was a longtime police informant. He said that one day, officers John Cichy, Matthew Hudak, and Terrance O'Brien gave him drugs to sell, narcotics the officers had confiscated from other busts. The informant brought them the proceeds, and the officers then split the cash.

I told my strike force guys to get the informant to make some calls.

"Let's cover the phone calls," I said. "He should call the guy he thinks is the leader. Just get him talking."

A couple of days later, they came into my office with a handful of audiotapes. Calls. Good ones, the guys said.

They popped one into the machine. One of the cops was so stupid he jabbered on to the informant about literally ten or fifteen deals they've done together.

"OK, let's set him up," I told them. "But first let me clear this with some people."

First I talked to Bob Berlin, the state's attorney in DuPage County. Then I ran it by Shapiro and Powers. "Look, I think this is low-level. I think it'll be over in a couple of days, and from what we can tell it's not systemic in the PD; it's just these three idiots," I said.

"OK. Go ahead and do it. See what happens, and we're available down the road should you choose to go that way," Shapiro said. "And, Jack, you have to bring an FBI agent."

That wasn't a problem. We had some of those in the strike force.

So we were ready.

The informant said the bad cops did much of their dirty business at a self-storage lot on the edge of town. The policemen kept an eye on activities there, because dope dealers often stash their inventory in storage units. When the threesome suspected a storage space had drugs, they'd break in and steal the dope, and whatever valuables they found there.

We had the informant tell the cops that somebody had three hundred or four hundred pounds of marijuana in there, and a load of cash.

The cops got a search warrant to look for the dope. They went to the storage facility three times. The first time they opened the unit and saw that yes, the story was true. Lots of drugs, lots of money—money we could get back easily enough. We had all the serial numbers and had photographed the bills. If they took the marijuana, we'd move.

But the cops left without the dope or the money. We waited. And they went back again. By then we'd taken the marijuana out of there, but we left behind $22,000 in cash. One of the guys opened the bag, saw the money, and they left again. Then the ringleader came back a third time, counted the money, and took it. What we found out later was he doled a little bit out to his two stooges, and gave the informant $5,000.

We had them.

I briefed my guys before we arrested the cops. The room was strangely silent.

"Look, this is a hard thing to do. This is harder for me than you'll ever know. But we're going to kick their asses today, because this shit, their shit, is on everybody in here. We're going to do this the right way, we're going to do it professionally, and then we're going to let the courts decide what happens to them," I said.

Arresting them was kind of tricky because, at that point, I didn't know whether these three had somehow figured out that we were after them.

We were going to make believe we were hitting a Schaumburg house that had a hundred kilos of coke, and we needed all the local guys to help us with the seizure. It was all bullshit, but I wanted to get them where we had them covered. I mean we're cops, trying to arrest cops with guns. And I'm hoping that the minute we turn on them they know it's over, and they go quietly.

We agreed to gather at a parking lot near the Woodfield Mall.

"When they show up, we'll tell them we're going to hit three different locations," I said. "We're going to have five DEA guys, five coppers, and an FBI guy on each team. When Cichy, Hudak, and O'Brien arrive, I want you to break them up. Assign each one to a different team."

"What if they don't want to do that?" someone asked.

"Tell them, 'If you're not on that team, and that team hits $1 million, your department can't put in for the assets,'" I said.

It was all bullshit, but they were so stupid I knew they'd believe it.

"Well, when are we going to know when to jump on them?" someone asked.

"I'll be there and give a bogus briefing to everybody, and then you guys do your team briefs because you're going to different locations. So what I ask you to do is just separate. You go to one corner of the parking lot, you go to the other one, you guys stay here, and I'll yell 'Go Irish.' And when I yell 'Go Irish,' you guys jump on them."

We assembled around 11 a.m. Cichy, Hudak, and O'Brien arrived as expected. I gave a make-believe briefing and when I was finished, the teams began moving into position. Everything went according to the plan. Then I yelled, "Go Irish!"

And with that, the teams turned on the cops.

But Cichy, Hudak, and O'Brien didn't go quietly. They fought back. It turned into a twenty-minute melee of kicking, punching, and rolling on the ground. We had our biggest strike force guys there, but those three were like wildcats, or cornered rats.

Finally, two of the guys were pinned and cuffed, but not Cichy. He was a big man, about six-foot-three, 250 pounds. He was fighting, swinging wildly, homicidal.

I ran over to him and screamed: "Stop fighting. It's over. We don't want to hurt you."

When he wouldn't stop, I whacked him. But it didn't faze him. I cracked him in the face again and by then he was out of breath. He fell backward to the ground. I kneeled over and stared in his eyes. "I said stop fighting."

After we cuffed him, we found his gun strapped into an ankle holster. I had no doubt he was trying to get to his gun.

Once Cichy was in custody, I walked over to O'Brien, who was crying like a baby. I looked at him with contempt: "Shut your mouth. You were acting like a man before. Act like a man now."

That was it.

Facing drug and misconduct charges, Cichy, Hudak, and O'Brien resigned shortly after their arrests. Cichy's charges were later dropped because the informant had lied about a meeting.

This case wasn't about the cartels, or Chapo, at least at first appearance. But in a way it was. So many people were making so much money with drugs—it was so out in the open in some parts of the city—that if you didn't have a good moral compass you could lose your way. You wanted to get a piece of that action.

And that's what happened with these guys.

But I also knew it was a bullshit excuse. In my career, I worked with hundreds of good DEA and FBI agents and cops, guys who would never do this: Tony, Comer, Cronin, Corcoran, Keefe, and more. And I knew someone else who always did the right thing: Leon Lacey, a young agent who had worked in my office, a guy I had taken under my wing.

Lacey was a badass new kind of DEA agent. He could take down bad guys in a dark alley like an old-time cop, but he had all the geeky computer skills of the new tech-savvy agents.

I remember the first time I met him. I had heard a lot about him, but he worked at our office at Chicago Midway International Airport, so our paths hadn't crossed since I'd returned to Chicago. We had a big drug bust out there, and after a news conference I walked over to him. "You know, you look like you should be playing football for Notre Dame," I joked.

He glowered at me. "I can't stand Notre Dame." Then he cracked up. I laughed with him.

We got on like we were old friends. Lacey was a Chicago guy, rode Harleys, played softball, and lifted weights. He had a big network of family and friends. And, most importantly, he was passionate about his job.

Over time I got to know him better. He came into the office to lift weights on his off-hours; he'd stop by my office to chat, and sometimes bust my balls.

"Hey you're getting a little paunchy there," he'd say, pointing to my stomach. "So how much can you bench-press?"

It was always in fun.

Whenever I thought we were just spinning our wheels, that our job was hopeless, I'd think about guys like Leon—honest, intelligent guys who just got up in the morning and did the right thing. Leon wanted to be with his partners and do his job.

And that is why it hurt me so much when I found out Lacey had lung cancer. It was like someone hit me in the stomach with a sledgehammer. I thought, *How could that happen?* Leo didn't smoke. He was so young, and so fit. He was in the prime of his life. How could he get cancer? I tried to stay optimistic, but over time, the cancer spread.

I was there with his family, sitting by his hospital bed, talking to him, encouraging him to fight. His buddies in law enforcement raised money to help with his treatment. I remember the last time I saw him I looked at the figure in the bed, and couldn't believe this was the strapping young man who would come into my office and bust my balls about lifting weights. This was the guy with the Harley and the big laugh, who loved wrestling with bad guys.

He was laboring to breathe. I leaned over his bed and whispered, "I love you, Leon."

I walked outside to collect my thoughts, fighting back tears.

The next day, I got the call: Leon had passed away. He was just thirty-three years old.

A few hours later, his family asked if I could give the eulogy at the funeral. I agreed, but I wasn't sure I could do it without breaking down.

Monica and I arrived at St. Raymond Church on that cold, windy February morning and sat in the back row. I had all the agents sit together in a few pews. I had jotted some notes, but every time I looked at them I was overwhelmed with tears.

When the time came I walked to the pulpit and faced the hushed crowd of two hundred or so. My hands trembled. I put down the index cards and just spoke from my heart.

"Leon was my hero. He was a remarkable person, a family man, a friend to many, and a DEA special agent. He was full of life. Nothing, it seemed, could crack his positive spirit and life outlook," I told his family and friends.

I said that every time the Notre Dame football team would lose, I could count on Leon bright and early on Monday morning to stick his head in my office and let me have it. "I will miss those rants.

"Leon loved life and his job. He loved busting bad guys with his beloved partners and was damn good at it. He cared deeply for his fellow agents and police officers, and would do whatever was needed to help and take care of them. He never went home until the job was done."

My voice wobbled. I paused for a moment to steady myself.

"I once asked Leon if he would ever consider becoming a supervisor. He thought for a moment and said, 'No way.' He wanted to be with his fellow agents and cops and make cases. He had found his true calling. He lived his life as I wish I could.

"He fought his illness to his last breath. He loved his job and continued to work until his doctors ordered him to rest. I will never forget his sense of honor and duty. It was truly remarkable. He made my life and this world a better, safer place. It is because of men like Leon that we carry on with hope and optimism for the future."

Tears welled in my eyes, I swallowed hard.

"We in law enforcement have a phrase that is often used. That is, 'Do the right thing.' Leon did the right thing by his family, his friends, his fellow agents, and his country. And for that we will forever be in his debt."

I took a deep breath.

"Rest in peace, my friend. I will see you on the other side."

I put the index cards back in my pocket, and slowly walked back to the pew. Everyone in the crowd was crying. I held Monica's hand. This was one of the toughest days of my life.

At that moment, in a private moment with God, I dedicated the rest of my career to Leon's memory. I'd keep fighting—even on those days when I felt like I couldn't go on. I owed that to Leon—and all the agents who risked their lives every day.

And that's why I was so angry at those Schaumburg jagoffs. They tarnished the name of Lacey, and all the good cops who work so hard every day to get the bad guys. But there was somebody else who deserved the blame: El Chapo. He helped corrupt those cops. He was responsible for so much death and suffering in Chicago—and the United States. Yet nobody was really talking about him. That's why it was more important than ever to put a face to the problem. That's why I wanted my next move to really connect Chapo to Chicago.

For years, I'd said El Chapo was the most dangerous criminal in the world—and the man responsible for Chicago's escalating violence.

The Chicago Crime Commission agreed with me. So in 2013, we did something we knew would generate a lot of attention: We named Guzmán the city of Chicago's public enemy number one. That hadn't been done since Al Capone, another notorious gangster, terrorized 1920s Chicago.

The suits in Washington didn't like it, but I felt we had to make a statement. Since I had been in Chicago, I helped get all the federal law enforcement agencies, as well as Chicago and suburban and state police departments, to work together.

We had just gotten funding to open the new building for the strike force. Everything was clicking. We had so many tips and good intelligence that we were starting to make a difference. Now we could do something to really piss off Chapo.

Putnam originally came up with the idea, but I broached it with the Chicago Crime Commission, formed in 1919 to improve the criminal justice system. They ran with the idea, and we decided to make the announcement on the anniversary of the infamous St. Valentine's Day Massacre. The biggest mobster of his time, Capone ordered an attack on George "Bugs" Moran's rival gang at a North Side garage on February 14, 1929. Seven men died, including a doctor who liked to hang out with gangsters.

They were lined up along a wall by two men dressed as police officers, and massacred by two other men using Thompson submachine guns. That secured Capone's place at the top of organized crime in Chicago and the public enemy list.

The level of violence and corruption generated by Guzmán and his cartel far exceeded that of Capone.

"In my opinion, Guzmán is the new Al Capone of Chicago," I said at a news conference, adding that it "wouldn't even be a fight if the cartel were pitted against the Chicago mob.

"His ability to corrupt government officials and perpetrate his reign of terror with his endless supply of revenue is more powerful than Chicago's Italian organized crime gang," I said about Guzmán.

I reminded everyone that Chapo had been on the run since 2001, when he'd escaped from a Mexican prison. Chapo went right back to work, and was now the country's highest-profile trafficker, hauling tons of marijuana, cocaine, methamphetamine, and heroin to US markets in trucks, on ultralight aircraft, and through secret tunnels.

Included on the *Forbes* list of billionaires, Chapo has been indicted in the United States in abstentia on dozens of charges of racketeering and conspiracy to import narcotics. Washington posted a $5 million reward for his capture.

I reminded everyone that the Sinaloa cartel had trafficking networks throughout the Midwest, and was waging an all-out war for turf with the rival cartels south of the border, stoking drug violence that had killed tens of thousands in recent years.

The border might be a thousand miles away, but El Chapo's network was so embedded here that Chicago police might as well be working in El Paso. The cartel was the city's major drug supplier, generating tens of millions of dollars and an ongoing wave of violent crime.

Chapo was still out there. More shipments of dope were on the way to Chicago and the Midwest.

But I wanted to send a message to El Chapo: I am still out here, too, and I am closing in. You can run, but you can't hide. It's just a matter of time before you're behind bars. This time in the United States.

CHAPTER 14

LONG-DISTANCE RUNAROUND, 2014

Even though I was the SAC in Chicago, I still took an interest in the hunt for El Chapo. No one knew more about the asshole than me—his history, his patterns, his habits. I had so much to do just being the SAC in Chicago—juggling meetings, investigations, personnel issues in five states, and more than a dozen field offices. But I tried to be in on all the phone calls, the meetings, everything related to Guzmán and Sinaloa. Agents called with the latest tips. SOD was coordinating our Chapo hunt in Mexico, and several of our DEA agents down there were getting good information from an array of sources.

I called Cronin just about every day at SOD. We'd bounce ideas off each other about Chapo. No, I wasn't leading the investigation. I couldn't because I was heading up the Chicago DEA office—and that took up most of my time. But Cronin and other agents, intel guys, too, called me dozens of times, looking for advice and suggestions as we tracked him down.

"Jack, this is really your case. You were talking about Chapo before anyone even heard of his name," Cronin said.

I knew that, but this was in the hands of the Washington folks, and that made me a little uneasy. They needed to push the Mexicans. The question was this: Would they?

Meanwhile, the best leads of all came from a device that most people tossed years ago in favor of the iPhone: the BlackBerry, a Canadian-made cell phone with a physical keyboard at the bottom of the screen.

Chapo was a creature of habit, and the BlackBerry was his communication device of choice. He never left home without one. For all his logistical brilliance, Chapo was suspicious of American-made mobile phones. He thought the United States government could easily track him and get information about him via iPhones and Android devices.

I think Chapo believed he was safe using a BlackBerry, in part because it was a Canadian product. Canadians don't do that shit to people, right? What he didn't realize was that we could use high-tech devices to monitor his BlackBerry communications, and geolocation technology to triangulate his signal. In other words, if he used his BlackBerry, we could figure out where he was.

And we used another strategy, one that paid dividends in tracking and killing Osama bin Laden in Pakistan in 2011. We put together a list of people who might have contact with Chapo. His gardener, cook, laundry service, and driver. Soon we were mapping their cell phone hits, tracking daily movements, creating a pattern of life.

Of course, we needed Chapo to come off the mountain and use his phone. Sometimes the grid went dark. But, lately, Cronin and others were telling me that we were getting more and more reports of Chapo sightings.

And we knew why: Guzmán loved women. All kinds, from beauty queens to housewives to hookers. We knew he used Viagra. We even knew which porn movies he watched.

In February 2012, from all the traffic, we believed he was headed to the coast, possibly Los Cabos. It was the perfect spot.

Los Cabos, at the southern tip of the Baja peninsula, is one of the safest places in Mexico. There Hollywood stars and thousands of US tourists still could enjoy Mexican beaches, cuisine, and hospitality.

Drug lords liked it, too, but they tended to leave their guns and henchmen at home when they vacationed in Los Cabos. In 2006, the US Coast Guard arrested Francisco Javier Arellano Félix, head of the Tijuana-based Arellano Félix gang, as he was sport-fishing off the coast of Los Cabos.

Clever Chapo came to town right alongside some of the world's most powerful elites. Secretary of State Hillary Clinton and dozens of other foreign dignitaries were attending meetings in Los Cabos for the G20 nations, the world's twenty top economies. The place would be bristling with security.

Chapo probably thought he could hide in plain sight.

I knew we had him in our crosshairs. The people around Chapo were chattering away on their phones, giving us exact locations to pass along. They were clearly on the move. The only downside was, we didn't know if we could trust the Mexican federal police. We'd have felt better working with the Mexican Marines. My agents in Mexico told me they could be trusted. But I wasn't in a position to push that. That had to come from higher up.

We tracked Chapo to a mansion in Los Cabos. We pinpointed the exact address. But when the federal police showed up, he was gone. Just like that. Slipped out the back door. You couldn't make this stuff up.

When I heard he got away, I cussed and screamed. The fix was in. Someone who knew, someone in law enforcement, had made the call.

"We just can't trust these bastards," I told Cronin.

We didn't say anything about the botched raid, but a few weeks later, word leaked out.

The Mexican government finally acknowledged that it was their screwup. What they didn't say was that at some point someone told Guzmán that we were tracking his mobile device. He passed his phone on to a fall guy. The police, unaware of the handoff, chased the signal around Los Cabos until they finally pounced on Chapo's flunky. Meantime, Guzmán made it into the desert. A private plane picked him up and flew him back to the safety of the Sierra Madre.

Typical Chapo. Typical Mexican government response.

The lesson in 2012 was that we had to push the Mexicans harder. Now, in February 2014, we had Chapo in our sights again.

It seemed that I had been on the phone nonstop for two weeks. We were closing in on Chapo. Intelligence said he had left a safe house in the mountains and was in Culiacán, the biggest city in Sinaloa province.

There were a million things to think about, and I talked for hours to Assistant US Prosecutor Mike Ferrara, Cronin at SOD in Washington, and our DEA counterparts in Mexico.

"We're getting close," Cronin assured me.

I could feel it. Again, I wasn't in charge of the investigation. Our Washington folks were—and they had the final call on every move. But everyone inside the agency knew about my Chapo obsession. They knew how I pushed to get him on the radar. How I made the connections between Chapo, the cartels, and the street gangs.

So agents in the field and intel people were leaning on me—just as I leaned on them. I read all the intelligence reports, called and emailed SOD for updates. Everyone I talked to—from Cronin to Comer to Tony and Keefe—the subject was always Chapo.

And I didn't hesitate to call agents or intelligence folks at any hour, asking for their angle on a new lead, a theory, a new point on the map. I prodded and pushed, made sure they dotted every *i* and crossed every *t*. I was a pain in the ass. But now they were calling me in the middle of the night, too.

Because of my relentless lobbying, agents in Mexico had infiltrated parts of the Sinaloa cartel, mostly on the money-laundering side of the business. I kept pushing our folks to make sure Mexican Marines were involved in the hunt. They were the only agency I could really trust—they took out Arturo Beltrán Leyva, the leader of the Beltrán Leyva cartel, in a shootout 2009. Every other part of the Mexican government was riddled with people on the take. We just didn't know who was on Chapo's payroll.

We barely missed nabbing him in 2012 in Los Cabos.

I hoped that wouldn't happen again. Yes, I wasn't running this operation, so it was hard to tell what would happen. But I can tell you this: I wanted so much to be in the field to grab him! I wanted to look the scumbag in the eye—just as I'd done with Zambada.

But for now, I'd have to be satisfied with getting the latest updates from SOD. Everyone knew how being on the sidelines was killing me.

Even with everything going on in Chicago, I made sure I knew every move, every detail of the Chapo hunt. I made sure the charges lodged against him were still active, so as soon as he was caught, Ferrara could start working to extradite him to Chicago.

"This is where he should be tried," I told Ferrara. "We proved we could do it with Zambada, so why not Chapo?"

"Jack, let's cross that bridge when we get there," he said.

Meanwhile, in Mexico, Chapo was popping up in public more frequently. We had put together a list of all of his associates using the same surveillance tactics the CIA used to track down Osama bin Laden. Osama might not pick up his phone when you called him, but you could track the people closest to him.

And that's what we were doing with El Chapo. Few people had direct access to Chapo, but we were working our way up the food chain, keeping close tabs on his underlings, hoping Guzmán would call them up and we could follow them to his front door.

Chapo and his people were sharp. They bought burner phones, used them for a while, then tossed them. Early on, everyone changed phones at the same time. Their network would go dark and send us scrambling. But lately Chapo and the cartel were getting sloppy. They weren't throwing their phones away all at once, and Chapo developed a text-message habit. His telephone sent out hundreds of messages, and we started running the pings from the cell towers through SOD computers. The patterns told us where he was, more or less.

And each text message had a nugget of information that we could use to track him.

"I wish you could see it," Cronin told me, about a marked-up map of Sinaloa in his office. He was putting together a pattern of life, a list of all the places where Chapo could be hiding. "He thinks no one is reading his text messages."

We took all the text messages, all the hits from cell phone towers, and, using satellite images, we pinpointed several of his safe houses in the mountains outside Culiacán.

172

We even had a satellite photo of Chapo himself walking into a big tent for a family gathering.

"I knew it," I said to Cronin. "You can stay underground, live a simple life like El Padrino, stay disciplined for only so long. But at some point, you're going to want to go out and have some fun. You're going to want to see your family."

Cronin laughed. "Everyone makes mistakes."

I was delighted to see that these days, Chapo was making plenty.

We knew where he was, more or less. Everyone agreed that this was it. We had to go after him. I called the DEA office in Mexico City and talked to John, the lead agent.

"We have to tell the Mexican Marines to take action now. I'm not sure when we're going to have a better chance," I said. We had several agents on the ground there, working with the Mexican elite unit. They had praised the unit, saying they didn't believe Chapo had gotten to them.

John agreed, but reminded me gently that those orders had to come from Washington.

"Jack, they're onboard, but no one wants to go into Culiacán. We're hoping we can get him someplace else."

I understood that. Culiacán was Chapo's home territory, the belly of the beast, a city with a "narco cemetery" where dead drug lords spend eternity in golden mausoleums. The holiest church in town was not the cathedral, but a chapel dedicated to Jesús Malverde, a bandit killed in 1909 and honored now as the cartels' patron saint.

El Chapo was the same kind of folk hero. He'd be protected by just about everyone in the city. He'd have lookouts on every street corner. The police were in his pocket. Culiacán wasn't the place to grab him, but we would go in if we had to. It wasn't often that Chapo ventured out in public like this.

Again, I was frustrated. An SAC in Chicago doesn't give orders about an international operation to land the world's biggest fugitive. But I just couldn't help getting involved. "I don't want a firefight and people getting caught in the crossfire," I said. "We should make sure a DEA agent goes along with the Marines to the site. But they shouldn't go in with the Marines. I wouldn't want to put them in danger."

The days dragged on. I was on the phone constantly, looking for updates, pressing our people for more information, relaying whatever details we had.

SOD was monitoring all communication, including text messages coming in and out of the area. They passed along critical information to our agents on the ground.

After all these years, all the time pushing the higher-ups to recognize that Chapo and Sinaloa were threats to our national security, we were so close.

Now I was going to nab him. No mistakes. Our man was finally in the crosshairs, and I was going to make sure we got him.

A few days later, a convoy of Mexican Marines rolled into Culiacán in armored vehicles and spread out to cover all the safe houses. Several DEA advisers went along just to be sure we got him, to snap photos, to make sure we had the right guy.

We expected the worst—maybe a firefight between the Marines and Chapo's loyal bodyguards. We would take Chapo dead or alive. The town was abuzz. Word quickly reached El Chapo.

Then we got a break.

"We got one of his top lieutenants," one of the advisers on the ground told me.

"Are you working him?"

"Yes. He told us where Chapo is."

I pumped my fist in the air. "Yes!" I calmed down for a moment. "Let me know what happens. Everything."

I hung up the phone and waited. I started pacing. Shit, I wanted to be there! Time moved so slowly. "Come on!" I said to the telephone. "Call me!"

I couldn't focus on anything else. When the phone rang, I picked it up on the first ring. It was Cronin.

"Jack, he got away," he said.

"What happened?"

The Chapo lieutenant led the Marines to the right safe house. It took several minutes to breach the metal front door. When they finally got inside, they couldn't find anyone. They went room to room, guns raised, looking. But he was gone. He'd activated an escape hatch underneath his bathtub that led to a tunnel.

"What the hell!"

Apparently, when Chapo pushed an electrical outlet by a bathroom vanity mirror, it engaged a hydraulic lift and the bathtub rose from its tiled frame. He then fled down the passageway and into a network of tunnels that connected to six other houses.

"Down the tunnel, like a spider, like a rat," Cronin said.

A tunnel, a Chapo trademark. Now he could be anywhere.

The news wasn't all bad. El Chapo left behind a handsome cache of cell phones, money, and drugs, and several of his security people were in custody.

"You'll have to comb through everything. We'll have to get everything," I said.

"We are," Cronin said. "Jack, we'll get him."

"I know we will," I said. "It's just frustrating as hell!"

I called Ferrara and we went over all the details. "I don't know what else we could have done," I said. "The guy has people and escape routes all over the place."

We agreed that we had to keep leaning on the Mexican government to keep looking for Chapo. We were already in Culiacán.

After I hung up, I looked at the calendar on my desk. A few weeks earlier, I had made plans to go to Washington to talk to DOJ about additional funding for the strike force. Chapo or no Chapo, I couldn't cancel the trip. I sent out an urgent memo to all our agents: Work 24/7 on the wiretaps in our five-state region. It was critical. Turn all information over to SOD.

Again, as we triangulated all our facts, I was sure we'd figure out where he was hiding. He could be anywhere in Mexico by now, but we'd posted a $5 million reward. Some of his men were flipping.

With Mexico's cooperation, we had hunted down Chapo in the hills.

Working hand in hand, the DEA and the Mexican Marines had closed the net on Chapo.

I was more optimistic than ever that we'd get him. Still, I knew a sunny outlook was one thing, and actually having him in custody was something else entirely.

My body was in meetings in Washington, but my mind was in Mexico.

I touted the strike force with my cell phone in my pocket, set on VIBRATE. Everyone already knew we'd been working together for years and that our model could be put to work in other cities. I reviewed our success stories, showed charts with budget totals, drugs, contraband, and cash seized. My phone kept vibrating. *Damn!* I thought. *This could be it! Maybe we have El Chapo!*

But when I checked my messages during breaks, they were only updates. No arrest.

We had gotten what could have been a big break the day before, February 20. Cronin told me one of Guzmán's bodyguards used a BlackBerry, and we'd traced its signal to Mazatlán, a resort city 130 miles south of Culiacán. A good place to escape to.

"We gotta get there," I told him.

"We're already on it," he said.

My bosses asked me if I thought we'd get him, and I didn't hesitate: "Hell yeah," I said.

I was pleased to see they were interested. Not long ago, when I brought up Chapo and the cartels, many people had rolled their eyes and told me, "Jack, you're obsessed with this guy. You're obsessed with the cartels." Nobody could believe the Mexican criminal organizations could wield such power. But now everybody knew how far the narcos' tentacles reached into the United States. They could see what a shrewd businessman Chapo was, turning America's appetite for opioid painkillers into an opportunity to sell more heroin.

I left Washington, but I didn't go straight home. I had to make a quick stop in South Carolina. I was fifty-six years old. Monica and I had been thinking about the future, and where we'd like to live once I left the agency. We found a quiet place in a lakeside community in South Carolina, and were about to start building a new home there. I had made plans to meet with the builder long before the latest developments in Mexico.

Cronin phoned. I thought hard about canceling my plans.

"We have Mexican Marines, DEA agents, Homeland Security guys, and US Marshals gathered in Mazatlán. The BlackBerry signal comes from a condominium building called the Hotel Miramar," he said.

"We're going in tomorrow morning."

I hung up the phone and called Ferrara. We had to make sure the Mexican Marines made the arrest, he said. Our guys would stay back. It was the Mexicans' show. As soon as they had Chapo, we'd take his photo and make sure the man in custody was indeed Guzmán.

There really wasn't much more I could do. In a perfect world, I would be in the command center, overseeing every move. But that was Derek Maltz's job. Still, I knew everything had to be perfect. We had to take Chapo and his men by surprise. We couldn't give him a chance to escape. His guards had every kind of weapon at their disposal, but we couldn't let them start firing. A firefight would give Chapo a chance to flee. We didn't know if he had an escape hatch or tunnels at the Miramar. With Chapo, we'd learned to expect the unexpected.

Meanwhile, I called our guys in Chicago and told them again: Pass along any information from informants, wiretaps—anything they got—to SOD. I was tethered to my phone. I made it to South Carolina that night, but I didn't hear a thing. I stayed up most of the night, but heard nothing. I wanted to call Ferrara or Cronin, but stopped myself. I had nothing to add. I knew they'd call as soon as something happened.

I kept my appointments with the builder—life goes on, I told myself. I was in a store picking out a washer and dryer for the house when a call came in, but I missed it—I was in a dead zone. I only noticed it in the parking lot, a message. Headquarters. I called the number. Cronin picked up. "We're about to go in," he said. "I thought you oughtta know."

"Is he in there?"

"We think so."

"OK. Call me as soon as you hear anything."

I sat in my car in the mall parking lot in South Carolina. *Damn!* I thought. I want to be down there, with the guys going in for the takedown. Twenty years I'd been waiting for this. The silence was excruciating. It wasn't like a ballgame where you could hear the play-by-play action, and that's what I wanted. I made sure my phone had service, was fully charged. I stared at the screen, willing it to light up.

Then I saw an email from Leonhart: Chapo was caught.

"YES!" I shouted.

But I wanted to know more. Then my phone rang and I answered on the first ring.

"We got him," Cronin said.

He gave me a quick rundown: The Marines found Guzmán's armed bodyguard protecting the entrance to one of the Miramar apartments. He realized he was outnumbered and surrendered quietly. The Marines stormed the apartment.

Inside they found Chapo with his wife and young twin daughters, a personal chef, and a nanny. The drug lord ran into a bathroom, but gave himself up moments later. No shots were fired.

Cronin said he'd email a photo of Chapo as soon as he had one. "It's over," he said.

I hung up the phone and took a deep breath. I called my office.

"We have Chapo," I said. "It will go public pretty fast. Once that happens, I want you to pay close attention to the phones. The bad guys might panic, make mistakes on the phone and the street, give us a chance to grab them, their dope, and money and guns. We needed to be ready."

Chapo's photo arrived a few minutes later. He wore dark jeans and a pale long-sleeved shirt, and sported a formidable mustache. The finishing touch to his ensemble was a fine pair of silver handcuffs.

I was elated. After all these years, there he was, being led away.

Word leaked out. Yes, the Mexican Marines got Chapo. But I knew it was US-supplied wiretaps and surveillance that allowed the Marines to capture El Chapo and his crew.

My next step was pushing the Justice Department to seek extradition of Chapo to the United States. Despite all the fanfare, Mexican jails were evidently no match for Chapo's money, influence, and tunnel engineers. At least in the United States, I knew he'd be locked up with no chance of escape.

For now, it was enough to let the Mexicans bask in the glory. It was enough for us to say "We got him" and move on. It was just a matter of time before someone else came along and to fill the void. The next El Chapo was already out there.

We pieced together a picture of Chapo's final days of freedom.

In keeping with his low-profile lifestyle, Chapo and his family had arrived in Mazatlán in disguise, without any bodyguards or fanfare. Emma Coronel, his beauty-queen wife, had rolled him into the condominium building in a wheelchair. They stayed with their twin daughters on the fourth floor of the ten-story, pearl-colored building. Their apartment was a small, simple, two-bedroom unit with white tiled floors and cheap furniture. A balcony overlooked the Pacific.

When the Marines stormed the apartment, Guzmán had scrambled out of bed in his underwear and darted into a small bathroom.

Emma Coronel had screamed, "Don't kill him! He's the father of my children!"

The standoff only lasted a few seconds, with the Marines bellowing and Coronel screaming. Then Chapo shouted, "OK, OK, OK, OK!" and extended his empty hands through the bathroom doorway.

The nearly thirteen-year manhunt was over. The man who supplanted Osama bin Laden as the world's most wanted felon was handcuffed and led away to a cell to await justice.

Now people were stepping up to take credit. Mexican Attorney General Jesús Murillo Karam said some US agencies had helped in capturing Guzmán, but his country had taken the lead.

Others knew better. For years we'd strongarmed and sweet-talked Mexico to take action. Bribery was built into Chapo's business model, and countless Mexican officials were on his payroll. Still, this was a significant victory of Mexican President Enrique Peña Nieto. It put to rest any lingering questions about whether he shared his predecessor Felipe Calderón's commitment to take on the cartels.

I didn't much care who got a medal, as long as the dirtbag was safely locked up.

Getting El Chapo was huge. I was overwhelmed with joy and satisfaction. He was the number-one drug trafficking figure in history, the world's biggest criminal fugitive.

This was a huge win for the rule of law—not even a billionaire can escape justice. But I wasn't naive. Happy as I was, I didn't believe the drug trade would disappear just because El Chapo was out of the picture. I didn't want anyone else to think that, either.

McCarthy, the Chicago police superintendent, said it best: "Obviously, [Chapo] is an arch criminal. But it won't fix what's wrong. When demand exists, supply will show up."

The Sinaloa cartel was a well-oiled machine, engineered to survive even the loss of its CEO. Its global supply chain and flexible distribution network were spread throughout the United States and the world. It wasn't going away.

El Mayo, Chapo's bosom pal, had addressed that in a Mexican news magazine interview.

"Say one day I decide to turn myself in and go before the government firing squad. My case would be exemplary, a lesson for all. They shoot me. Euphoria erupts. But when all is said and done, nothing would really change," Mayo said. "Drug trafficking involves millions of people. How can anyone control it? As for the bosses, whether locked up, dead, or extradited, their replacements are already out there."

He was right. But that didn't mean we shouldn't fight them like hell.

Chapo was in custody in a maximum-security prison in Almoloya de Juárez, outside Mexico City. I wanted to see him extradited as soon as possible to the United States. For a Mexican drug lord there were few fates as terrible as life in an American prison. He can't bribe his way out, he has no cell phones to continue running his operation, his girlfriends can't visit him in his cell. He's thousands of miles away from what he knows as life.

I didn't believe El Chapo would ever be secure, even in the most high-tech Mexican prison. Extradition was going to be a tooth-and-nail battle. Chapo would drag it out as long as he could.

"I think [the United States] has the strongest case against him," I said at a news conference in Chicago. "I fully intend for us to have him tried here."

Extradition would take a while, and deciding where he would be tried would be another battle. Chicago was one of seven US jurisdictions that had indicted Chapo on charges ranging from cocaine and heroin smuggling to racketeering, organized crime, and murder.

If Chapo made it to the United States, Attorney General Eric Holder would ultimately decide where Guzmán was prosecuted. I was determined to see the trial take place in Chicago.

The drugs Guzmán's cartel supplied were the key factor driving gun violence in the Windy City. Twins Pedro and Margarito Flores provided vital evidence that linked Chapo to the sale of drugs on Chicago's streets. What better place than Chicago to show how Guzmán's Sinaloa cartel exported violence, along with tons of drugs from border cities like Tijuana and Ciudad Juárez straight into the American heartland?

Guzmán escaped Mexican custody in 2001. For the following thirteen years we tracked his movements throughout Mexico's "Golden Triangle," a mountainous, marijuana-growing region straddling the northern states of Sinaloa, Durango, and Chihuahua. We had telephone records of calls, receipts, manifests, and recordings ready to go.

I wasn't the only one who wanted to bring Chapo to Chicago. Lorino urged me to fight.

"We have a whole bunch of seizures, both dope and cash, that track straight to the cartel. We have the [Flores] boys and all their recordings with Chapo...We could literally put the cartel on trial," Lorino said to me.

I agreed. I made an urgent plea to federal prosecutor Zachary Fardon, who had taken over after Pat Fitzgerald left the federal prosecutor's office in Chicago.

"There's no case currently in the country that's as strong as our case," I told him. He was not optimistic.

Federal prosecutor Loretta Lynch was pushing for Chapo to be tried in New York, he said. He'd have to talk with some people.

That wasn't good enough. I kept just hammering him and hammering and hammering him. You could tell he just didn't want the case. He'd go to meetings and talk tough, but it was bullshit.

"You've got to come out swinging. You've got to get on TV and you've got to apply some political pressure," I told him.

But Fardon was uncomfortable. "Oh, I don't know if I can do that," he said.

I'd just shake my head in disgust. "Zach, you'll be retired before this guy is brought to trial, but you got to do the right thing by the agents and your prosecutors who did this case, and Pat Fitzgerald who oversaw this thing. You just can't abandon it," I said.

"Oh, well, it's not my decision," he said.

I wished Fardon would see how important this case was to Chicago. I don't think he understood what trying the case in another city would do to us all.

In the end, I knew it was about security. The DOJ would make the final decision. They'd probably combine all the evidence and try Chapo in one place. But if there was ever a place where Chapo should face a jury of his peers, it was Chicago—a city on the front lines, a city that lost so many people to the gang-related violence and drugs he shipped north to us.

When I least expected it, Leonhart dropped another of her bombs on my life. I wasn't sure how to take the news. I was being appointed to one of the DEA's top posts, in Washington again. This, she said, was the reward for my achievements.

I suspected that I didn't have a choice, not if I wanted to stay in the agency. I wasn't sure what to do. Chapo was behind bars, but if we didn't extradite him soon he'd escape again. Monica and I were building a retirement home in South Carolina. Kevin had just graduated college and was ready to start his career in sports management.

I loved Chicago. I'd settled into my old hometown, and I didn't want to leave.

"Give me a day or two to discuss it with my wife," I told Leonhart. She agreed.

I told Monica that evening that I was going to be the DEA's new chief of operations, the agency's number three position. I would oversee all agency enforcement activities, all over the world.

I could tell that Monica didn't want to move again. But she also knew that I had worked my entire career to get here. "In Washington, you'll be in a better position to extradite Chapo," she said. "You can't turn it down."

So I accepted the job. Friends called to congratulate me. Tony said I was crazy to leave Chicago. I did the rounds of local media, reflecting on everything that had happened since I came back to town in 2010. It was a good chance to review what had changed, and where things were going. Mexican cartels were now strongly entrenched in the Midwest. Chicago was still a wholesale drug hub. But the city now had the Chicago Strike Force to fight the cartels and street gangs selling heroin, cocaine, and other drugs.

Heroin and opioid addiction were major issues that nobody was really talking about. When I went to Washington, I promised I'd raise public awareness of the problem. But, more importantly, I'd order our agents to go after heroin traffickers the same way they went after Chapo. If I had to go, I wasn't going to waste my opportunity.

CHAPTER 15

THE SUIT

I was chief of operations, DEA, Washington, DC.

I had been mentally preparing myself for weeks. In Chicago, I had free rein. Yes, I was responsible for five states, but Leonhart left me alone to run my own show. I did the job, got the bad guys, and generated positive publicity for the office. In fact, when I left, one of the newspapers said I was the most famous federal agent in Chicago since Eliot Ness—the "Untouchables" guy who got Al Capone.

This was the Big League. As third in command of the nation's drug-fighting agency, all United States and international DEA operations would be under my command. I always thought street work was my strength, but I could handle the administrative side, too. I was good at managing people, getting the best out of them. I would do the same here, but on a much larger scale. I would be responsible for nine thousand employees.

The agency was undergoing significant changes.

Deputy Administrator Thomas Harrigan, the DEA's number two, had announced that he'd be stepping down soon. Several key positions stood empty, including intelligence chief and human resources director. My boss was under fire. DEA agents in Cartagena, Colombia, had reportedly participated in sex parties with prostitutes paid for by drug cartels. Lawmakers were pushing for Leonhart to testify about the scandal.

It wasn't all doom and gloom. I had a beautiful corner office, with a view of the Pentagon. I already knew many of the people in the building. Some of the people I knew at SOD were gone. My friend Cronin was now the resident agent in charge in Springfield, Illinois. Derek Maltz had retired. But he was replaced by Larry, a tough, relentless agent, one of the agency's rising stars. Larry and Cronin were both instrumental in creating the map that led us to El Chapo.

And Chapo was another issue I'd have to tackle. He was awaiting trial in a Mexican prison. He wasn't safe there, or anywhere in Mexico. I had to get him transferred to US custody before he managed to break out again. The Mexicans had promised that wouldn't happen, but he'd done it twice already. I didn't believe them.

Chapo was no fool. He'd probably already figured out how to escape, and where he'd go to hide. Twenty years of studying Chapo, hearing his voice on wiretap recordings, tracing his travels on maps, hearing testimony about him, seeing the outcomes of his criminal genius...I had never met the man in person, but I felt I could read his mind. He was sweating it down there, knowing the clock was ticking, knowing extradition meant the end of all hope for freedom.

He was supposedly under twenty-four-hour watch in Mexico's highest-security prison. No easy payoffs here, no convenient laundry baskets. If he escaped this time, it would be through a tunnel—Chapo's trademark. He had the money. He had the engineers. All he needed was time. I know it sounded paranoid, but for Chapo, nothing was impossible.

Leonhart stopped by my new office to welcome me.

My first order of business was Afghanistan.

The US military was drawing down there, withdrawing to a heavily protected "green zone" before packing up and moving out. The DEA compound was the last federal agency outside the wire. Leonhart was concerned about our agents' safety.

"I want you to go and have a look, and give me an honest assessment. Do we pull out? Dig in? What do we do?" she said.

Damn, I said. I was looking forward to putting together my team so we could tackle domestic issues, starting with heroin and opioids. I reluctantly agreed to go to Afghanistan.

And while I was there, I was to meet with leaders to see what they were doing to stop the cultivation and sale of drugs.

With all the issues swirling around me, I had to pick one thing and get that right. So, for the next few months, I focused on Afghanistan. At one time, the DEA had five counter-narcotics groups, called Foreign-deployed Advisory and Support Teams, or FAST. One was deployed to Afghanistan. The elite group helped the US military find and destroy heroin labs whose profits financed the Taliban and terrorist groups.

In 2009, the unit had fought alongside Special Forces in Operation Siege Engine, a battle that lasted for nearly a week. The Taliban massed fighters and attacked the badly outnumbered DEA agents and Special Forces soldiers over and over again. But with the help of air cover, the Americans blunted each wave. The FAST unit went on to help destroy one of the world's largest drug operations. They recovered more than $1.2 billion worth of black-tar heroin and 300,000 pounds of poppy seeds.

Drug trafficking continued to destabilize Afghanistan. Heroin, morphine, and opium have fueled conflict, terrorism, and insurgency there for hundreds of years.

"Opium wars" erupted between China and England in the mid-nineteenth century, as English traders forced farmers in their Indian colonies to grow opium to sell to China. Chinese authorities banned the drugs, and the resulting trade wars turned violent. In the United States, especially after the Civil War (1861–1865), medical and recreational users of morphine and laudanum often became addicts. Great fortunes were made meeting the voracious demand, and ruthless criminal syndicates and lily-white pharmaceutical companies took full advantage.

In the twentieth century, South America, particularly Colombia, saw tremendous internal conflict due to the massive illegal drug trade with the United States. The ability to produce and move narcotics into free and open Western societies has provided a source of spectacular wealth, and the twenty-first century is proving that drug money can be used to maintain human conflict forever.

Repressive religious rulers in Afghanistan had overseen production of drugs such as opium, heroin, and hashish, so drug traffickers made only modest money through the twentieth century. The terrorist attacks of September 11, 2001, led the United States to overthrow the Afghan Taliban, and tear all controls off the Afghan drug market. Traffickers, the Taliban, and other terrorist groups smelled opportunity, and put their cell phones, computers, and modern agricultural methods to work to build a network of worldwide drug production and trafficking organizations. Conflict anywhere in the world can now be funded and fomented with relatively small groups of fighters financed with drug money.

Known as the "graveyard of empires," Afghanistan became the US military's longest-lasting war. Its massive drug trade was funding conflicts in Pakistan, Iran, Yemen, Somalia, Libya, and eastern Europe, as well as terror cells all over the globe.

Monica didn't like me heading into a war zone, but I assured her it wasn't any more dangerous than the West Side of Chicago.

My trip was scheduled for early 2015. By then, Afghanistan wasn't nearly as hazardous as it had been in previous years. As President Obama promised, we were pulling out troops, but I knew we'd continue to maintain a presence there. If all our soldiers left at once, the country would collapse.

But with fewer American troops around, DEA agents had less protection from local warlords and insurgents. I had to make sure our people were safe.

I wasn't going to spend more than a week in Afghanistan. I asked Jon DeLena, my executive assistant, to come with me. We'd travel light, with no security team. I'd be OK with DeLena there. He was an aggressive agent, an Italian guy from Boston. We got along right away. He had been at headquarters for a while and knew the protocol—where I should sit during meetings, whose hand to shake first, things like that. He knew all the key players, and how to get things done.

DeLena was a born fixer. When I started in Washington, the desk in my office was an old, beaten-up relic—someone probably had made a quiet trade during the interim. I didn't complain about it, but one day when I arrived, there it was: a sleek new conference table. "Where did this come from, Jon?" I asked.

Jon just smiled. "Don't worry about it," he said.

It was a long, long trip. When we landed in Kabul, the airport was like a scene out of a war movie: People with guns running everywhere, total chaos. We waited in the plane for a convoy to show up and take us to the US compound. I took a good look at the scene outside on the tarmac, and asked some US soldiers to explain what I was looking at.

About a hundred British airplanes, basically small C-130s, were parked in neat rows. These were meant to move Afghan troops, but they just sat in the airport all the time, the soldiers said. In a nearby lot, there had to be about two hundred brand-new Toyota Land Cruisers. They didn't move, either, because no one had any gas. I recognized eradication equipment, which was supposed to be used to destroy the nation's countless poppy fields. But like the other equipment parked there, it was never used.

So why did we give the Afghans all this equipment?

Finally, our ride arrived, in what looked like a delivery at the mint: three armored cars.

The agent in charge of the Kabul office, Craig Wiles, showed me to the first one.

"What the hell is this?" I said.

"You've got to get in this car."

I jumped inside. An agent put a black Kevlar vest on me, and handed me an M4 carbine, which I had no idea how to use. I was a little uncomfortable with the big gun. I turned to DeLena and gave him a look. "I'm a cop. Just give me my handgun."

I must have looked like a clown, because I could see DeLena trying hard not to laugh his ass off. "I could shoot somebody with this, but it would probably be somebody here in the car," I joked.

The agent briefed us. "Before we leave, listen. If there's an explosion on one side of the car, we're going to push you out the other side. And your job then is to get to the vehicle behind us."

What the hell? I thought. I felt as if I'd fallen into a movie. We headed through the city streets. More armored vehicles, men with guns everywhere.

"Who are they?" I asked.

"Oh, they're warlords," Wiles said. "We gotta stay away from them."

We were supposed to go the US Embassy, but we stopped first at Camp Liberty, the US military compound. It was nothing but a bunch of huts, with Marines training Afghans. I got out of the vehicle. It was cold. Somehow, I'd imagined Afghanistan was going to be hot.

I went into the hut where our guys were stationed, but most of them were out back by a bonfire. I went outside. The landscape was like El Paso, barren, flat, and scrubby. There wasn't any wood, so they kept warm by burning old tires. I introduced myself. Someone handed me a flask. It was whiskey, and man did it taste good.

These guys were part of DEA FAST. Right off the bat they started talking, and made a compelling argument as to why DEA needed to stay in Afghanistan. We'd invested so much—we'd lost three agents in a helicopter crash, and another had lost his eyesight when he was shot in a skirmish. The men shared battle stories, yarns of going after bad guys, destroying drug rings that backed the Taliban, fending off attackers alongside military units. I smiled, I listened. But I thought: *I've gotta get these guys outta here. We're cops, not soldiers.*

Then I addressed the men.

"Look, it's an honor to be here with you. You guys are my heroes, and I'm proud of everything you have done, everything you guys have accomplished in Afghanistan. You guys are warriors. I just want you all to know that," I told them. We passed the flask around. An attaché approached me and said Afghan military leaders were coming to the base to meet with us over dinner.

"Did you know anything about this?" I asked DeLena.

He shrugged. "No." I was exhausted, and didn't know where our luggage was. We'd been wearing the same clothes for two days.

When the time came, we walked into a room crowded with Afghan officials and Marine and Army generals decked out in their dress uniforms. Local officials were there in their suits, and a government minister presented me with a beautiful Afghan hat and scarf.

I was glad for something warm to wear, but I didn't give a damn about the formalities. I wanted to ask some tough questions. After dinner, I launched in. Did anyone know if any aerial spraying was being done? We'd been leaning on President Hamid Karzai to continue that program, we'd sent in everything needed to get the job done. If we eliminate the crop, a large part of our problem is solved, I said. We literally nip it in the bud.

"You know the money they're making from the opium is fueling the insurgency," I said politely. But their faces showed no emotion. It looked like everyone in the room had heard this argument a hundred times, but nothing registered. It was mind-boggling. Their country was being undermined by the drug traffickers and terrorists. Where did they think the money was going?

I asked other military and civilian leaders the same questions, and they responded the same way. Then it clicked. I'd heard that Karzai's government was corrupt, that drug lords were bribing politicians. This was just like Mexico, but with a big difference: Chapo and the cartels weren't trying to overthrow the Mexican government.

It should have been in Karzai's self-interest to eradicate poppy production and destroy the heroin processing plants. So why wasn't the government doing it? The only thing I could think of was Karzai and his cronies were crooks.

I told one general, "Look, this equipment is going to waste. If you don't want to spray the fields, we'll do it." Again, silence. It was no use. Finally, I had to get to my bunk or I was going to collapse from exhaustion.

The day finally ended. When my body hit the cot it shut down instantly. I slept like a stone. I was supposed to see P. Michael McKinley, the US ambassador, the following day, so I got up bright and early, put on my gray suit, and went out to meet the convoy that would take me the ten miles to the embassy in Kabul. But McKinley said no.

"They know you're here now," he told me and a troop of Marines. "No convoy. You have to air-bridge."

Some State Department guys flew over in an old Huey helicopter from the Vietnam War. Just before I got on, a guy threw an eighty-pound bulletproof vest on me—right over my suit. I staggered under the weight, and had a hard time getting on the helicopter. DeLena glanced at me and laughed his ass off. I put on a pair of headphones so I could hear the pilots. "It should be a two-minute flight. You don't want it to be any more than that. You don't want to be up there too long," a voice said.

But that's exactly what happened. As we neared the embassy, I saw that it didn't have a helipad. We had to wait to land because of other air traffic. The pilots started circling around over the countryside, over downtown Kabul. They were worried about drawing fire from down there. I was stunned: It was January 2015, and the military still didn't have control of Kabul.

Frustrated, our pilot said, "Look we either got to go down or we're going back because we can't keep floating around here." We were circling over territory that the government didn't control, waiting while a small plane landed.

These guys weren't DEA. If they were our pilots, they'd have said, "No. We're outta here. We're not doing this." But these were retired military guys, private contractors making money for flight time.

When the traffic finally cleared, we landed on the embassy's soccer field. They hustled DeLena and me inside the building. McKinley was waiting to greet us. After exchanging pleasantries, I told him why I was there. "Sir, I'm here to figure out what to do with our thirty-six agents in the compound."

He didn't hesitate. "Get them out," he said. "This country does not have the will to fight narcotics. It doesn't have the will to do anything."

I could tell he was burned out. He wanted our agents back in the green zone, an area inside the embassy, in two weeks' time. "You cannot stay out there. We cannot take another Benghazi," he said, referring to the coordinated terrorist attack on US government facilities in Libya that ended with a US ambassador and three other Americans dead.

Now McKinley is an Obama guy. He talked to the president almost every day. If he was telling me to move my people, I knew that was the right thing to do.

"OK, then. That's all I need to hear. We'll be back in the Green Zone," I told him.

We talked a little bit more. Wiles, the DEA Kabul chief, stormed into the room with a worried look on his face. He turned to the ambassador and shook his head.

"Pardon the interruption, but that helicopter can't stay on the ground any longer. We have incoming flights," Wiles said. "We gotta get them out of here."

I shook hands with the ambassador and we ran out to the waiting helicopter. Back at the base, an ICE agent met us. He would take us by convoy to the back of the Kabul airport so we didn't have to go through the terminal, he said. Then we'd board a plane to Dubai.

We grabbed our bags and jumped into the armored vehicles, but when we got to the airport, two Afghan guards wouldn't let our convoy through a checkpoint. Our military guys started to get worried.

"We can't sit here very long. We're stuck. They can come up behind us and we've got nowhere to go," one of the soldiers said.

The ICE guy decided he'd get out of the car and talk to the Afghans, but couldn't speak the language. He flashed his badge. If it was the right color, they'd let us through. It wasn't.

As the ICE agent walked back to the vehicle, he asked one of our DEA guys, "Who's in the car?"

He didn't know who I was. And when the DEA agent said I was the agency's chief of operations, he flipped out. "Holy shit. We have to get you out of here."

They jumped into the vehicles and started backing up, knocking into garbage cans, turning around, and speeding to the front of the terminal. By this point I'd had enough.

"Just get me outta this car. We'll figure this out," I said.

The DEA agent shouldn't have let us go. Before he left, he told an Afghan national to help us. When we got inside the chaotic airport, he asked us for our diplomatic passports. I knew that was screwed up, but what were we going to do? He whisked them away to an office, and we just sat there in the airport terminal, waiting to board a plane without tickets or passports. There were only two flights to Dubai each day, and if we missed this one, we were really in trouble.

"I don't have a good feeling about this," I said to DeLena.

I spotted the Afghan walking toward us. "You're good," he said. He handed us our passports and took us to the back of the ticket line. There were five people ahead of us, but when the ticket agent got to us, he said, "Sorry, we are closed." He walked away.

"Dammit! We're not going to make this plane!" I said. "The pilots don't want to stay on the ground any longer than they have to."

We didn't know what to do. We were standing there, stunned, when another guy came up behind us, dressed in civilian clothes. He was military, a colonel, a big guy who'd played football at West Virginia. We told him we were in a fix.

"I know what's going on," he said. "Put your hand on my belt."

I grabbed the back of his belt and he just started shoving people aside, knocking a few of them over, dragging and pushing us onto the jetway and into the plane. It worked. We got on the Airbus, but the plane sat there on the tarmac for two stressful hours. I thought we'd never get out of there.

Back in Washington I told Leonhart that Afghanistan was a mess. Poppy fields were flourishing. The city was still full of armed warlords. I told her I agreed with the ambassador: We should get our agents to the embassy. I recommended we keep only six agents in Afghanistan, and take a couple out of Pakistan, too, because they were doing nothing there.

Then I brought up another subject: El Chapo. I told her I wanted DOJ to push for his extradition. Our agents were picking up information that Chapo was preparing to escape from prison. This was serious, credible information.

"Did you pass along the information to the Mexican government?" she asked.

"Yes, but they just blew us off," I said.

He was being held in Altiplano Federal Prison, a maximum-security facility, and they said no one could escape from there.

"Do you believe them?"

"No," I snapped.

I decided to take matters into my own hands. I'd been invited to a mid-March meeting with Mexican law enforcement in Mexico City. I knew that high-ranking officials, like Enrique Galindo, the commissioner of the nation's federal police force, were going to be there. It was the perfect opportunity for me to personally warn them about Chapo. I had to go.

I went down with only one DEA guy: DeLena. I didn't take any security with me. I didn't want any attention, but I did tell Leonhart before I left. We flew down on a midnight flight on Air Mexico. I wanted to get in and out under the cover of darkness.

I had one goal: to make sure they took this threat seriously. The last thing we needed was for El Chapo to escape again. We had spent months trying to dismantle the rest of the Sinaloa cartel. New players were coming on the scene. But if Guzmán escaped, all hell would break loose.

When we walked into police headquarters at about 9 a.m., just about every key Mexican law enforcement official was there, along with our DEA agents and supervisors stationed in Mexico. But before we could began, they took me on a tour of the building to show off their high-tech equipment. At one point, they even took pictures. DeLena didn't think that was a good idea. "I don't think you want to do that," he said.

"Well, it's a goodwill gesture," I said.

After the tour, we went into a conference. Even though I wasn't sure I could trust all the Mexicans in the group, I shared the information.

"Chapo's planning to escape. I want to know what you're going to do about it," I said to Galindo, point-blank.

I knew Galindo couldn't speak English, but I suspected he could under-stand it. He looked incensed at my remark. A man at the table translated his response: "That's not going to happen. We're taking care of it."

"Really," I snapped. "What are you doing about it?"

He couldn't answer the question. All he said was there was no way Chapo could get out of that prison. "Look, I'm telling you he's getting ready to go," I said. I was getting tired of repeating myself. This guy just didn't get it. "We have credible information that his people are working to get him out."

"How?"

"We're pretty sure it's a tunnel," I said.

Galindo smirked. No. That's impossible.

I was really starting to get pissed off. I stared into his eyes and said, "I just want you to know, if this guy escapes, it's on you. You knew in ad-vance. If you were to tell us that a prisoner being held in the United States was getting ready to break out, we would do something. Move them. Lock them up. Do something. Instead, you're blowing this off."

Galindo didn't say another word. And, by doing so, he was essentially saying, "You gringo bastard, how dare you tell me how to do my job?"

We adjourned the meeting, but DeLena knew how angry I was. He tried to calm me down, but I was beside myself. We'd worked so long and hard to get Chapo. Now, we had good information about his plans and the Mexican government was sitting on its hands.

When we got back to Washington, I filled in Leonhart. "He's getting ready to go," I said about Chapo. "We need them to take this threat seriously."

She agreed that we had to keep pressing the Mexican government on this.

We decided to contact Tomás Zerón, the chief investigator in the attor-ney general's office, because he was close to Mexican President Enrique Peña Nieto. He'd also played a lead role in Chapo's capture the previous year.

I told Zerón the same thing I had said to Galindo. And his response?

"That's not my job. Contact the federal police." I couldn't believe he wasn't interested in the information, either. It was unbelievable.

When I wrote up a report about the meeting in Mexico City, I put in every detail, how key people in Mexican law enforcement ignored our information. I put it in writing.

Meanwhile, I threw myself into my new job. I started every morning with a full briefing at 8:30 a.m. in our command center. Each one of the section chiefs reported on activities in their part of the world.

At every meeting I stressed how important it was to continue going after the Mexican cartels, even though El Chapo was in jail. Afterward, I'd brief Leonhart, if needed, and then start the day. It was usually one meeting after another. I was in meetings or on the phone all day, and sometimes until late at night.

In April, Leonhart announced her retirement. Leonhart was on her way out, but DOJ still hadn't hired anyone to replace Harrigan. So, in effect, when Leonhart left, I was the acting head of the DEA.

Then Holder announced that he was leaving, too. The president appointed Loretta Lynch, the federal prosecutor in New York, to take his place. I was stuck in limbo. Everything would have to go through her, and it would be a while before she got up to speed.

Then, on May 13, 2015, I got a call from Daniel Grooms, deputy attorney general at DOJ. He said they'd picked a guy named Chuck Rosenberg to replace Leonhart. "He's going to take the load off you," he said.

That was great news. And within hours of his appointment, I was named the acting deputy administrator—the number two position in the DEA. It was something to add to a celebration we'd already planned for that weekend. Monica and I were going to Columbia, Missouri, for Kevin's college graduation.

I didn't know Rosenberg from a hole in the wall, and right then I didn't give a damn. I was going to my kid's graduation. While we were in Missouri, I got a call from Rosenberg. It was a gracious hello. He said he was looking forward to working with me.

Rosenberg was an attorney. Even though he didn't have a drug enforcement background, I felt at ease for the first time in a long while. I relaxed and enjoyed a memorable weekend of family celebration.

Rosenberg met me when I returned. "I'm all yours today," he said.

He was great about that. I pitched right in with an explanation of my philosophy about interagency cooperation. I told him we had to fill the vacancies in the agency. We discussed metrics. I said it was a bad way to judge whether a DEA office was doing its job.

"You still have some DEA SACs who say, 'You've got to get me thirty arrests and I need you up on five wires for the stats.' Chuck, none of that means anything. I want to know what they did in their area to hurt Sinaloa, or Gulf, or the Zetas. I don't want to hear about how much dope or money they seized. Yes, those are important indicators, but what did they do to damage the organization? Who went to jail? Consequently, how did that criminal organization fail? That's not always easy to get across," I said.

Rosenberg nodded his head.

"But before we do anything else, there's one thing that's most important of all," I said. "We've got to repair our relationship with Congress."

He agreed. How could we do that? he asked.

We had to meet with key members of Congress, explain our mission, highlight our successes, and ask them for help not only in battling the cartels, but in addressing the opioid crisis.

Rosenberg was all-in, and the guy had connections on Capitol Hill. He was a former federal prosecutor who served as counsel to then–FBI Director Robert Mueller. Later, he became chief of staff for then–Deputy Attorney General James Comey.

Over the years, Rosenberg had taken part in prosecuting 9/11 plotter Zacarias Moussaoui; the dog-fighting case against NFL quarterback Michael Vick; and the corruption case against US Representative William Jefferson, the Louisiana congressman whose freezer was full of bribe money.

He returned in 2013 to work for Comey, who had just taken over as FBI director. This time, Rosenberg was Comey's chief of staff and counselor. Rosenberg and Comey were good friends. And they were both friends with Pat Fitzgerald.

Rosenberg knew how to do this job. "Jack, I'll handle all the political stuff," he told me. "You worry about the day-to-day operations." That was fine with me.

My friends all busted my balls, saying, "If you hang around long enough, anything could happen." Yeah, maybe they were right. I had been with the agency thirty years, but I was getting promoted because of my record, not my longevity. I was one of the few street agents to make it this high up the ladder. Most of the DEA administrators were political appointees. I didn't like the politics, but I knew I could try to change the culture. I did that wherever I landed, and it got me to where I was.

With Rosenberg in place, I started spending time on another front. Washington was finally noticing the explosive growth of opioid and heroin abuse I had been haranguing them about for years.

During my time as SAC in Chicago, I saw step by step what happened to the city. Chapo and the cartels flooded the market with fentanyl-laced heroin as Americans became more and more addicted to prescription opioids. Families fell apart as moms, dads, and children lost jobs, savings, health, and hope in pursuit of the next high.

More and more of them were losing their lives.

But somehow this crisis just hadn't registered on the national scene. I can't tell you how many public officials had discounted my warnings. Painkillers like OxyContin were legal, pushed by the big pharmaceutical companies, so maybe that made it OK. Time and again, I was asked, "What does pain medicine have to do with the influx of heroin?"

The answer was simple: Heroin and opioids had a similar effect on the body. Both were highly addictive. And with the price of opioids skyrocketing because of the crackdown on pill mills, and doctors becoming reluctant to prescribe painkillers, addicts were turning to heroin.

The cartels—Chapo's Sinaloa, in particular—had exploited the problem.

I had testified before Congress a number of times in 2015 about the crisis. At first, I was shocked at how little our elected officials knew about the DEA. One time I was trying to explain the enforcement issues to a California congressman, when he said, "How do you guys have time to do that? Don't you inspect meat?"

I said, "No. That's the USDA." What an idiot.

But that's partly our own fault. We cannot expect people to know us if we aren't talking to them. It's just like dealing with the media. You have to develop relationships. I used to tell guys who run small DEA offices that cover fifty counties, "Look, you'd better know every police chief and sheriff. They don't have to like you, but they got to know who you are. Otherwise, you're done. You're finished."

Probably 80 percent of the state and local agencies we routinely dealt with didn't really understand what our job was. No matter where I worked, I'd make it my personal crusade to sit down one on one with these people and try to win them over as friends. And in Congress I did the same thing. I was up front with lawmakers, especially when I testified before committees.

During a US House Judiciary Committee hearing in July 2015, I used a detailed map of North America to illustrate how opioid abuse was a national health and security crisis. I think that map was a real breakthrough.

It showed the reach Sinaloa had into every corner of the United States. It showed Chapo. It showed Mayo. It showed which cartel was where in Mexico. And overlaid on that map were their allied street gangs.

"They are in your neighborhood. They're selling dope to your kids. I don't care where you live. And here's where they are and who they are," I told the representatives.

Our intelligence people didn't want me to make the map public at first, but I insisted. "It's not classified," I pointed out. "But we've never done it before," one of them said. I snapped. "Just do it."

Every member of Congress on the committee wanted to examine that map, to see what the hell was going on in their district. It brought it all home to them.

Judiciary Chairman Bob Goodlatte, a Republican from Virginia, said, "I've had a chance to see these charts. How would you describe these?"

And I said, "The Sinaloa cartel is one of the most serious national security threats we face. You have the largest, most well-funded criminal entity probably the world has ever seen, run by—in my opinion, since Osama bin Laden's been taken down—the most dangerous criminal in the world. And what has Chapo done? He's built a toxic business relationship with hundreds of thousands of violent street gang members."

The map didn't lie. We tied every street gang to a cartel. We got that information from either drug seizures or informants.

That got their attention, and dominated the discussion.

I kept the focus on the big picture, not individual arrests or specific issues. "The drug cartels are a major priority, because they are a threat to our national security," I said.

And I would say the same thing to the US Senate's Committee on Homeland Security and Governmental Affairs.

New Hampshire Senator Kelly Ayotte opened the hearing by calling prescription opioid and heroin abuse a public health issue that was "devastating New Hampshire communities and families.

"Law enforcement is working tirelessly to take these drugs off the streets. But we can't simply 'arrest our way out of' this problem. I've actually heard from law enforcement in New Hampshire that key pieces they need to confront this public safety issue are more prevention efforts, more treatment options, and more support for individuals in recovery," she said.

She'd helped reintroduce bipartisan legislation that would expand opioid abuse prevention and education efforts, and make Narcan, an opioid antidote, available to first responders and law enforcement.

"We must take a multipronged approach to this problem and ensure that local, state, and federal officials are working in partnership to ... help save lives and take back our communities," she said. She spoke my language.

Manchester, New Hampshire, Police Chief Nick Willard told the committee about life on the front lines of the epidemic.

"Every single day, our officers are dealing with overdose victims. They are dealing with drug traffickers. There's also the intangible 'quality of life' issue that drug abuse presents to us…Sadly, the quality of life in Manchester is suffering from the scourge of prescription opioid and heroin abuse," he said.

I felt a kinship of sorts with New Hampshire, and Manchester in particular. DeLena was now the ASAC in Manchester. He'd filled me in on the crisis there. He was building partnerships with Willard and other cops and federal prosecutors to fight the problem.

When it was my turn, I touched on the same issues, saying this was the worst drug epidemic I had seen in my thirty years with the agency. I noted that 5,900 Americans died from heroin overdoses in 2012. In 2013, the number spiked to 8,200. I offered more grim statistics: Of the 120 drug overdose deaths seen per day in the United States, more than half were from heroin and prescription painkillers.

"Overdoses are the leading cause of injury-related death here in the United States. These are our family members, friends, neighbors, and colleagues," I said.

And I knew who to blame.

More than half the heroin in the United States was smuggled across the southwest border by Mexican cartels. They were taking advantage of the connection between painkillers and heroin, I told lawmakers. The cartels have "seen the spread of prescription drug use, and they know at some point that availability does cease."

I said the DEA was addressing the threat both internationally and domestically, and prioritizes its efforts by targeting the world's biggest and most powerful drug traffickers. We don't target individual users or pushers—that's what policemen do. We go for the big fish, the wholesalers.

Drug trafficking is as much a threat to our nation's security as any Middle Eastern terrorist group, I said. We attacked cartel-controlled drug-distribution cells within the United States with an alphabet-soup of agencies and programs, but that wasn't enough.

As doctors wrote more prescriptions, more patients became addicted. The doctors' orders ran out. The new addicts couldn't get a fresh supply of pills or couldn't afford them. Withdrawal symptoms set in quickly. Anguished addicts learn that heroin has the same effect as their pain pills, at a fraction of the price.

Similarly, recreational drug users reach for the most intense high for the best price, and also quickly become addicted. America's appetite for opioids and heroin was voracious.

Heroin overdose deaths were increasing in many cities, but particularly in the Mid-Atlantic, New England, New York/New Jersey regions, parts of Appalachia, and the Midwest.

I predicted the epidemic was likely to get worse before it got better, noting that most of the heroin bound for the United States originates in Mexico.

"The DEA has seen a 50 percent increase in poppy cultivation in Mexico, primarily in the state of Guerrero and the Mexican 'Golden Triangle,' which includes the states of Chihuahua, Sinaloa, and Durango. The increased cultivation results in a corresponding increase in heroin production and trafficking from Mexico to the United States, and impacts both of our nations, by supporting the escalation of heroin use in the United States, as well as the instability and violence growing throughout areas in Mexico," I said.

I told the lawmakers that we were convening an interagency task force of more than twenty-eight federal agencies, to confront the heroin and opioid threat. The task force would have a strategic plan in place by the end of 2015, I promised.

It was a long and exhausting day. When I finally wound up my testimony, I felt like a revival preacher after he's shouted the last *Amen*.

Lawmakers came to shake my hand and offer their support. After all these years, opioid and heroin abuse was finally making its way into the public consciousness. We had to find a way to end the scourge.

But even as I looked for ways to address the opioid crisis, Chapo was always in the back of my mind. I was going to ask DOJ to once again push for his extradition. We were still getting credible information that Guzmán was planning an escape. I told Rosenberg about the tips, my Mexico trip, and how the Mexican government had blown me off.

"Chuck, this guy is tunneling out as we speak," I said.

"You don't know that for sure," he said.

"Can I give you the exact details? No. But it's happening, and the Mexican government doesn't want to believe it. They believe he can't get out. But I'm telling you it's going to happen," I said.

Rosenberg agreed that we had to keep pressing the Mexican government on this. He promised he'd bring it up with DOJ and the State Department.

That's all I wanted. And I really hoped I was wrong. I hoped that all the information we had gathered was nothing more than speculation from drug dealers.

But when I got a late-night phone call from my son, everything changed.

CHAPTER 16

SHORTY REDUX

El Chapo was gone. Just like that. My son told me first, at 2:30 in the morning. He saw it on Twitter.

I was still half asleep. "Is it true? Chapo escaped?" he asked.

It didn't sink in at first. Chapo? Escape? But then it hit me. "Oh my God," I mumbled. I knew I had to get off the phone. "I'm on it," I said to Kevin. "But I gotta go."

I turned on the television. It was true. It was all there, on the cable news channels: Guzmán escaped, through a tunnel that his men built to his cell. He must've held a press conference on his way out.

I went ballistic. Chapo had been on the lam for hours, and no one had thought to tell me. I picked up my phone and called our command center. I needed to talk to the acting chief of operations. "Patch me through to Jim Solis," I said, trying to hold back my anger.

A minute later, he picked up his phone. "What's going on?" he said, sleepily. He didn't know, either.

I couldn't hold back my temper. "Get the hell out of bed!" I shouted. "What the hell is going on down there? Chapo got out last night!"

"I don't know what you're talking about," he said.

"You don't know what I'm talking about? It's on CNN," I shouted.

"I don't think that's true. Let me call you back," he said.

When he did call, he said, "Chapo is out, boss."

"I know that. Everyone in the world knows that. My question is: How the hell did that happen?" I yelled at him.

"I'm trying to find out now."

I slammed the phone down and called Rosenberg.

"Chuck, we got a problem. El Chapo has escaped," I said.

There was silence, followed by, "Tell me again, who's El Chapo?"

Really? You don't know who Guzmán is? I knew Rosenberg was new to the agency. Still, I can't tell you how many times I had talked to him about the drug lord...I took a deep breath and regained my composure. "El Chapo, the head of the Sinaloa cartel. The world's most notorious drug lord."

That jogged his memory. "What do you mean he got out?"

"I don't know the details," I said.

He paused for a moment, then said, "Well, you'd better be prepared to go up on the Hill and explain how this happened."

Rosenberg was quiet and I started feeling guilty. I started blaming myself, even though I had warned the Mexican government. So I thought, *All right. I guess that means ultimately I'm responsible.*

But when I thought about it, I got angry. Chapo probably paid millions of dollars to tunnel out of his cell. We saw it coming, and I flew down and warned the Mexicans in advance. I pushed our people to extradite him from Mexico so this wouldn't happen. So why did I feel responsible? I had done everything humanly possible to keep this from happening. I just had to push those feelings aside.

I started working our people for information. My guys scrambled. Soon I knew.

Chapo's men had built a mile-long tunnel from a construction site just outside the prison walls to a shower stall in his cell. The tunnel was thirty feet underground. It was two feet wide and five feet high, tall enough for him to walk standing almost upright.

When the time was right, Guzmán went into the shower stall, which was the only place in his cell without surveillance cameras. When his men broke through the shower floor, Chapo squeezed through the hole and descended a ladder to the tunnel below. By the time the guards knew he was missing, Guzmán was long gone.

It was just incredible. I thought about the effort that went into moving that amount of dirt—nearly four hundred dump trucks' worth. I thought about the planning it took to tunnel below a maximum-security prison without anyone seeing or hearing anything. I thought about the sheer audacity of it. This was pure Chapo, a brilliantly executed plan. It had to be flawless. One wrong move and they'd have been discovered.

But it worked. Now we had no idea where he was. And the reporters were calling us for comment.

Rosenberg was traveling, so I was running headquarters. At first, DOJ said we should hold off commenting for a few days, but Earl Wayne, the US ambassador to Mexico, appealed to us to issue some kind of statement. Everyone was calling him for comment, and he didn't know what to tell them.

"Someone up there has to say that we're working with the Mexicans to recapture him," he said. "I can't speak for you."

DOJ finally gave me the green light to talk to the media, and give them a positive message. I called a news conference.

"Let's not talk about how Chapo got out," I said. "That was beyond our control. But we've caught him before, and we're going to get him again. We're working together with the Mexican officials. It's just a matter of time."

The ambassador called later, and said the Mexican government was pleased with our response. I heard from a Mexican general who said they were working hard to find him.

"This is a national embarrassment," he said through a translator.

I could have said, "I told you so," but I didn't. It wasn't the right time.

I just kept thinking, *How long would it take to get him this time? Another decade? Twenty years?* I didn't know.

As the number two guy at DEA, I had the full resources of the agency behind me. We were going to get the dirtbag. I promised myself I wouldn't retire until we did. No, I'd stay at the DEA until I was ninety, but I was going to bring him in, and see his ass extradited to the United States. Only then would I think about leaving.

I set up a war room in DEA headquarters. I called together my best people. I made sure SOD was involved right away. Yes, there were other investigations, other things going on in the world, but this was important. Imagine if the Navy SEALs hadn't killed Osama bin Laden. Imagine if they had him in custody, only to find out he escaped from Guantánamo Bay? Heads would roll. We needed to find Chapo as quickly as possible.

But, first, I had to explain to Congress what had happened.

There were so many rumors floating around, and I had to separate fact from fiction. A few Mexican officials were trying to blame us, saying we'd never warned them. I was apoplectic when I heard that. I had the memo, and a ton of witnesses. DeLena and other DEA agents had been in the room that night in March. They'd heard me tell Galindo to his face that Chapo was planning to escape.

It appeared to me that Rosenberg wasn't as upset about this as I was. He should have said, "Look, we shared our intelligence with Mexican law enforcement, but they didn't heed our advice." But he left it all to me.

Washington is all about politics—who gets the credit when things go right, and who gets the blame when the shit hits the fan. I think John F. Kennedy said it best, after the Bay of Pigs fiasco. Kennedy took the heat, saying, "Victory has a thousand fathers, but defeat is an orphan."

No one felt worse than me about Chapo's escape. My agents knew that. We were doubling down on our efforts to get him. Still, the questions remained. The tunnel was perfect. It was as if whoever designed the prison sold the blueprints to the Sinaloa cartel. It was an engineering marvel.

I told Cronin that there were no deviations in the tunnel; they hadn't made a left turn and thought, *Oh, shit, we should've gone right.* That thing went straight as an arrow right up into Guzmán's shower. It was almost satellite-aided, GPS.

Surprisingly, I didn't get much pushback from Congress. I think our leaders knew the escape wasn't our fault. I turned my attention to getting our Chapo operation up and running.

Guzmán's network went dark. We didn't know where he was, but informants said he was once again running Sinaloa. For many people in Mexico, he was back and better than ever. His legend as a Jesse James–style folk hero grew even greater. Musicians were writing new songs about the heroic narco-terrorist.

That's why we had to get him, I told my team in the SOD command center. It was time to go back to basics, the core principles we used to capture El Chapo in 2014, I said. Teamwork. Details. Intelligence. Phone signals. Satellite maps.

"We have to concentrate on everybody who may have legitimate or illegitimate contact with him. We need to track the communication of the people around him. That's how we'll get him," I said.

In the weeks following his escape, Chapo didn't make calls or send text messages, but the mutts around him did. They were supposed to use burner phones, then toss them. They weren't supposed to call or text him, but that wasn't happening.

It started slowly, with photographs. An airplane being unloaded. A panel truck at a border stop. They did it for legitimate reasons, to show the boss, "Here's the dope. We're not stealing it." But every photo could be tracked. So at SOD, we began plotting the points on a map. I knew it was just a matter of time before we'd start seeing patterns of life, clues that, with time, would eventually lead us to Chapo.

And some of the mutts were lazy. They didn't throw away their burners. They kept them long enough for us to get hits from cell towers. Again, they became critical pieces as we tracked the cartel's movements. We suspected that Chapo was still using a BlackBerry. If you could get into that BlackBerry, you could get everything. But it was still too early to tell if he had one.

"We're going to use every tool in our toolbox," I told the guys in the war room. "You have all these expensive toys. It's time to use them—every little switch and trigger."

Those included predator drones, which can hover in the air for hours. They have wonderful cameras. There were a couple of operations where I actually watched the live video feed in my office as we caught the bad guys.

I spent long hours with our guys, going over new information and strategy. I read everything that SOD and our guys in Mexico sent. I spent time with our Mexican counterparts, too, reminding them to stop trying to get Chapo personally. That may have sounded counterintuitive, but that wasn't the way to find him.

"Instead, get everybody around him," I'd say. "You got to get the cooks, the doctors, his girlfriends, the guy who brings him porno movies. All of those things. That's how we need to go, because once we can figure them out, we can see the network."

We really weren't trying to get Chapo on the phone. We just wanted to know where he was, try to approximate his location. Then we'd have to go to that location and stay in the field, narrowing things down, until we found him.

And that's where the physical surveillance would help us. We needed to find a cluster of cartel-owned buildings or homes that were connected by either a sewer or a human-made tunnel. If cornered, that's how Chapo would get away. It had helped him in earlier escapes, but now that we knew how he worked, it would be easier for us to track him down. All we needed was a location, a general area in a village or town or city.

My media campaign started paying dividends. I did interviews and updates, drummed up attention for the manhunt, hoping it would piss off Chapo enough to make a mistake.

"We've got him on the run. He's looking over his shoulder," I said on TV. "We are making it as hard on him as possible."

Mexican police had set up checkpoints on major highways around the country, distributed 100,000 photos of Guzmán to tollbooths, and put ten thousand agents of the Mexican federal police on high alert. DEA and FBI officials were in daily contact with our counterparts in Mexico.

In one interview, I called El Chapo and Sinaloa "the world's biggest drug trafficking organization, and the source of much of the heroin pouring into the United States." That had to make him feel good. "I was going to retire, until this bastard escaped," I said. "Now, I'm in it for the long haul."

Chapo was back in the saddle, and was opening up new markets on the East Coast, using inner-city street gangs to distribute drugs. In turn, that fueled the heroin epidemic that was causing a spike in murders and overdose deaths across the country.

In one interview, I recounted that Chapo hated me so much that he'd placed a bounty on my head while I was in El Paso.

The journalist asked how I reacted to that. I paused for a moment before answering.

"What bothers me the most is I did exactly what that dick wanted me to do. I got scared, and I started looking over my shoulder. And that's what he intended for me to do," I said. "And that's why I hope he's feeling the same thing right now."

"Is he still after you?" the reporter asked.

"We have informants coming in all the time . . . We'll debrief somebody in Durango, and they'll say, 'They want to know where Jack Riley is.'"

It was true. After all these years, I was still on Chapo's radar—just as he was on mine.

In a way, we had the same traits: We were both relentless, organized, and held a grudge. The big difference was that he sold dope and settled his disputes with guns. I settled mine with handcuffs, and years and years of prison time.

The media weirdness was hitting Elvis levels as the hunt for El Chapo dragged on. Sightings filled the news on both sides of the border. At one point the internet was abuzz with a story that the drug lord had ordered a hit on GOP presidential candidate Donald Trump because the New York billionaire promised to build a border wall.

That was pure horseshit. There was absolutely no intelligence to suggest that. It was probably planted by Trump's campaign. Still, we got phone calls about it from people who actually thought it was true.

I was tied up running the manhunt, but I still made time to talk to re-porters, saying things I knew would get under Guzmán's skin. They knew the hunt was personal. An ages-old grudge makes great news copy.

I did more than a dozen interviews, including one with Meghna Chakrabarti, host of National Public Radio's *Here and Now*. I wanted to get the word out. Chapo was in our sights, and we weren't giving up or going away.

Chakrabarti resurrected the story of the Chapo plot to decapitate me while I was working on the border.

"Decapitate an American DEA agent?" she asked in a stunned voice. She asked if the Sinaloa cartel had the resources and the reach to pull off something like that.

"I took it as a badge of honor, because it signified to me that our efforts were really causing his organization some trouble," I said.

"Were the threats credible?" she asked.

"We were never really able to find out. But certainly his organization, Sinaloa, has the ability to corrupt, they have the resources to do some-thing like that. That obviously got our attention, and we paid close attention to it."

I didn't mention the night I might have been chased by the hit men. I'd never told my wife about that, and I didn't want her to learn about it on the radio.

Chakrabarti asked me why I was obsessed.

It's the violence, I said. The terror and the corruption that Chapo and the Sinaloa cartel sowed on both sides of the border.

"I want to caution you," I said. "This is a marathon, not a sprint. We're in it to win and the Mexicans are in it to win and I certainly look forward to retiring the day that we get him. And we will get him. I promise."

But as Chakrabarti told her listeners, "It's also personal, because Jack Riley is unflinchingly clear about his feelings for Chapo. He says he hates him."

I responded. "If I ever took this badge for a reason, it was to lock this guy up. This is truly good versus evil. And we need, collectively, as a law enforcement community, to do whatever we can to get this guy back in prison."

"Do you worry about your own safety, given the threat he made against your life?" Chakrabarti asked.

I didn't hesitate. "You know, I used to worry about things a lot. Now, I worry about our people on the streets all over the world and our Mexican counterparts. That's what keeps me up at night.

"One of the best days I've had in my thirty years on the job was a year and a half ago when he was finally captured. That was just a great day. And one of the worst was when I heard he'd escaped.

"Clearly, I was exposed to him for many, many years," I said, adding that I knew what his organization had done to innocent people in Mexico but what his heroin in particular had done to the Chicago area and the Midwest.

"For me, he is the number one bad guy in the world," I said.

"The Sinaloa cartel is probably the number one criminal enterprise in terms of its viciousness, its finances, and its reach globally...What that organization has been able to do to capitalize on the prescription drug problem, the ties to heroin here in the United States, is unprecedented."

I said that taking down Chapo had a profound impact on Sinaloa. Imagine suddenly removing the founding CEO of a major corporation— chaos would ensue. The same thing had happened to Sinaloa.

"Alliances began to break down...and we had an opportunity to do serious damage to the organization," I said. "What we're doing now is what we did a year and a half ago when we first caught him. We're reconnecting the dots. We're using all the intelligence information we have available from here. We are targeting Sinaloa, but also working on the ground with our Mexican counterparts using every legal tool possible. We'll do everything we can do to help them."

I ended the interview with a warning. "If I was Chapo, I would be looking over my shoulder, because Mexican law enforcement people are as committed as we are to seeing this guy locked up," I said.

It was true.

We spent hours every day poring over reports from informants, wire-taps, and surveillance photos, triangulating hits from cell phones. We watched video feeds from our drones. The technology had advanced amazingly since 2001, when Chapo made his laundry-cart escape. Now we had great tools, and much-improved cooperation with the Mexican government.

We worked on the case full time ourselves, and other federal agencies were pushing hard, too—from US Marshals to the Central Intelligence Agency. They were pushing their sources and sharing the intelligence they collected.

At my request, the Mexicans dedicated an elite Marine unit to track down Chapo. For me, they were the only Mexican law enforcement unit I could trust: a bribe-proof corps of tactical Marine fighters trained by US Special Forces.

Small in relative numbers—there are only sixteen thousand Marines—they rarely stayed in one place long, racing from fire to fire. We needed the Marines to stay out in the field until they found him. I knew the Mexicans weren't going to get Chapo without this unit, without them hunting him every day.

The Mexican government, thoroughly embarrassed by Chapo's latest escape, stepped up. Once again, as we did in 2014, we followed the cooks and drivers who served Chapo. Pings from their phones suggested that Guzmán was in the hills, moving nightly between a cluster of farms in and around the rugged terrain of La Tuna.

On October 2, 2015, more than a year after he'd escaped, about a hundred elite Marines were in place at the base of a wooded mountain, waiting for the order to go.

It took us at least three months to figure out for sure that Chapo was up on that godforsaken hill. And from the video feed from our drones, I knew why he chose this place. There were eight buildings in the compound with heavily armed guards on the perimeter.

It wasn't up on a mountain, but it was in a valley on the way up to the peak. It was extremely rugged. And because we'd gotten burned so

many times with helicopters—they could hear you coming a mile away—
the Marines decided to go in on foot. They even had some ATVs to get
up the hill.

So the Marines had found a place they could bunk down for one
night and then start the ascent. We had the photos. The location. Now,
all the soldiers had to do was go up and find him. In the war room in
Washington, we waited anxiously.

"OK, boys, this is it," I said.

On the commandant's orders, they'd swarm up the hill and surprise
him. Several DEA agents were stationed with them, but I'd ordered them
to stay in the rear.

An order came. But not "Go."

"Stand down, stand down, stand down!" came over the order—in language that said it was a decree from the top of the Mexican government.

We had no idea what had happened.

"What the hell is going on?" I said. "Why the hell did they call it off?"

We didn't get the answer until a day later.

While the Marines took up positions around the remote hill, two people
had unexpectedly rolled up at Chapo's compound at the top: Hollywood actor Sean Penn and Mexican actress Kate del Castillo—a woman
famous for playing a drug-cartel queen on a Mexican TV series.

I was furious: "Are you kidding me? Who are these people? What the
hell are they doing there?" I shouted at our agents in Mexico. "How the
hell did they get there, and why didn't I know? Why didn't we know about
this?"

We quickly discovered that some people knew Penn was in Mexico,
planning to interview Chapo for a freelance story he was writing for
Rolling Stone magazine. They just didn't know where or when the interview
would take place.

I was livid. I couldn't believe it. I couldn't understand why this guy was
there in the first place. I knew he was an actor, but I couldn't remember
any of his damn movies. *Fast Times at Ridgemont High*, right? *Mystic River*?
Wasn't he married to Madonna for about an hour? He certainly wasn't a

journalist. And he certainly wasn't relevant anymore. Was that why he was doing this? For publicity? To resurrect his sagging career? Was he going to make a Chapo movie, with this Castillo woman playing the love interest? How did Penn even know her? How did she know El Chapo? Damn, I just couldn't understand any of it, except that this Hollywood asshole had just undone months of hard work.

After Chapo escaped in 2014, we had to push the Mexicans to keep looking. Normally, we'd give them the best information about his location, and if he slipped away, they'd just give up. They didn't keep up the pressure. We couldn't let that happen this time. Not now. We didn't want them to go back to their barracks just because of a freak thing like this.

I told them, "Go where we want you, go with the right amount of people, do the right thing. We'll do everything we can to help you. But if it turns up negative, let's go to the next place. Let's go to the second best place. Let's just keep the pressure on. That's how we'll find him."

Apparently, the Mexican government had heard rumors that Castillo was setting up the Sean Penn interview with El Chapo. They even spotted Penn and Castillo at the Mexico City airport, but lost them. They suspected the couple went to a private hangar and were whisked away in a Cessna.

No one had seen them, but Mexican authorities suspected they were in the Chapo compound. They didn't want to attack until they knew for sure. If they were in there, the Marines would hold tight until the couple left.

When I found out the details, I recommended going in. "The Marines are moving in! If those people are stupid enough to get in the way, the hell with them. I mean, let's not go up there to kill them. But if someone's shooting at the Marines, the Marines are going to shoot back. And if you're hanging out with El Chapo, so what?"

But my bosses—and the Mexicans—didn't want celebrities caught in the crossfire.

Everyone weighed in about what to do.

Some said Chapo knew he was about to be hit and would use Penn and Castillo as human shields. I discounted that theory. To me, Castillo was there because Chapo wanted to get into her pants. And Penn? Maybe Penn could help get a heroic movie produced about his life story. It was all a great ego massage.

Meanwhile, the Marines were out there in the bushes, waiting.

And, sure enough, Penn and Castillo were in the compound all along.

They watched them leave, and the Marines began getting ready again. But just as we feared, the locals tipped off Chapo.

So, Mexican officials changed their plans. Instead of scaling the mountain on foot, which would have taken eight or ten hours, they went in by helicopter.

They lost the element of surprise.

As soon as the helicopters approached, Chapo's men scattered. The helicopters started firing, but by the time they landed and secured the compound, only Chapo's gardener remained.

The soldiers searched the perimeter. They thought they had him. One of the commanders called us and said, "Well, he's got to be within this square-mile area." Apparently, Chapo was using his telephone. My guys took the information, and pinpointed the coordinates. They called me every few minutes. "We're closing in," they said. "We think he's caught. He can't get out."

So I called Rosenberg and told him we'd have him by the end of the day.

Radio traffic said Chapo had apparently injured his leg. He was holed up inside a house, trying to get his people to come and get him.

Meanwhile, the drone video showed five people scurrying down a remote trail. The terrain was brutal, the canopy was so thick they almost blended into the scenery. Looking closely, I thought one of the guys fleeing—the guy toward the back—was Chapo. He had a child in his arms.

"Permission to fire?" a Mexican pilot called to his commander. "The child!" came the answer. Chapo was using the toddler as a shield. The people disappeared into the bush.

We all were crushed. We had Chapo, right then. But the child, but the celebrities, but goddammit all to hell.

The Marines stayed out there for a few more days, searching, trying to tighten the noose. But Chapo was gone. Finally, the Marines pulled out.

I called Rosenberg to let him know. He was not happy and he let me know it. Unbeknownst to me, he had called the attorney general and said we had Chapo.

Again, the escape pointed to Chapo's genius for organizing and preparing. I remember Zambada saying Guzmán used to have fire drills. When they moved to a new safe house, they'd all know who was to cover the doors, where the tunnel was, how to work the controls, and all the other shit. He'd say, "OK, let's go! They're here!"

His mutts would go to the door and get blasted. But Chapo and his girlfriend or his wife, whoever was with him at the time, would scurry like cockroaches down the spout.

We were all angry. We wanted to get to the bottom of what happened. The information started coming in fast, including how Chapo met Castillo.

Guzmán had long fancied himself a folk hero. So when he decided that he wanted a movie made about his life, he turned to Castillo. Guzmán had been watching her on Mexican television for years, where she stared in telenovelas on Telemundo. Her biggest role was as a drug lord in a sixty-three-episode telenovela: *La Reina del Sur*, or *The Queen of the South*.

She was beautiful and famous, so he had a thing for her. Chapo loved beautiful women. Through his attorneys, Chapo approached her to produce the movie. Castillo lived in Los Angeles, and already knew Penn. She asked him if he'd be interested in backing the movie.

But Penn played her like an idiot. He said he'd do it, but he really had no intention of backing a movie. All he wanted was to meet Chapo so he could write an "explosive story" for *Rolling Stone* about the war on drugs, and rebrand himself as some kind of intrepid investigative journalist. Castillo didn't know that. She began texting Chapo. He agreed to meet them. Guzmán's son helped set up the meeting.

But the whole thing backfired.

When we interviewed Castillo, she said she never thought they'd really meet Chapo. Really? Who the hell was she kidding? As for Penn, he wouldn't talk to us unless he was subpoenaed. He made up some bullshit excuse in interviews that he was acting as a journalist and wanted to write about drug policy. Right.

But you know what? They did their interviews, they played their publicity game. And they put a lot of Mexican Marines and DEA agents in danger. They compromised a carefully planned law enforcement action.

Tony Williams, who just took over as my chief of operations, knew what it took to get the Marines out there. They get paid like crap, but they were risking their lives. They cooperated with us. It took us years to build up this trust. And then they got screwed. Now Chapo escaped again, and it had become a national embarrassment for them.

"This was wrong," Williams said. "They screwed up everything."

I agreed. I pushed for Penn and Castillo to be prosecuted for obstruction of justice.

"Those Marines could have gotten killed, and it was all because of this moron Sean Penn, so-called journalist, and a TV star," I told Rosenberg. "We have to indict these people."

"Well, it's under review. He was under the protection of being a journalist," he said.

No one wanted to listen.

I brought it up again after a meeting with Deputy Attorney General Sally Yates. She threw a bucket of water on my ideas. "I know what you're going to say," she told me. "We've already made our decision."

I said, "These two people knew they were going to go meet the most wanted guy in the world. Someone who's indicted in federal court in eight districts, who's a fugitive from the Mexican authorities. How can that not be obstruction?"

So it was back to square one. We knew Chapo was in Sinaloa. We knew he couldn't have gotten too far. We knew we'd have to turn up the heat.

But this time when we found him—and I knew we would—we wouldn't hesitate. And if Sean Penn was up there again, to hell with him. Nothing was going to stop us.

* * *

The headlines said it all: "Raid at Mexican Ranch for 'El Chapo' Turns Up Empty."

"No shit," I grumbled.

We didn't want any publicity, but word had leaked out about how Mexican forces had Guzmán cornered on his mountain hideout, but he escaped. Their information was surprisingly accurate: Chapo had injured his leg evading capture. The operation by Mexican Marines was mounted after US drug agents intercepted cell phone signals suggesting he was hiding at a ranch near Cosala in the Sierra Madre mountains. Marines raided Guzmán's ranch hideout in helicopters, but were driven back by Guzmán's security force. Soldiers entered the camp on foot and found cell phones, medication, and two-way radios. Guzmán and his accomplices apparently fled on ATVs. But no one knew about Sean Penn and Kate del Castillo. Somehow, we had managed to keep that secret. More importantly, no one suspected how important the seized equipment was to our ongoing investigation.

"Sixty BlackBerries are on their way," Larry at SOD told me.

Once they were at SOD, we'd be able to extract a bunch of important information from the phones, especially if they had been activated. Even after all these years, Chapo still used BlackBerries. It was like he had obsessive-compulsive disorder—he constantly changed locations, but he knew what he liked. He rarely changed his personal habits. We hoped that would help us as we tried to pick up his scent.

Meanwhile, more information was becoming public about his big jailbreak.

Authorities initially released surveillance camera video showing Guzmán stepping behind a shower-stall partition, blocked from view, in making his escape. But the images did not include any audio.

The broadcasting company Televisa later aired the audio portion, which created more of a public stir. Despite several notably loud noises at the time of the escape, there was no reaction from guards. For almost two hours before his escape, the video showed Guzmán on his bed watching a video on a computer tablet with the volume cranked up.

At 8:46 p.m. a drill can be heard for almost six minutes over the sound from the tablet. At that point, Chapo got up and walked over to the shower area.

"Boss?" came a voice from the tunnel and Guzmán replied, "I'll help you."

He then bent over in the shower area, which was blocked from the camera's view, and apparently helped remove a piece of the concrete floor. Within a few moments he was gone. No one noticed anything until 9:17 p.m., when two guards were sent to the cell to check on why nothing was moving.

"Commandant, there's a hole in the shower," one called out.

"How big?" was the response.

"Big, commandant, big."

"But the prisoner isn't there?"

"No, commandant, he isn't."

It was not until three hours later that a code red emergency was declared.

A newspaper report noted that loud noises had been heard in the Altiplano prison for as long as a week before the escape, but that prisoners in that part of the penitentiary didn't complain because prison officials had threatened them.

A few weeks after Chapo's escape, Mexican Attorney General Arely Gómez González announced that twenty-four people, all but one a government employee, had been arrested in connection with the breakout.

We already had the video and audio, so this wasn't news to us. But it reminded me how we'd warned the Mexicans that Chapo was planning to escape, and how they'd ignored us.

Now, after yet another cliffhanger Chapo escape, we were hunting him again. But this time the Mexicans seemed totally focused, really committed to the job.

We knew Chapo loved his unfashionable BlackBerry phone. He didn't mind some discomfort. When he was in the rugged mountains, he was like the Unabomber, living ascetically in a small house with few luxuries. When he came down from the mountain, and eventually we knew that would happen, it was a different story.

He lived in clusters of modest one- or two-story homes, connected by sewers. If his house was raided, he'd run to a special room in the house, and activate an escape hatch above the sewer system. And while his gunmen battled police, he'd descend a ladder into the sewer and escape through the muck.

About half the confiscated BlackBerries had never been activated, but Larry thought he could put together a pattern of life from what we did have.

That was great news.

So while Larry and his team conducted their research, I once again tried to get under Chapo's skin. When reporters called, I told them Guzmán was a rabbit on the run and he soon would make a mistake. Our Mexican counterparts were ready to strike, as soon as he put his head out of whatever hole he was hiding in.

Informants made it clear that Guzmán knew who I was, and hated me enough to want to kill me. He followed the news. But I also understood his psychology: He thought he'd never get caught again. He thought he was invincible. When that happens, the suspect gets careless. That's what I was banking on.

Not only that, I was on the telephone with our Mexican-based agents, making agreements on tactics. The next time we narrowed Chapo to an area, the Marines would go in and conduct undercover surveillance. They couldn't just show up and raid a place and go home. This wasn't a military operation, it was undercover work, a police tactic. They agreed.

Two months passed. Larry gave me the news: All our information pointed to Los Mochis, a scruffy sweatbox of a coastal city in Sinaloa state, in northwest Mexico. Los Mochis was home to about 250,000 working-class people, a great place for Chapo to blend in when he came down from the mountains. Despite millions being offered for his capture, no one would betray him there. He was a local hero, one of their own.

We had global satellite images of the area, old schematics of the sewer system, and information on how many and which homes were actually connected to it. Things like that. It would help us narrow down possible safe houses where El Chapo would stay if he spent the night in the city.

I talked to our agents in Mexico and they spoke to Admiral Carlos Ortega Muñiz.

"This is what we need to do," I said. "Let's hit the architectural designs for this area and find out what the status of the sewers are. Look around, see if anyone is fortifying houses. We need people in the field doing under-cover work," I said.

I told my guys this was like Notre Dame playing Alabama for the fifth time in five years. "I can guarantee you I know what plays they're going to run," I said. "We just have to prepare."

I knew this was where the Marines couldn't fall asleep on the job. They couldn't go out there for a few days, then fall back. No, they had to stay in the field. They had to do surveillance as well as go undercover and collect information. They picked right up on it, too. They looked at new homes, but quickly focused their full attention on a half-dozen condo develop-ments undergoing aggressive renovation, with loads of steel and concrete arriving daily.

They all seemed to fit the profile: They were clusters of units that all connected to sewers. They were new, but not ornate, nothing that would stand out or attract attention.

One particular place seemed perfect. A cluster of homes connected by large sewer drains. Construction activity taking place at all the houses. A front door at one of them was being heavily fortified. That was critical. We'd found these metal doors at other raids. Just getting through them was a pain in the ass, and by the time the soldiers got inside, Chapo was gone.

The Mexicans placed all the locations under twenty-four-hour surveil-lance. We had DEA agents in the area, and monitored the activity from Washington.

Meanwhile, Marines went undercover, eating at local restaurants, shop-ping at little bodegas near the construction sites, keeping their ears open for conversations between the locals. The people working on one home kept saying they had to get the place ready soon because "Papi is coming," "This is for Papi," or "Papi wants this done on time."

"We keep hearing that, over and over," a Mexican official told me.

"Focus on that one," I said.

I turned to Larry and my guys.

"This is exactly where he's coming. I just know it," I said. Everyone felt the same way. It was just a matter of time. If he showed up, it was all hands on deck. Anyone who was within twenty to thirty miles of the place had to be on call.

So the days dragged on. We focused on the various locations, keeping in touch with our agents on the ground. Even though I wanted to be with my men, I couldn't be in the command center all the time.

I had a commitment on January 8, 2016. I had to attend a ceremony in Quantico, Virginia, to help present badges to a class of new agents. I put my cell phone on VIBRATE when the ceremony began. Soon it began growling in my pocket. Something was up, but I couldn't answer the phone. It wouldn't be right. I had to focus on the ceremony. This was our next generation of agents, after all.

Soon as it was over, I ducked out and picked up the calls. It was the news we'd been waiting for: The cops had El Chapo!

Undercover Marines had been keeping vigil across the street from our main target house. They saw a white van leave with three men inside. One of them looked like Chapo. "They were going out for burritos and porn," the agent told me.

Before dawn, Marines stormed the condo. Inside was a maze of re-inforced doors designed to blunt and confuse them. By the time they crashed the right one and shot Chapo's gunmen, he'd bolted barefoot down an escape hatch inside a closet.

Accompanied by a lieutenant and chief assassin called "El Condor," Chapo slogged for a mile through thigh-deep sewer water. No one was there to scoop him up when he emerged. Chapo jacked a car, ordered its occupants out at gunpoint, then raced south through town.

He made it a couple of miles before police cut him off. The prolific killer went meekly. For years his men fought and died to protect him, but when the time came, El Chapo surrendered without a shot fired—like the coward he is.

Still, I refused to believe it until they sent me proof. I wanted pictures of that prick in cuffs. I hurried back to headquarters, where I paced back and forth for an hour until a photo came through: Chapo sitting disheveled in a dirty wife-beater T-shirt, his hands bound tightly behind him.

I pumped my right fist in delight. "Yes! We got him!" Cheers broke out in the war room. After all the hard work, all the planning, we'd gotten him. I'd do everything to make sure he'd never escape again. We had to get him out of Mexico, and see him face justice in the United States.

The headlines from all over the world shouted the news: EL CHAPO CAUGHT!

Few people believed we'd be able to nab him so quickly. But, then again, few knew how much information we had collected about the drug lord over the years. We knew so much about him, his habits, houses, his inner circle, his tastes in food and entertainment. Burritos and porn are what did him in.

It was a case of US agencies cooperating with each other and our Mexican counterparts. In the end, the Mexican military came through. With our crack intelligence, high-tech equipment, intelligence-gathering techniques, and plenty of prodding, the Mexicans made the catch.

With Chapo in custody, the world could revel in the details of his capture.

The *New York Times* recounted how El Chapo was "captured again after a fierce gun battle near the coast in his home state, Sinaloa, Mexico."

"Mission accomplished: We have him," President Enrique Peña Nieto announced.

The capture was an immediate boost to Peña Nieto, who had struggled with corruption scandals, drug violence, and the humiliation of the escape the year before by Mexico's most famous prisoner.

In a televised address from the national palace, Peña Nieto shared the credit with Mexico's armed forces and intelligence services.

What he didn't say was how his nation was aided by the United States, or that DEA agents risked their lives every day to get Chapo.

I didn't expect Peña Nieto to credit the United States. This was his moment in the sun. But the fact is, we forced Mexico to take action. Another fact: I personally dedicated my career to making sure everyone knew about El Chapo and the devastating impact the Sinaloa cartel had on American life. I had hounded that sonofabitch into the ground.

My agents knew it. My bosses knew it. And what really mattered was that we had the most dangerous criminal in the world behind bars.

Now we had to keep him in there.

My bosses promised that we'd push for extradition, but that could take up to a year. I knew I wouldn't rest easy—or retire from the DEA—until his ass was in a high-security cell on US soil.

The US government wanted Chapo on a multitude of pending charges in American courts. They tried for extradition when he was caught in 2014, but Mexican authorities refused. It was a point of pride for them to prosecute their most important criminal in their own judicial system. They put him in Altiplano, an "escape-proof" prison, to await trial. And look what happened.

But that was then. We could learn from that, maybe.

Attorney General Lynch said Guzmán's capture represented "a victory for the citizens of both Mexico and the United States, and a vindication of the rule of law in our countries." She later called her Mexican counterpart, Arely Gómez González, to congratulate her.

I left the crowing and strutting to the politicians. I wanted to go over the whole action with my agents in Mexico. I wanted to hear every detail, and they were more than ready to tell the story, over and over again.

The Mexican authorities put their prized criminal on display. I smiled as I looked at the pictures. After all these years, there he was.

My phone was blowing up. Friends called to congratulate me. Tony was amazed. "Man, you really got him. Again!"

I informed Rosenberg, thanked my Mexican Marine counterparts, then rounded up my boys to celebrate. We all piled out to a bar in Crystal

City, a dozen senior DEA agents roaring like pledges at the final keg party of rush week.

News of Chapo's capture flashed across the television. From then on, none of us could pay for drinks; fellow patrons bought toast after toast. We were badly overserved. I was so excited that I did it again the next day, and the day after, and the day after that. Finally, my wife said enough already. "Chapo never managed to kill you, but keep this up and you sure will kill yourself," she said.

Still, Monica and Kevin were happy for me. They paid the price for my obsession. I always tried to be there for them, at all the important events in our lives. But how many birthdays or Sunday dinners did I miss because I had to work late? How many times did I sneak away from the celebration to make another telephone call? The late nights, waiting to go until I read or wrote another intelligence report, or took a call from another agent far away.

El Chapo's capture was a perfect illustration of what could happen when agencies worked together. If I was celebrating a little too hard, so be it. I knew I'd come back to earth soon enough.

Drug trafficking wasn't going to magically disappear because one man was in jail. No, as long as people wanted to get high, some mutt would step in with something to sell. Maybe the Sinaloa cartel would simply continue to operate as usual under El Mayo Zambada. Maybe it would devolve into smaller groups. And if the Sinaloa cartel did fragment, would it produce more violence or lower the death toll?

No one knew the answer. We'd never been here before.

Meanwhile, a day after Guzmán's capture, Sean Penn's *Rolling Stone* article came out. Now everyone knew he had interviewed El Chapo. What a badass hero!

Perfect timing, right? I thought.

I really didn't want to read it, but I had to. Just in case anyone asked me questions about the Hollywood dickhead.

"Tell me that's not *Rolling Stone*," Larry said when he saw the magazine in my hand.

I shrugged. "Yeah, well...I need reading material in the bathroom."

"A waste of time."

That was the truth. I won't get into the writing, the stream-of-consciousness crap. But the story was a paean to a stone-cold killer drug lord. I'm not exactly sure what Penn was trying to do. There was nothing in the piece that we didn't already know—how he got there, what happened. We picked up all that stuff in wiretaps, surveillance, emails, text messages. Penn spent a day or so at the compound, then sent El Chapo questions.

He gave Guzmán editorial control over the story. The bastard got to pick and choose what was said about him. So much for journalistic principles. For me, the Q & A was the most interesting part. Forget about the fact that Guzmán is a mass murderer. Forget that he's a ruthless thug. Forget the softball questions or the lack of follow-up or even the bull-shit reason Penn gave for wanting to talk to El Chapo: "My only interest was to ask questions and deliver his responses, to be weighed by readers, whether in balance or contempt."

Yeah, right. I understand that Penn is not a journalist and was clearly intimidated by that piece of shit.

But despite the interviewer's lack of professionalism, Chapo answered several of the questions with unapologetic honesty.

He told Penn, "I supply more heroin, methamphetamine, cocaine, and marijuana than anybody else in the world. I have a fleet of submarines, airplanes, trucks, and boats."

Penn asked Chapo, "Do you think it is true you are responsible for the high level of drug addiction in the world?"

Chapo's response: "No, that is false, because the day I don't exist, it's not going to decrease in any way at all."

And when asked, "What is the outlook for the business? Do you think it will disappear? Will it grow instead?"

Chapo responded: "No, it will not end because as time goes by, we are more people, and this will never end."

And when Penn asked, "What is the relationship between production, sale, and consumption?"

Chapo's response: "If there was no consumption, there would be no sales."

That was a simple, true answer.

Mexican officials, however, were still angry. They let the world know that Penn's and Castillo's escapade helped them track down the fugitive, even if he slipped away from the initial raid. So not only was Penn exposed as an exploitative asshole, *Pee-wee's Big Adventure* led to El Chapo's capture.

It couldn't have happened to a nicer guy.

Chapo was right. He was in jail, but heroin, fentanyl, and opioids kept right on killing Americans. Congress kept pressing me for answers: What were we doing to address the ever-growing crisis?

I was spending more time than ever up on Capitol Hill, appearing before congressional subcommittees, talking to lawmakers about drugs, especially heroin and fentanyl.

They praised us for our role in capturing Guzmán, but demanded that more be done at home. We knew that. Arresting Guzmán was a significant victory. We were breaking the Sinaloa cartel into pieces. New blood was coming up to fill the void, but we had developed critical techniques to take on these new enterprises.

We had time enough to look over what we'd done, to get some perspective.

If anything, Chapo set up the infrastructure for the cartels. He was like President Dwight D. Eisenhower, building the US interstate highway system in the 1950s. Now, we were setting up tollbooths and speed traps to slow down the drug traffickers. We had to keep focusing on the choke points, attacking the street gangs at the exit ramps.

Thirty years ago, we didn't understand how cartels worked. We didn't know the alliances and business models. Many people in law enforcement didn't believe cartels existed, just as the FBI in the early days didn't believe that Mafia crime families controlled organized crime in the United States. Those days were over, thanks to SOD and agents like me who pushed hard to publicly expose these criminal enterprises.

That was something I was still trying to convey to lawmakers. Despite all the information and statistics we continually spouted, some of them couldn't seem to grasp the extent of the crisis. But as heroin and fentanyl inundated what once were drug-free communities, some were starting to get the picture.

Every time a celebrity died of a drug overdose, it drew more needed attention to the problem. In April 2016, the musician Prince died of a fentanyl overdose in his home in Minneapolis. The public suddenly started asking questions about fentanyl, the opioid-style painkiller made in laboratories.

A staggering number of stories described it as a new drug, when I had been warning people about fentanyl for years. The cartels, especially Sinaloa, had been amping up their heroin with fentanyl to make it stronger.

Rosenberg asked me to talk to the media about fentanyl.

But what was I going to say that I hadn't already said?

Still, I told reporters that the drug that killed Prince had become a favorite of Mexican cartels because it was extremely potent, popular, and profitable.

Mexican cartels produce fentanyl in their own labs, or import it in bulk from China. They distribute it through their vast smuggling networks to meet rising American demand for painkilling opiates and pharmaceuticals.

"It is really the next migration of the cartels in terms of making profit," I said. "This goes to the heart of the marketing genius of the cartels. They saw this coming. They got in on the ground floor."

It was unclear how Prince obtained the drug. Doctors can prescribe fentanyl, a synthetic opioid, for cancer patients and for palliative care, including end-of-life treatment.

But illicit fentanyl was surging to levels not seen since 2006, when a string of heroin overdose deaths in the United States was connected to a single fentanyl laboratory in Mexico.

The potentially deadly drug was now mainstream. You could buy it in the streets of the smallest towns and cities in the most rural states. It was a natural progression: First there was methamphetamine, followed by Oxy-Contin. Then came heroin, and now fentanyl. And fentanyl was deadliest of all.

A Centers for Disease Control study said death rates from synthetic opioids, which included fentanyl, increased by about 72 percent nation-wide between 2014 and 2015. In Pennsylvania, for example, there were 349 fentanyl deaths in 2014. A year later, 913 users died. In Florida, fentanyl deaths were up nearly 70 percent from 2014 to 2015. In Massachusetts they were up 20 percent during the same period.

Fentanyl is deadly because it is so concentrated. It is eighty to a hun-dred times stronger than morphine, and twenty-five to forty times more potent than heroin. Contact with just a few grains can be fatal.

The DEA sent out to police departments around the country a video warning, with my voice-over narration, featuring two investigators from Atlantic County, New Jersey, who accidentally ingested the drug after a bust.

"I felt like my body was shutting down," one of the officers said. DEA agents must wear cumbersome protective suits with oxygen tanks when making arrests and raiding buildings where fentanyl is stored or produced.

Behind all the statistics are communities like Manchester, New Hampshire, where the opioid epidemic has hollowed out the entire community.

DeLena asked me to be part of an ABC news show looking into the epidemic in his community. He had adopted my philosophy: Be open with the media, get the word out about how the DEA was cooperating with other agencies to fight drug abuse. DeLena lived at ground zero for the fentanyl epidemic. I was happy to help him spread the word in New England.

Like me, getting the bad guys was something personal to DeLena. He was raised in a bare-knuckle suburb of Boston called Revere, and had worked narcotics for years.

DeLena knew about drug addiction firsthand. His father was a user who deteriorated into a junkie who betrayed, and later abandoned, his family. I knew that a couple of his former classmates overdosed on opioids. So he had taken it upon himself to issue public warnings about fentanyl.

"Best move I made was getting you up here," I told him.

"Thanks, Jack. We're working together with the local cops. But it never ends."

I nodded in agreement. New Hampshire had even taken a blow in the 2016 presidential campaign. Republican presidential candidate Donald Trump claimed the nation's border was so porous that heroin and fentanyl had spread into small towns across America. He used New Hampshire as an example, calling it a "drug-infested den."

"We have a massive drug problem where kids are becoming addicted to drugs because the drugs are being sold for less money than candy," Trump said.

But I wasn't there to talk about politics. Politicians have no idea what happens on the front lines. They live in their safe suburban worlds where they don't have to worry about street gangs, shootings, or drug dealers moving in next door. If, by some chance, their kids are caught smoking weed or popping Percocet, they have the resources to send them to rehab, unlike most Americans. No, they were clueless about what real people went through. They saw things through the smeary lens of the Beltway. They thought the DEA inspected meat. They didn't know we risked our lives every day to stop drug dealers from destroying lives.

We climbed into a police car with a camera crew, and talked about the local drug problem as we surveyed the city streets.

New Hampshire is not a big place. There are typically less than twenty homicides a year in the state. But in 2015, more than four hundred people died from drug overdoses, and around 70 percent of those were linked to fentanyl. In 2016, 437 people died of drug overdoses.

Timothy Pifer, director of the New Hampshire State Police Forensic Laboratory, supplied more statistics. The spike in overdose deaths began in 2014, Pifer said. "I've been involved in the forensic field here in New Hampshire for twenty-seven years. And I lived through the crack and methamphetamine epidemics, but we've never had deaths like we do now."

The state lab receives about 750 new drug evidence submissions every month, but can only process about 550. "Some days it feels like we're shoveling sand against the tide in terms of getting the cases out," he said in a news article.

"It's all true," DeLena said.

While the Northeast has been hit hard, fentanyl is rapidly spreading across the United States. "If anything can be likened to a weapon of mass destruction in what it does to a community, it's fentanyl," I told the journalists. And the people producing the drug saw it as just another product in an ever-evolving market.

"Just as people in Silicon Valley are working on the next iPhone, I think the Sinaloa cartel is working on the next drug they're going to market to their addict customer base in the United States. That is just how sophisticated they are, how hell-bent they are on making a fast buck. And I got to tell you, across the country, they don't care who dies," I said.

Fentanyl is cheaper and easier to make than heroin, which requires a growing season.

I praised New Hampshire's work, and admitted that I had never seen anything as insidious as the opioid crisis. "It's in every corner of the country, but I think the Northeast, in particular New Hampshire, is ground zero," I said.

After the interviews, I talked privately to DeLena. "Just when we have something under control, it's something else," I said. DeLena agreed. "That's why we can't give up."

I smiled. He sounded just like me. "Damn straight. We can never give up. Otherwise, the bad guys win."

I'd been pestering Rosenberg and the Justice Department about El Chapo's extradition. We couldn't let him stay in a Mexican jail. We knew all too well what would happen if we did. Guzmán's attorneys in Mexico, of course, had been working to block his extradition.

Now Rosenberg said he felt optimistic. Mexico didn't want another embarrassing breakout. They were sure, like us, that it would happen. Guzmán had too much money and too many connections.

Finally, in May 2016, a Mexican judge ruled that Guzmán could be extradited to the United States to face money laundering, drug trafficking, kidnapping, and murder charges.

But Mexican President Peña Nieto wasn't sure he supported the move. In the United States, Chapo would face the death penalty.

After much debate, the DOJ quietly dropped the murder charges—the biggest hurdle to extradition. Peña Nieto then pledged to send El Chapo to the United States to stand trial.

That was huge. The Mexican government had never been willing to let El Chapo leave Mexico. Yes, Guzmán's attorneys would continue to fight, but I could see a light at the end of the tunnel.

"We expect (Guzmán's extradition) in January or February 2017," a Mexican official told a television crew.

The back-and-forth continued. I looked at my calendar. If everything went according to plan, I'd retire at the end of the year—if El Chapo was on a plane headed back to the United States. If not, I'd stay. I promised myself a long time ago that I wouldn't leave until he was in a US jail—and I meant it.

It's a wonder anything ever gets done in Congress.

I was a cop on the streets. I ran DEA offices. I worked closely with federal law enforcement agencies to get the bad guys. We took care of business for the good of the American people.

But Congress? These guys couldn't get a damn thing done.

For years, lawmakers in both chambers of Congress had offered multiple bills aimed at curbing drug trafficking and rampant opioid use, but none had become law.

And then there were the members of Congress who couldn't understand the nation's drug crisis.

We had too many guys like James Lankford, a junior Republican senator from Oklahoma. Before he was elected to the Senate, he was a congressman from the fifth district for four years. He asked me to come to his office for a meeting one day.

I arrived with my intel analyst, and we sat down with a huge mural of Lankford's beautiful blond wife and their two kids staring down at us. The congressman asked me to explain how the cartels were affecting Oklahoma. I explained. It was clear he was not listening. He looked at me suddenly and said, "Aren't you a little too old to be doing this job?"

Whoa, that stopped me for a second.

I was in my late fifties, but I knew of a few congressmen in their eighties and nineties.

"Well, sir, I'm committed to this job," I responded. "There are people dying out there. I'm not walking away."

The idiot sat there in silence. I went back to explaining the problem in his state, but he interrupted again. He wanted me to beef up our presence in Oklahoma City, he said.

When I told him we only have so many resources and we had to place them where they could be most effective, he blew a gasket.

I tried to calm him down.

"Every member of Congress I meet wants more resources. It takes money. Currently, sir, we're down almost 400 agents from our ceiling of 5,200. And, just so you know, we operate in sixty-four countries, in addition to every major city in the United States. That doesn't go a long way. We're restricted by Congress on how many task force positions we can have with the funding we get," I said.

But he didn't give a damn. He just wanted more people for his state.

It was like that with just about every lawmaker. Then you'd get someone like Jason Chaffetz, a former Utah congressman, who was a total idiot.

Back when I was in Chicago, I got a bonus one year for all the good work I did. Chaffetz had a problem with that.

"You know, the American people—we're $19 trillion in debt and I'm sure he's a good, capable person—but it's just unimaginable that we can somehow justify handing out bonuses by the tens of thousands of dollars," Chaffetz said.

This dickhead had no idea how hard I worked, or even what DEA agents did. No, this guy made three times as much money as the average DEA agent for a fraction of the work. You want to know what's wrong with Congress? Look at people like Lankford and Chaffetz. Lawmakers are out for themselves. They don't act in the interest of the American people. They're quick to accept credit when things go right and quick to blame others when things go wrong. They have no backbone, and they refuse to work together to solve problems.

We're facing the biggest drug abuse epidemic in this nation's history and they look the other way. But the hardworking agents in the DEA, the FBI, and other federal agencies see problems and try to solve them. We're in it for the good of the nation.

I was getting fed up. And the presidential campaign was getting ugly.

Trump and Democratic presidential candidate Hillary Clinton were embroiled in a bitter campaign. No matter who won, it wasn't going to be pretty. The government was split in half, more partisan than ever.

We needed bipartisan leadership if we were going to solve the drug problems that were ripping apart our nation. I didn't see that anywhere on the horizon.

The political side of Washington disgusted me, turned me off. It made me realize how blessed I was to serve the country in the job I had. I got to make so many great things happen as a cop.

I saw that now was a good time to leave.

It was time for me to retire in peace.

Everyone who works knows this day will come eventually. Some people count down the days. Others dread it. It's like death—you know it will get you, but you try not to think about it.

But now here it was, my last day of work. I was sad.

Friends had been calling for weeks. Some like DeLena, Cronin, and

Comer begged me not to go. Others like Tony said, yes, it was time. Get out while you still can enjoy life.

I was leaving as the nation's number two drug cop, having been at or near the center of nearly every major mission to catch foreign kingpins since the early 1990s.

I was a member of the squad in Washington that built the intel platform to bring down Pablo Escobar in Medellín, Colombia; that helped catch the leaders of the Cali cartel; and, later, the overlords of the Mexican mobs.

I spent my first years on the Chicago streets, working undercover.

Through it all, since I'd first heard his name, I tracked down a total jagoff named El Chapo.

Now, the drug kingpin was boarding a plane in handcuffs, bound for a tiny cell in a Manhattan jail. I could retire in peace.

The DEA threw a big retirement party. More than 250 people were there, guys I started with who had retired, and new guys like Larry. We all stayed around, drinking and telling stories of the glory days, like that old Springsteen song.

They made a video with snippets from some of the journalists and fellow agents I'd made friends with over the years. Of course, they got in some good-natured shots.

"You never failed to answer the bell when we needed someone to talk to the media," the DEA spokesman said. "I always tell folks the most dangerous place in the room is between Jack Riley and a microphone."

They all mentioned that I made capturing El Chapo my personal crusade.

I worked with Geraldo Rivera a few times, and he recounted how we once met in a pub at 2 p.m. to discuss a story.

"And by six in the evening we forgot what we went there to talk about," Rivera laughed, adding that, "He was a great cop. He kicked El Chapo's ass. He's the best dope-fighting cop in this country."

CBS investigative journalist Armen Keteyian remembered a piece we did for the show *48 Hours* about drugs and Chicago. He called it one of the highlights of his career. "I got to ride along with a real lawman as part of that piece," he said.

Pete Williams of NBC news first joked about Notre Dame football, then turned serious.

"We can definitively say that retirement has done what the Mexican cartels never could: Get Jack Riley the hell out of DEA," he said. "Jack, you're the real deal, a shining example of what it means to be devoted to public service."

Country singer Toby Keith said retirement meant I'd have more time to watch Notre Dame football.

It was all in good fun.

And by the end of the night I heard it again, "This place is never going to be the same without you."

Bullshit, I thought. *The minute I walk out that door, someone's going to come in and steal my desk chair and my beautiful Notre Dame sofa cushions.*

It reminded me of one of the funniest gags I ever saw on *The Johnny Carson Show*. Evel Knievel came on, dressed in red, white, and blue leather and a $50,000 diamond-studded cane with a motorcycle on the handle. He was there to promote the Snake River jump attempt in Idaho. Comedian Richard Pryor was already there, and sat patiently on the couch as Knievel gave his whole spiel about patriotism, don't do drugs, but a little booze will take the edge off. Then he starts hyping the jump. Pryor doesn't say a word. He's just looking at that cane. And when there was a lull in the conversation, Pryor leaned over and said to Knievel: "If you don't make it, can I have the cane?"

It was great.

That was my career: Great. But now it was over. It was time for someone else to take my cane and whack some ass.

WRIGLEY FIELD

I sat in a sold-out Wrigley Field, enjoying hot dogs and baseball with my family and friends on a sunny Sunday afternoon. I am not usually a gloomy guy, but a statistic floated across my mind, and the reality it represented hit me like a ton of bricks.

This historic stadium with the ivy-covered outfield walls seats 41,649 people. It was too small to hold all the Americans who died of drug overdoses in 2018.

That's right. Some 51,000 men, women, and children—brothers, sisters, mothers, fathers, aunts, uncles, and friends—lost their lives to drug overdoses. A large percentage of the dead were killed by heroin, fentanyl, and prescription drugs.

All of a sudden the ballgame didn't seem so important.

Even though I've been retired from the Drug Enforcement Administration since January 2017, I still can't stop thinking about those lost souls. That's what drove me as a street agent. That's what motivated me when I helped create the DEA's Special Operations Division. That's what pushed me all those long days and nights during my thirty-two-year DEA journey.

Yes, I'm retired. I have a beautiful house near a quiet lake in South Carolina. I have a wonderful life with Monica, and our son Kevin visits all the time. We're surrounded by good friends. I am a lucky man, blessed even.

But I am haunted by thoughts of the families whose lives have been destroyed by illegal drugs. And I know who to blame: Joaquín "El Chapo" Guzmán Loera, infamous drug lord, head of the deadly Sinaloa cartel.

Every day, I read more stories about Chapo, who spends twenty-three hours a day sitting in a twenty-by-twelve-foot cell on the tenth floor of the Metropolitan Correctional Center in New York City. His racketeering and drug trafficking trial is expected to begin in early 2019.

The case has been surrounded by so much damn hyperbole, with journalists calling it the trial of the century. A judge has refused to order Guzmán released from solitary confinement, where his court-appointed lawyers say he faces needlessly harsh and restrictive conditions that make it difficult for him to mount his defense. The silence is too much for him. He says he's having auditory hallucinations in the form of twenty-four-hour "Mexican music."

Prosecutors say his trial is expected to take two to three months. The court has heard that evidence includes fifteen hundred recordings and ten thousand documents.

Since his arrest and extradition, Chapo's life has been sensationalized in the US and Mexican media. He's been the subject of multiple television series and documentaries. He's the most infamous gangster in history—bigger than John Gotti, Al Capone, and Pablo Escobar.

Every move is recorded, documented. The public appetite for El Chapo seems to be insatiable.

For me, it's surreal. I chased his ass for nearly thirty years and I don't think he deserves this kind of attention.

But, then again, maybe he does.

El Chapo didn't "invent" drugs or the concept of drug trafficking. There have been traffickers—gangsters who transport illegal alcohol and drugs—for centuries. But Guzmán was a logistical genius, a mobster who found new ways and means and routes to bring his deadly products to market.

He created a criminal enterprise that outstripped anything Charles "Lucky" Luciano could have imagined in the 1920s and 1930s. And, as a result, this second-grade dropout became so rich that he ended up on the *Forbes* list of the wealthiest people in the world. It's been estimated that Guzmán, who grew up a shack with a dirt floor and an outhouse, is worth billions—maybe not as much as Bill Gates, but certainly more than Donald Trump.

What separated El Chapo from ordinary drug lords was his ruthless zeal for both violence and planning. He paid meticulous attention to logistics, and was truly innovative in the many ways he found to smuggle dope into the United States. He never hesitated to use violence when battling rival cartels for territory and influence.

Crime families in the United States knew violence drew unwanted attention to their illicit activities, but Guzmán never shied away from that kind of attention and had no scruples about killing innocent people to achieve his goals. He built terror into his business plan.

As a result, thousands of innocent Mexican citizens were killed or maimed by crossfire. Drug money fueled corruption, reaching a point where no one could trust Mexican government officials.

For me, that was the conundrum: Mexicans were among the most loving, yet terrified, nation of people in the world.

I chased Guzmán for years. My family paid the price. Now my old quarry sits in a Manhattan jail awaiting trial on a litany of charges.

He's in there because of the hard work of DEA agents and cops from the Federal Bureau of Investigation; ATF; Internal Revenue Service, other federal agencies and local and state police departments that joined forces to find the connections that led to his downfall.

At first, I was like a voice in the wilderness. Some people thought I was crazy for blaming El Chapo and the Sinaloa cartel for so much of the drugs and the gang violence that blighted the streets of US cities, especially Chicago. They thought I was a bore, harping about how opioids were turning ordinary Americans into junkies and how Chapo was behind the trend.

I can't tell you how many times people said, "Jack, back off. How can this one mope control all the methamphetamine that's turning good folks in rural communities across America into 'meth heads'?"

But early on, agency intelligence showed that Chapo—this scumbag with a criminal degree in logistics—was the mastermind behind the explosive growth of America's drug addiction.

He found new routes and creative ways to bring drugs across the border, digging multimillion-dollar tunnels to move marijuana, cocaine, methamphetamine, heroin, and fentanyl. He built a criminal marketing enterprise—and relationships with street gangs—that rivaled the best multilevel marketing companies.

And, for the most part, he stayed in the background. Later in his career, perhaps during a midlife crisis, he bought into his own legend. He started appearing openly in Mexican cities. And that would ultimately be his undoing.

What Chapo didn't count on was police agencies in the United States and Mexico talking to each other and sharing information. And he certainly didn't count on an Irish cop from Chicago dedicating his career to tracking his every move.

While I believe that many are responsible for our nation's drug crisis, including unscrupulous doctors, pharmacies, wholesale drug distributors, drug companies, and the banking industry, none played a bigger criminal role than El Chapo.

Guzmán was a sociopath and a mass murderer. But he was also one hell of a corporate CEO. It was Chapo who recognized the growing abuse of prescription drugs in the United States, well ahead of many law enforcement officials.

Most of these prescription drugs were opioid-based. As American demand began to escalate, Chapo seized on a business development windfall: He directed his criminal empire to prepare a new product line for market. He ordered the increase of poppy production in Mexico, heroin processing labs, and a surge of illicit fentanyl.

In 2010 he stockpiled his cocaine supply on the Mexican side of the border, which created scarcity and raised prices. Meantime, cheap, high-grade heroin flooded into US cities and towns. No matter which poison he chose, the American addict put his money into El Chapo's pockets, right up to the day the addict died.

Chapo built a retail empire through toxic alliances with American gangbangers. They became his salesmen, going door to door peddling death, misery, and a cheap high.

I'm simply a cop, not a politician. I am sworn to enforce the laws of the United States. So, for me, this boils down to good versus evil. I can think of no one on the face of the earth more evil than Guzmán.

It is true. I hate Guzmán and his Sinaloa bastards. And it was Chapo who turned this into a personal battle.

In 2007, while I was in El Paso as the DEA special agent in charge, he put a bounty on my head. One night, his henchmen chased me down to an isolated parking lot and were ready to shoot me. But for some reason I will never know, they backed off before any shots were fired.

I saw what he did in Mexico, killing thousands of innocent people and corrupting virtually every corner of the Mexican government. Later I saw firsthand what he did to my beloved Chicago and other cities across the country.

In the DEA, you do nothing by yourself. The agency is a family of brave warriors, and it became my second family. I did not single-handedly end Chapo's murderous reign. No, I was honored to lead and work with hundreds of heroic DEA special agents, police officers, prosecutors, and our foreign counterparts as we risked everything to put Guzmán on trial, and behind bars, in the United States.

Regardless of your views on America's "war on drugs," there is no denying that drug abuse is tightly bound to evil and death. In fact, the term *war on drugs* drives me crazy.

A war has a beginning and an end. I never expect to see an end to our battle against illegal drugs and deadly addiction. Let me repeat this: We as a society will likely be dealing with illegal drugs, addiction, and its accompanying violence and death for the remainder of our existence.

How we choose to confront this enduring evil, and the criminals who profit from it, is the key to ridding our society of people like Guzmán and his deadly henchmen. Guzmán is a murderer of historic proportions, who has profited immensely from our never-ending addictions.

Sitting in the stands that day in Wrigley Field, I thought about what we should do. More treatment programs to get people off drugs? Definitely. More educational programs so people don't get started in the first place? Yes. Making sure we stop glamorizing drug use so people don't get started in the first place? Absolutely.

But remember this: Drug addiction is not a socioeconomic condition. For so long, we were told it was mostly the poor and lowly inner-city dwellers who were addicted to drugs. But drug addiction cuts across all socioeconomic boundaries. Bankers and rock stars and suburban house-wives are addicted to painkillers, heroin, and fentanyl, just like poor African-American and Latino teenagers from some of the toughest neighborhoods.

But what I have learned in thirty-two years of chasing bad guys is that the problem belongs to every US citizen, institution, and community. I'm talking about educators, policy makers, ministers, parents, athletic coaches, pharmaceutical companies and distributors, doctors, dentists, and pharmacists. We are all key players in how we confront this never-ending evil.

We used every legal tool at our disposal to take down Chapo and the Sinaloa cartel, but our most powerful weapon against crime is quite simply cooperation. Its success depends on the willingness of law enforcement agencies to effectively communicate with one another in real time.

As a society, we cannot stick our heads in the sand and hope the drug problem goes away. We have to attack, attack, and attack criminal organizations wherever they hide. The outstanding relationships the DEA and other US agencies built with our Mexican counterparts that led to Chapo's demise must be a model for all to strive for.

Leadership starts at the top. I wish our current president would heed my warning. Words matter in the foreign law enforcement arena. Years of bridge building can be destroyed in one thoughtless public outburst—or tweet.

President Trump's 2016 campaign rhetoric included promises to some-how attack the current opioid crisis, but very little has been done to date.

I would be shocked if the president has even had a DEA briefing on one of this nation's most pressing dangers. In July 2018, he named a new acting head of DEA: Uttam Dhillon, a White House lawyer with little or no knowledge of the DEA or its operations. In his first teleconference with SACs, he said something that ran counter to everything my mentors taught me, everything I had been preaching for years: "We need more arrests." He had gone back to metrics. We're going to be arresting addicts again.

Let's not think for one minute that drug lords will limit themselves to drug trafficking. If Chapo and others like him had joined forces with terrorist organizations, we might now be looking down the wrong end of a gun, an American Afghanistan.

So how do we stop our people from using drugs? I know from my years of dealing with drug addicts and traffickers that there is no easy answer, no Nancy Reagan "Just Say No." Yet, education is part of it. People like El Chapo will always be there to exploit our weaknesses, to entice us with drugs that make us forget our troubles for right now and enslave us later on.

I've watched mothers abandon their children and sell their bodies for another hit. I've watched men lose their jobs and become homeless, leaving behind families as they search for their next high. I've watched people steal from their employers—their parents—to support their habit, while people like Guzmán got richer and richer.

Until he was caught. Chapo was right when he said the United States will still be craving drugs long after he's gone from the scene. "The day I don't exist, it's not going to decrease in any way at all," Chapo said in his star turn in *Rolling Stone*. While he's right, it doesn't mean we should stop trying.

I believe Chapo's biggest fear—the biggest fear of all drug traffickers and terrorists—is being stuck in a tiny cell with no access to the outside world. That's where he is now, awaiting a trial that could put him away for the rest of his life.

I believe that, in the end, it's fear that will reduce drug trafficking—

the fear that the United States can, at any time, reach out and find you. No matter where you hide, no matter where you operate, we'll shut down your cartel and bring you to justice.

In the end, this is a fight about our national security. Stopping the Guzmáns of the world is just as important as finding the terrorists planning their next attack. A brother, sister, son, daughter, or parent killed by drugs is just as dead as a loved one killed by a terrorist. I don't want another person in my country to attend another drug-related funeral.

But to do that, we have to keep fighting—fighting the next Guzmán. Our nation's future is at stake. We can't let the bad guys win.

ACKNOWLEDGMENTS

When I retired from the Drug Enforcement Administration, I had no intention of writing a book. But my family, friends, and former colleagues encouraged me to write about my life and career. With the glorification of El Chapo and the drug crisis, I felt compelled to do so.

There are so many wonderful people that I'd like to thank, people who have had a profound impact on my life and contributed to my story.

My deepest thanks to "Tony" my partner, navigator (both literally and figuratively), and great friend. To Joe Keefe and Joe Corcoran for your support, guidance, advice, and friendship.

Many thanks to my lifelong friends and fellow DEA warriors, including Jon DeLena, Joe Cronin, John "Steve" Comer, Sheila Lyons, Sherod Jones, Spider, Dave Grant, Owen Putnam, Kevin Powers, Van Quarles, and Lori Mays, who, by the way, deserves an award for keeping me in line. And thanks to Frank Main at the *Chicago Sun-Times* and Paul Solotoff.

My undying gratitude to "Chicago's Finest," including Nick Rodi, Leo Schmitz, Joe Gorman, and the late John Moran, as well as all the heroic police, agents, and prosecutors that I've worked with over the years.

My deepest thanks to Mitch Weiss, without whom this book would not have been possible, and to my editor, Amanda Murray, and the great team at Hachette Book Group.

To my sisters, Barb and Joan, for believing in me when no one else did.

To the brave men and women, past and present, of the Drug

ACKNOWLEDGMENTS

Enforcement Administration for allowing me the honor to serve by your side.

To my son, Kevin, who provides me with a higher purpose in life.

But most importantly my heartfelt gratitude to my wife, Monica, the true rock of our family, for her unwavering support and love through all the ups and downs of a thirty-two-year career as a DEA agent.

INDEX